A GUIDE TO
PHOTOGRAPHING
ROCKY MOUNTAIN WILDLIFE
BY WELDON LEE

THIS BOOK IS DEDICATED TO...

Linda

who shares my tears
and my dreams

Scot and Buck

who allowed me
to share their early years

Dillon Walker

and the future

to those

who are fighting the good fight
to preserve wildlife

and

to the Grizzly

he must win
yet I too must win
there can be no draw.

International Standard Book Number: 1-56579-155-X
Photographs copyright Weldon Lee, 1996. All rights reserved.
Text copyright Weldon Lee, 1996. All rights reserved.

Published by Westcliffe Publishers
2650 South Zuni Street
Englewood, Colorado 80110
Printed in Hong Kong by Palace Press International

Publisher, John Fielder
Production Manager, Patricia Coughlin
Designer, Ann Green
Editor, Dougald McDonald
Proofreaders, Catherine Goetz and David Zimmerman
Indexer, Brooke Graves

Library of Congress Cataloging-in-Publication Data

Lee, Weldon, 1937-
    A Guide to Photographing Rocky Mountain Wildlife / by Weldon Lee.
        p.   cm.
    Includes index.
    ISBN 1-56579-155-X
    1. Wildlife photography—Rocky Mountains. 2. Rocky Mountains—Guidebooks.
        I. Title.
    TR729.W54L44   1996
    778.9'32'0978—dc20   96-24106
                                                          CIP

To receive a free color catalogue, call Westcliffe Publishers at 303-935-0900.

PREFACE

Wildlife issues are a concern to many of us. However, we must go beyond concern. We must educate ourselves about our subjects and about the impacts we have upon them. And, we must work to educate others.

As the human population increases, more pressure is placed on the remaining islands of wilderness and the species residing therein. As wildlife photographers, we have a role in educating the general public and making changes. First, however, we must educate ourselves.

I hope this book will reinforce your concerns about wildlife and add a little something to your understanding of our brothers and sisters of the wild.

While conducting research for this book, I spoke with someone who said it is important to protect people from wildlife. My first reaction was that just the opposite is true — we need to protect wildlife from people. But, this person explained, when people are injured by wildlife, it is the animal that pays the price.

Along similar lines, Thomas Hurd, a fauna specialist for Banff National Park, made a point that really started me thinking. He said, "Even non-consumptive uses (of wildlife) are not without their costs." As an example, he referred to the wapiti that have taken up residence near Banff Townsite. They realize they are safe from wolves as long as they stay in town. As a result, many are killed by automobiles every year. These animals, along with the many deer that are killed, could have been food for the wolves.

What kinds of costs do we, as wildlife photographers, exact from the very subjects we love? Only through knowledge and understanding will we find the answers to these questions — and ultimately lessen our impact.

Weldon Lee

Canada Lynx

TABLE OF CONTENTS

INTRODUCTION

Throughout the Rocky Mountains, from New Mexico to British Columbia, almost unbelievable opportunities await wildlife photographers in their quest for the ultimate image. Whether you're a first-time visitor to the Rockies or have lived here all of your life, *Photographing Rocky Mountain Wildlife* has something for you.

This book presents specific information on how, when, and where to photograph more than 60 species of birds and mammals. For each species, an average of five photographic "hot spots" is highlighted.

A hot spot is a location where you should have a good opportunity to photograph your target species. However, there is major difference between a hot spot for mountain goats, which sometimes walk right up to a photographer, and one for bobcats. I can promise that a bobcat will not come walking up to you. A hot spot for bobcats is simply a location supporting a reasonable population of these creatures. By applying the information in this book, you stand an above-average chance of getting the images you came after.

Chapter 3 describes 28 special locations, including state and national parks, national forests, and national wildlife refuges, that support an especially large population and diversity of wildlife. These range from the Platte River Valley of central Nebraska, guest to half a million migrating Sandhill Cranes every spring, to the Snake River Birds of Prey Area, west of Boise, Idaho. Well-known wildlife preserves such as Yellowstone National Park are highlighted, as well as little-known cornucopias of wildlife such as Kelly Island, near Missoula, Montana. All of these places are worth making a special trip to visit.

The species included in Chapter 4 were selected as a broad representation of Rocky Mountain wildlife. Many were chosen because they're frequently observed, some were chosen because of the interest they hold for wildlife photographers, and a few were included because of their high-profile status.

Species such as bighorn sheep, mountain goats, and Trumpeter Swans, while not common throughout the entire region, are easy to photograph in certain locations. On the other hand, mountain lions and wolves, which nearly everyone wants to photograph, are very difficult to photograph in the wild. However, they can be quite easily photographed at one of the game farms in the region.

With this book, it is my hope that beginners will discover new, invaluable techniques, and that professionals will learn about previously unknown locations, and, as a result, add thousands of new images to their stock files.

Regardless of who you are, I hope you have fun and enjoy the book.

Note: Bird names in this book are capitalized in accordance with American Ornithologists Union practices.

Gray wolf

300mm lens allows mountain goat to be photographed from a comfortable working distance.

Chapter 1

ETHICS

A baby hippopotamus in the Congo was chased from its mother by a photographer. Why? The photographer wanted to catch the baby hippo being eaten by crocodiles.

In the Serengeti, an impala was shot and killed by another photographer. One end of a rope was tied to the impala, and the other end to the back of a Land Rover. The carcass was dragged around for miles, then placed in an acacia tree. Concealed in a blind, the photographer waited for a cheetah to zero in on the dead animal's scent, so he could take a picture of a "cheetah making a kill."

These incidents were reported in *Currents*, the official newsletter of the North American Nature Photography Association. The initial reaction of most wildlife photographers to these incidents might be one of outrage, followed by the feeling, "I'll never have the resources to do something that bizarre." These situations seem so remote and improbable to most photographers that the lessons to be learned from them are usually forgotten.

But what about the unthinking photographer who is determined to get that close-up shot of a fawn? Without regard for the subject or other people, this person moves ahead of fellow photographers, fails to maintain a comfortable working distance, and disturbs the fawn, which gets up and runs off, destroying the photo opportunities for everyone.

Each of us has a set of ethics or rules for proper conduct. Even the most hardened criminals have rules they play by. Yet, some photographers behave unethically. Why? There are probably as many answers to this question as there are photographers acting unethically. To compound the problem, some photographers criticize unethical behavior while their own behavior violates ethics in others' eyes.

In order for all of us to act more ethically, and to stop pointing fingers, we must agree on a set of ethical standards to guide our behavior as wildlife photographers. This code should address three topics: consideration for subjects, image misrepresentation, and consideration for fellow photographers.

CONSIDERATION FOR SUBJECTS

Most wildlife and nature photographers agree that no photograph is worth more than the well-being of their subject. Beyond this point, however, there seems to be a substantial gray area for disagreement.

Certainly, separating the baby hippo from its mother so it could be photographed as it was eaten by crocodiles is a clear-cut case of an ethics violation. But what about baiting the cheetah? Could killing the impala be considered unethical? Whether or not we agree with hunting, impalas are listed as a legal game animal. If killing impalas or other animals is unethical, that issue needs to be addressed separately from the ethics of photography. However, implying the kill was made by the cheetah is unethical. This comes under the topic of image misrepresentation.

One of the most frequent ethical infractions is placing stress on wildlife by approaching too closely. Your subject will let you know when you are too close. When that happens, back off and do not go any closer. Respect your subject's comfort zone. If your subject wants to approach you, let that be the decision of the animal.

A high-powered telephoto lens will permit a comfortable working distance from your subject and allow you to get those frame-filling head shots.

Research and obtain as much information about your subject as possible. Only then will you know when you are putting undue stress on the animal.

Remember: No picture is worth more than the well-being of your subject.

IMAGE MISREPRESENTATION

With the widespread use of wildlife models and the advent of computer imaging, image misrepresentation is becoming more of an issue.

I tend to agree with one person I heard speak on the subject of computer images. He said, "I produce images which could be observed in nature but not photographed because of the limitations of photographic equipment." In my mind, there is no problem with creating such images. It is simply up to us to label these images as computer-generated.

The other issue is wildlife models. For a number of years, many species of animals have been photographed in zoos. More times than not, the images looked as though they had been taken in the wild — and no one said anything. Now, with the increased use of models, there is much debate over their use, and a few magazines even refuse to publish images of captive animals.

Where do we draw the line? Do we no longer publish images of pronghorn photographed in Yellowstone because they are "too tame?" As the number of species on this planet continues to dwindle, we will see more extensive use of captive animals and wildlife models as photographic subjects.

Models obviously are accustomed to being photographed. And, by using captive models as subjects, we relieve potential stress on wild animals As long as wildlife models are properly cared for, there should be no question as to their use.

We should focus on the proper labeling of images, regardless of whether they are taken at a game farm or at the zoo, or produced by a computer.

Wildlife photographers marketing their work might consider this subtle approach to captioning their images. A photograph of a mountain goat taken in the wild might be labeled, "Mountain goat in the Mount Evans Wilderness." An image of a captive goat would simply be labeled, "Mountain goat." In other words, eliminate any location names when captive animals are used and include a brief explanation of the circumstances on your delivery memo.

The bottom line is, don't represent an image as something it is not.

CONSIDERATION FOR PHOTOGRAPHERS

How many times have we had someone walk in front of our camera to get a close-up shot? Certainly, we all have our war stories.

Avoid cutting in front of other photographers. If someone moves in front of you, politely say something like, "Please don't go any closer. You could cause stress to that animal."

Showing consideration to other photographers is simply a matter of respecting others and putting ourself in their place.

CONCLUSION

If you want to use wildlife models or to enhance your images with a computer, all power to you. Simply use some labeling system to outline what has taken place. Show consideration for other photographers. Above all, remember that no image is worth more than the well-being of your subject, whether it is wildlife or some species of plant or mineral.

The last chapter has not been written on wildlife photography ethics. As times change, our ethical values will change, and rightly so. As long as photographic techniques, subject portrayal, and equipment are evolving, the ethics of photography will change too.

The North American Nature Photography Association

Principles of Ethical Field Practices

The North American Nature Photography Association (NANPA) believes that following these practices promotes the well-being of the location, subject, and photographer. Every place, plant, and animal, whether above or below water, is unique, and cumulative impacts occur over time. Therefore, one must always exercise good individual judgment. It is NANPA's belief that these principles will encourage all who participate in the enjoyment of nature to do so in a way that best promotes good stewardship of the resources.

Environmental: Knowledge of Subject and Place

Learn patterns of animal behavior.
Know when not to interfere with animals' life cycles.

Respect the routine needs of animals.
Remember that others will attempt to photograph them, too.

Use appropriate lenses to photograph wild animals.
If an animal shows stress, move back and use a longer lens.

Acquaint yourself with the fragility of the ecosystem.
Stay on trails that are intended to lessen impact.

Social: Knowledge of Rules and Laws

When appropriate, inform managers or other authorities of your presence and purpose.
Help minimize cumulative impacts and maintain safety.

Learn the rules and laws of the location.
If minimum distances exist for approaching wildlife, follow them.

In the absence of management authority, use good judgment.
Treat the wildlife, plants, and places as if you were their guest.

Prepare yourself and your equipment for unexpected events.
Avoid exposing yourself and others to preventable mishaps.

Individual: Expertise and Responsibilities

Treat others courteously.
Ask before joining others already shooting in an area.

Tactfully inform others if you observe them engaging in inappropriate or harmful behavior.
Many people unknowingly endanger themselves and animals.

Report inappropriate behavior to proper authorities.
Don't argue with those who don't care; report them.

Be a good role model, both as a photographer and a citizen.
Educate others by your actions; enhance their understanding.

Printed with permission of the North American Nature Photography Association.

C h a p t e r   2

THE WILDLIFE PHOTOGRAPHY SYSTEM

This chapter explains some tools and techniques that will enhance the wildlife photographer's time in the field and help produce higher quality images. Such basics as exposure, selecting the right camera equipment, and composition have deliberately been avoided. These subjects have been covered thoroughly in a number of good books.

EQUIPMENT

Flash bracket used for close-up work.

FLASH BRACKET

Certain species, such as lizards, frogs, and deer mice, can be difficult to photograph in the wild. One solution is a terrarium, which is nothing more than an aquarium set up to duplicate the subject's natural habitat.

Even in a terrarium, many species are highly active, and a hand-held camera is necessary to follow your subject. To stop the action and provide the lighting for your image, you need a flash. However, a camera-mounted flash results in light bouncing off the glass sides of the terrarium and into the lens, ruining the image.

The solution is a bracket that allows you to mount the flash unit away from the camera body. I prefer using a single flash mounted approximately 30 degrees above the lens. Kirk Enterprises manufactures just the right bracket for this type of photography. The bracket acts as a third hand, allowing me to direct all of my attention to focusing and tripping the shutter.

BACK PACK

Many devices have been designed for carrying photo equipment into the field, including padded pouches, camera cases, lens bags, fanny packs, and vests.

Like many of you, I've used most of these items, and I have positive comments about some of them — and some criticisms. With pouches, cases, and the like, some necessary item would always be back at my car. Often, I would simply sling my tripod-mounted camera over my shoulder and head into the field. I figured if I couldn't carry everything I needed, I might as well travel light. Photo vests were much better, and I still own a couple of them. The problem with vests is they're too hot in the summer, and they are never very comfortable.

I finally found the answer — a photo backpack. After examining the different models, I settled on Lowepro's Photo Trekker AW. It does not hold the back-breaking loads of some of the larger packs, but it's comfortable during an all-day trek in the field. It meets the requirements for airline carry-ons, and it even has a hideaway backpack harness.

This pack holds my 28 mm, 55 mm, 135 mm, 80-200 mm f2.8, 200-400 mm f4 (or your 500 mm f4), two camera bodies, an incident light meter, teleconverter, filters, batteries, and a six-month supply of film. (I'm only kidding about the film.) I have the option of replacing any two of my smaller lenses, along with my light meter, with a thermos of hot coffee, lunch, and a lightweight anorak. I selected the AW model because it has a built-in rain cover for foul weather.

Photo backpack used when carrying equipment into the field.

Johnny Stewart Bird and Animal Caller.

WILDLIFE CALLS

If you have never tried calling wildlife, you're in for some unforgettable moments. Predators are usually difficult to locate and photograph in the wild. When using a wildlife caller, however, you may become the hunted. Many predators respond to calling, including foxes, coyotes, bobcats, and, if you're lucky, even mountain lions.

Some birds also can be called, including turkeys, waterfowl, and owls. Even song birds respond to a screech-owl call.

When calling during nesting season, a few precautions must be observed. Do not keep your subject away from its nest for more than 10 minutes, and allow a 20-minute break between calling sessions. As long as these rules are observed, calling will not threaten birds' nesting success.

For several years, I've used the Johnny Stewart Bird & Animal Caller. It's rugged, portable, and weather-resistant. It even comes with a camouflaged carrying case. Johnny's latest addition is a battery-operated transmitter and receiver. The easy-to-use controls allow you to operate the speaker from up to 200 yards away.

WINDOW MOUNTS

Many wildlife species are easily photographed from a blind. Portable blinds and floating blinds are good, and a length of camouflage cloth, netting, or burlap thrown over your body works well. Even camouflage clothing can work when nothing else is available. However, many photographers overlook using their automobile as a blind. Your car makes a fantastic blind under certain situations.

Using a long lens from the car requires some support to keep the camera from moving. One economical solution is the traditional bean bag. However, bean

The Kirk Multi-Purpose Window Mount turns your vehicle into a four-wheel moving blind.

bags have two major shortcomings. They do not provide enough support for slow shutter speeds, and it is practically impossible to adjust a large zoom lens when it is resting on a bean bag. That leaves only one alternative: a window mount.

I prefer the Kirk multi-purpose window mount. Not only is this unit a first-rate window mount, it also functions as a camera mount for close-up macro photography. Add a focusing rail and you've got a winning macro platform that can be used on the ground or resting on a table. Rubber feet supply stability on rocks and uneven surfaces.

A solid window mount is one of the best investments you will ever make. I cannot begin to count the number of images made from my car window.

Remember to turn off your ignition. Otherwise, engine vibrations will be transmitted through your mount, or bean bag, and into your camera, causing blurred images.

LENS SELECTION

The most common question regarding equipment selection is, "What kind of lens should I buy?"

An almost unlimited number of variables make answering this question next to impossible. The final selection of equipment is very personal, and only one person can make that decision. Several factors should be considered: lens speed, fixed focal length versus zoom, and manual focus versus autofocus.

Is a "fast" lens — one having a wider aperture — really that important? Are zoom capabilities and autofocus important features, or are they something manufacturers contrived just to sell more equipment?

To answer these questions, it's important to understand why some of the images we make don't meet our expectations.

One reason is that most of us attempt to shoot when light levels are too low. The camera's shutter speed is slow, and we wind up with a blurred image because our subject moved as we were taking its picture. The solution is to purchase a faster lens — an f2.8 for example, rather than an f5.6. This should increase your percentage of "keepers."

Photographing small birds flitting about, a weasel nervously searching for food, or a raptor flying directly toward you typically results in a high percentage of throw-aways. This is simply because we are often unable to keep our subject in focus. The answer is autofocus.

A zoom lens will allow you to stand in one spot and crop undesirable elements from your image, thus reducing the need to move around, possibly disturbing an animal. A zoom also permits you to include your subject in a scenic composition in one shot, then, in a matter of seconds, zoom in for a tight portrait shot. This eliminates the need to change lens, a time factor that often results in lost images.

Wildlife photography dictates the use of a telephoto lens. Just how powerful depends on the subject and the shooting conditions. You can get much closer to a Canada Goose in a city park than one in a wildlife refuge. A captive grizzly can be photographed with a 200 mm lens. However, you certainly don't want to be close enough to photograph a wild grizzly using the same lens.

Your lens is your most important piece of equipment. Skimp on the purchase of a camera body, if necessary. Even purchase a slower lens if money is a consideration, such as a 400 mm f5.6, rather than a 400 mm f3.5 or f2.8. However, always purchase top-quality glass. If you later decide wildlife photography is not your cup of tea, it's easy to sell quality equipment.

TECHNIQUES

BACKGROUNDS

The single largest factor separating mediocre photos from fantastic, publishable images is the background.

Many backgrounds are too "busy." They compete with the subject for the viewer's attention. Every element of an image should enhance and reinforce the subject. The simpler the background, the stronger the image.

Several techniques can rescue an otherwise excellent image from an inferior background. The first and easiest method is to reposition your camera a few feet to the right or left, which often will place your subject against a more pleasing background.

Changing lenses can sometimes accomplish the same thing. A 200 mm lens, for example, has a wider field of view than, say, a 500 mm lens. If you were to switch from the 200 mm to the 500 mm, less background would be visible in the image, and distractions might be eliminated.

When using a flash, adjusting the flash level so your subject has about two stops more light than the background will make the background very dark, reducing the "busyness" of the image.

The last technique is to use a wider aperture to reduce the depth of field. This throws the background out of focus, and can often eliminate distracting details.

Contrast between the subject and its background is another important factor — unless you're attempting to portray examples of camouflage. Contrast can be provided using color or tonality. Examples would be red against blue, or light against dark. I generally favor the dramatic effect of a lighter subject against a dark background. However, a Bald Eagle or bighorn certainly looks good against a blue-sky background.

It's easy to get "buck fever" when your camera is pointed at a Boone and Crocket record-book mule deer. At times like these, the background is often the last thing that comes to mind. However, if you want that mule deer to adorn the cover of some magazine, you must pay attention to the background.

Three simple words of advice: Keep it simple!

THE EYES HAVE IT

Have you noticed that some wildlife images contain a tiny white speck in the eye of the subject? It's called catch-light. And you want it when you can get it.

As the subject moves its head to one direction or another, watch for the catch-light to appear. That's the moment you want to take the image. If you're not noticing catch-light when the subject's head moves, try positioning yourself as low as possible so you're shooting upward at an angle. This often produces catch-light when nothing else will.

Generally, you should focus your lens on the eyes of your subject. However, there are exceptions to this rule.

Have you ever taken a head shot of a fox or eagle and noticed how the eyes were in sharp focus but the beak or muzzle was so blurred the image was practically unusable? Sure, we've all done it. The problem was failing to take into account depth of field.

There are a few things we need to understand about depth of field. First, the more lens magnification we use, the shallower the depth of field becomes. Also, the closer we are to our subject, the shallower the depth of field. When shooting close to the subject or with a long lens, we need to be extra aware of depth of field.

The depth of field, or area of focus, extends both in front of and behind the focal point (twice the distance behind the focal point as in front of it). For this reason, when photographing a subject head-on at close range, we should focus about halfway between its eyes and the nose. That way, the animal's entire face should be in focus.

EXPOSURE

Obtaining the correct exposure is the most misunderstood aspect of photography. Most of the time, light meters read pretty accurately and no problems arise. However, that all changes when you begin shooting ptarmigan in their winter plumage nestled in a snowbank, or ducks swimming on a pond rippled by a stiff breeze and reflecting the sun's rays, or a head shot of a bison or moose.

It is important to understand the operation of your light meter. Light meters are designed to render everything 18 percent gray, or middle tone. Obviously, the reds in a scene stay red, and the yellows remain yellow; they're simply rendered an equivalent density of 18 percent gray. In other words, if the colors were reproduced in black and white, they would all look the same — 18% gray.

The secret is knowing what corrections to make and when to make them, based on the "tonality" of the object you metered on. Corrections for wildlife are unnecessary when they occupy only a small part of a scenic image. Corrections under these circumstances are only made for the scene as a whole, such as a snowy winter setting that just happens to contain a flock of Snow Geese. Exposure corrections for wildlife subjects should be considered only when the subject occupies roughly one-third or more of the viewfinder, and the subject is very dark or very light.

If we take our meter reading from a black or white object and do not make a correction, the object will appear 18 percent gray in the final image. For proper exposure when the reading is taken from a black object, reduce the amount of exposure by one-half stop. If the reading is taken from a white subject, open up one to one and a half stops.

For wildlife photography, I often find it more practical to meter on a middle-tone object, and then make the necessary corrections. If you like, you can use an 18 percent gray card for this purpose. In the field, I find it easier to meter on a middle-tone object such as grass or a tree trunk. If your subject is in the shade, make sure whatever object you select for a meter reading is also in the shade. Likewise, select an object in the sun if your subject is in the sun.

When metering from a middle-tone object, blacks will appear black and whites will be white in the final image. However, all of the details in a black or white subject will be lost if we don't make the proper corrections. To correct for a white subject, when metering from a middle-tone object, reduce the exposure by one-half stop. If the subject is bright white and in the sun, then reduce the exposure one full stop. For a black subject, open up one stop, allowing more light to reach the film.

These corrections apply to color slide film. If color print film is used and corrections are not made, many people probably will never know the difference. The reason is that a good lab technician can correct exposure errors as long as the images are not grossly over or underexposed.

Ultimately, you have a decision to make. What kind of feeling do you want the image to portray? Dramatic? Bright and cheerful? Moody?

Let's say you have a dark, back-lit subject, situated against a dark background. If you overexpose to show detail in the subject, you could miss out on a very dramatic image that could be portrayed by simply metering off a middle-tone object and shooting without any corrections.

Understand exposure, and then take control; don't be controlled by a set of arbitrary rules. Remember, you're the artist, and there is no right or wrong way to portray a scene.

SHOOTING UP

Normally, shooting up is illegal. Not so if you're a wildlife photographer. In fact, it's recommended.

Ninety-five percent of all images are taken from the standing position. However, by positioning yourself close to the ground and shooting upward at an angle, you will impart more significance and prominence to the subjects in your images.

Shoot from their level, if not lower.

SUNNY F16 SKY

A blue sky provides a simple and colorful background for your images. Too often, however, blue-sky backgrounds appear washed-out and faded.

The way to eliminate this problem is to use "sunny f16 sky" for your background. "Sunny f16 sky" is the northern sky when viewed looking up at a 45-degree angle. The deepest blue is found in this quadrant of the sky.

The name "sunny f16 sky" is derived from a rule for metering that many photographers remember. On a sunny day, while metering the northern sky at a 45-degree angle with your camera's aperture set to f16, the shutter speed should equal the ISO of your film, or as close to it as possible.

In any case, "sunny f16 sky" makes a good background. Just remember that front lighting — either direct sun or fill flash — will be important.

KNOWING YOUR SUBJECT

RESEARCH

If you intend to photograph a mule deer, your first priority is to locate a mule deer. Learning to think like your subject will help with this task. Where would you find food? What would you do after eating? Are you nocturnal? Put yourself in the deer's position.

A White-tailed Ptarmigan can be lifted from her nest and will show absolutely no alarm or distress. Yet a Red-tailed Hawk may abandon its eggs if approached too closely. If you wait until the eggs have hatched, it will demonstrate a little more tolerance. It's critical that wildlife photographers know this kind of information. Otherwise, we could cause a bird to abandon its nest.

Where is the best place to photograph brown bears feeding on migrating salmon? What is the best time of day to photograph this spectacle? What time of year should a trip be planned?

The only way you can answer these kinds of questions is to thoroughly research your subjects. This book is a good place to start. Beyond this, scientific journals provide a wealth of information.

Search the pages of *The Auk* and the *Journal of Mammalogy*. The American Ornithologists Union publishes a bimonthly series called *The Birds of North America*, featuring a different species each month. Inquire at your local public library and university library concerning these publications and others.

Regardless of the species — Piping Plover or monarch butterfly — the more information you have on your subject, the more successful you will be in locating it and making classic images.

NETWORKING

A wealth of information on wildlife is literally at your fingertips. Use your telephone.

Contact biologists working for state wildlife agencies or the U.S. Fish and Wildlife Service. Many county governments employ biologists, and don't overlook the personnel at state and national parks, as well as national wildlife refuges.

Natural history museums have a wealth of research information and scientists who can answer your questions. Universities conduct research year-round. Ask intelligent questions. If the person you speak with is unable to answer your questions, ask for someone who can.

Local Audubon clubs and ornithology organizations are good sources of information concerning bird species. CompuServe, America On Line, and the Internet provide unlimited contacts and resources.

Do not limit your queries to local contacts. New York and California are only as far away as your telephone. Directory assistance can help you with phone numbers.

When someone has performed "above and beyond the call of duty," follow up with a letter of thanks, and maybe even a photo. You may make a lasting friend.

PHOTOGRAPHING NESTING BIRDS

It's especially important to know your subject when photographing nesting birds.

Most birds will abandon their nests during the incubation phase if repeatedly disturbed. Many show more tolerance after their eggs have hatched. Personally, I feel the amount of stress birds experience is probably the same during incubation and during the nestling phase; they simply are more willing to endure the stress to protect their nestlings.

Do we, as humans, have the right to inflict high levels of stress on another species? I would have to say no. But nest photography is not a black-and-white issue. Among the members of a highly sensitive species, certain individuals are more tolerant than others. Likewise, to say all members of a more tolerant species can be photographed without any negative impacts would be unfair to shy and high-strung individuals. Only through observing our subject's behavior are we able to detect these characteristics. And, only then can we determine which individuals will allow access to this very private and sensitive moment in their lives.

Let us restrict nest photography to individual birds that show little concern over human presence, and, even then, let us exercise extreme care.

The following guidelines will help us insure the well-being of our feathered brothers and sisters:

1) Conduct photo sessions after the young have hatched, not before.

2) Erect your blind some distance away from the nest. Gradually move it into position over a period of two or three days.

3) Employ a remotely operated camera for sensitive individuals that will not accept the presence of a blind. Move a "dummy setup" into position over a period of several days before shooting with the real camera.

4) Abandon all efforts the moment any nervous behavior is detected.

5) Never cut or break distracting plants and branches. Tie them out of the way, and, after concluding your photo session, allow the plants to go back into position and provide cover for the nest.

GETTING CLOSE TO WILDLIFE — THE GRAZING APPROACH

In order to get tight, close-up shots of wildlife, you need to be close to your subject. One way is to employ a blind. However, this tends to be time-consuming. Two other methods can yield the same results: approach your subject, or allow your subject to approach you.

The latter is easier than it would appear. Determine the direction your subject is traveling, then place yourself in a position that will allow the subject to pass close by. I often use this method for photographing predators, although it can be used with other species.

When your subject is a member of the deer or sheep families, approaching it usually proves more satisfactory. Getting close to most wild animals requires finesse. I have taken the old "lost wallet" routine and refined it into a technique I call the "grazing approach."

This technique evolved from observing herds of wapiti. Within the herds, individual animals were constantly moving as they grazed. Yet it appeared the herd stayed in one general area. Wrong! The whole herd was slowly advancing in the direction of ungrazed areas. Their overall direction went unnoticed amid all the milling around. Adopting this approach, you can often walk quite close to your quarry.

The first step is to locate the subject. As you search, remain in the open. Avoid a walking stride. Take time to smell the roses. Simply stroll along, stopping often, and scrutinize the area with your binoculars. Your subject will be aware of your presence long before you are aware of it. The moment you attempt a stealthy approach, you send up a red flag. At that moment, you become a predator in your subject's mind. If you're with someone, it's all right to talk. You don't have to whisper; just keep the volume low. Avoid fast or sudden movements.

The unexpected is what causes most animals to flee. If your subject can anticipate your actions and determine that you present no threat, it usually will accept your presence.

When you sight your subject, it is not uncommon for it to run off. Don't worry. In all likelihood, it will not go very far. Continue what you've already been doing up to this point.

After the subject has settled down and begun to accept your presence, it is critical that you remain where the animal can see you at all times. It's all right to occasionally look at the subject, but avoid staring. Do not attempt to approach any closer. Sit down, mill about, even read a book, but remain where you are for at least four or five minutes.

Now you can begin your approach. Never walk directly toward the subject. Pick a direction that will take you past the animal. After going some distance past, turn around and walk past your subject again, altering your direction of travel so you pass a few feet closer. Continue this zigzagging until you are within comfortable photographic range.

During the zigzag approach, act as if you were grazing. This is critical. Don't worry, it won't be necessary to eat any grass, or even to pretend. The point is to go slow, stop often, mill about, and even rest on the ground a minute or two.

Watch for any change in the subject's behavior — for example, if it stops eating or looks up, or if the ears suddenly stand erect. The moment you see any change, FREEZE!

After your subject has learned to accept your presence, do not be surprised if it decides to approach you. One time in Denali National Park, after working a Dall ram for three or four hours, he walked up to me, stood no more than five feet away, and looked me in the eye before turning and walking away. In Rocky Mountain National Park, a mule deer lay down and went to sleep while I was photographing him. One sunny day on Mount Evans, I was taking five when a mountain goat walked across the slopes and lay down next to me.

When you're using the grazing approach, camouflage is not necessary. But avoid wearing light colors, such as white or yellow. Darker reds, browns, greens, and blues are fine — even purple is OK for you purple lovers.

Finally, it's important to remember that, regardless of any gentle actions the subject may display, you are working with a wild animal. Always exercise caution.

NATIONAL WILDLIFE REFUGES

The National Wildlife Refuge system, containing more than 90 million acres of wildlife habitat, stretches from the Florida Keys to Alaska, plus Puerto Rico and Hawaii. Refuges provide habitat for more than 60 endangered species.

You may have to work a little harder in a wildlife refuge for that image you want, but few other places provide the variety and sheer numbers of wildlife as refuges do.

It's always good practice for wildlife photographers to inform refuge personnel of their intentions. This should be your first priority upon arriving. However, don't drive up and expect the refuge staff to direct you to the closest endangered species and its nest.

If you're interested in photographing an endangered species, or one that's particularly sensitive, call ahead to inform the staff about what you would like to accomplish. You might consider mailing a brief "bio," letters of recommendation, or a list of references. Make sure these items relate to your qualifications for photographing wildlife conscientiously. They're really not interested in learning why you're qualified to dip ice cream at Baskin-Robbins.

Most refuges allow individuals to erect a temporary blind. However, permission is always granted on a case-by-case basis.

Refuge personnel generally are able to share information that can greatly assist you in your endeavors. Don't hesitate to ask questions. Just make sure you ask intelligent questions.

With more than 450 refuges nationwide, there's almost sure to be a refuge near you. Given all of the pressures on today's national parks, wildlife refuges are "sleepers" whose time has come.

CREATING ART

Examine where you are, photographically speaking. Are you a portrait photographer? Do you only photograph wildlife in scenic surroundings? Or, does your work reflect a balance between these two styles? What about lighting? Background? Could your work stand improvement? If so, where?

Study the paintings of the old masters or contemporary artists. When you find something you like, begin experimenting. Explore ways of incorporating these new findings into your photographs.

Explore the grain qualities of high-speed film. Experiment as you "push" your regular film by seven or eight stops. Examine the effects of different filters. Probe the realms of double exposures and slow shutter speeds.

Develop a fresh, new style. After you have perfected it, try something different. Never be satisfied with status quo. Constantly stretch your personal boundaries.

Learn the difference between making an image and taking an image. Begin creating art. Push the limits!

"Spirit Wolf". This double exposure of the gray wolf and caribou was taken in Alaska.

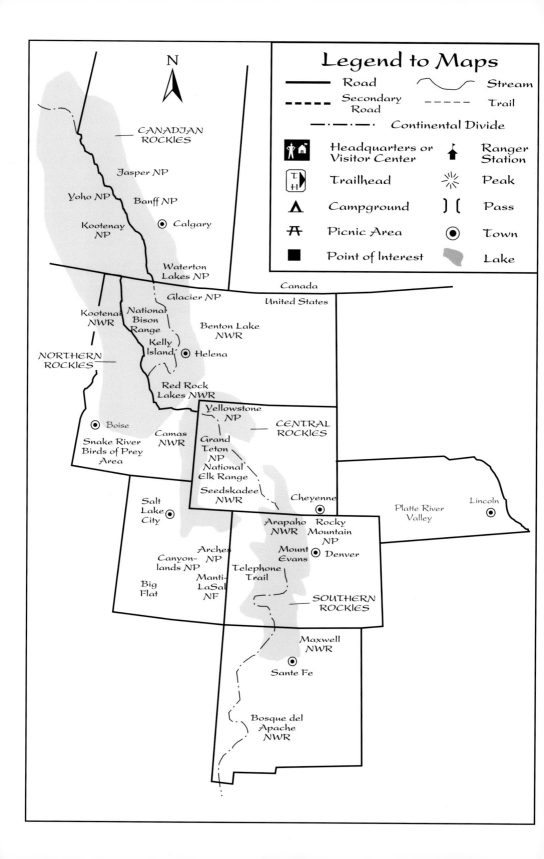

Chapter 3

REGIONS OF THE ROCKIES
The Best Wildlife Photography Locations

The Rocky Mountains extend from north-central New Mexico northward through western Canada and into the state of Alaska. This chapter spotlights some of the best wildlife photography locations within the Rockies and adjacent areas. Each of the 28 locations described below offers consistent opportunities to photograph wildlife that is reasonably approachable.

Use this chapter to see which species you may find in a given location, and how to get there. Then turn to Chapter 4 for detailed information on each species you hope to photograph. The information in these two chapters will help you make the most of the photography experience.

Within the United States, the Rocky Mountains are divided into three physiographic provinces: the Northern, Central, and Southern Rocky Mountains. In Canada, the range is called the Canadian Rockies.

Key to Animal Symbols

Snowshoe Hare	Moose	Red-tailed Hawk
Beaver	Bighorn Sheep	Golden/Bald Eagle
Fox Squirrel	Mountain Goat	Ptarmigan
Red Squirrel	Bison	Sharp-tailed Grouse
Coyote	Great Blue Heron	Ring-necked Pheasant
Gray Wolf	Sandhill Crane	Mourning Dove
Red Fox	Hooded Merganser	Great Horned Owl
Grizzly Bear	Northern Pintail	Hummingbird
Weasel	Wood Duck	Raven
Skunk	Trumpeter Swan	Black-billed Magpie
Elk	Canada Goose	Songbird
Mule Deer or Whitetail Deer		

Southern Rocky Mountains

The Southern Rockies, rich with wildlife photography opportunities, contain some of the best locations in the United States to photograph mule deer, bighorn sheep, mountain goats, and wapiti.

This portion of the Rocky Mountains extends from the Sangre de Cristo Mountains in north-central New Mexico to the Laramie Mountains, immediately south of Casper, Wyoming.

COLORADO

ARAPAHO NATIONAL WILDLIFE REFUGE

Arapaho National Wildlife Refuge, located in a 1,500-square-mile intermountain glacial basin known as North Park, is home to pronghorn, mule deer, elk, and moose, as well as a variety of birds and small mammals.

LOCATION — 8 miles south of Walden

OPEN — All year (daylight hours)

BEST TIME TO VISIT — Late spring through fall (peak waterfowl migration in late May)

ECOSYSTEMS — Sagebrush, prairie wetland, willow riparian

ADMINISTRATION — U.S. Fish & Wildlife Service

KEY SPECIES — Moose, pronghorn, white-tailed prairie dog, waterfowl, shore birds.

Moose and elk can be found among the willows along the Illinois River, while pronghorn and mule deer prefer the sagebrush country. A 6-mile Self-Guided Auto Tour takes the visitor through a series of ponds and wetland habitats, providing photo opportunities for several species of waterfowl and wading birds, including American Avocets, Common Snipe, Canada Geese, Mallards, Gadwall, Northern Pintails, American Wigeons, Northern Shovelers, and Green-winged, Blue-winged, and Cinnamon Teal. White-tailed prairie dogs and Richardson's ground squirrels also can be photographed from the auto-tour road.

The refuge also hosts a Black-crowned Night Heron rookery. In the winter, Rosy Finches flock to bird feeders around the refuge office.

In addition to the Self-Guided Auto Tour, several refuge roads are accessible to photographers. Explore these roads for additional photo opportunities.

Stop by the refuge headquarters, open 8 a.m. to 4:30 p.m. on weekdays, and identify yourself as a wildlife photographer. The refuge personnel can be very helpful. The Self-Guided Auto Tour is located 3 miles south of Walden along State Highway 125, on the west side of the highway. Headquarters is another 4 miles south. Turn east at the refuge entrance onto a gravel road, and follow the signs to headquarters.

For information, contact Arapaho National Wildlife Refuge (970-723-8202).

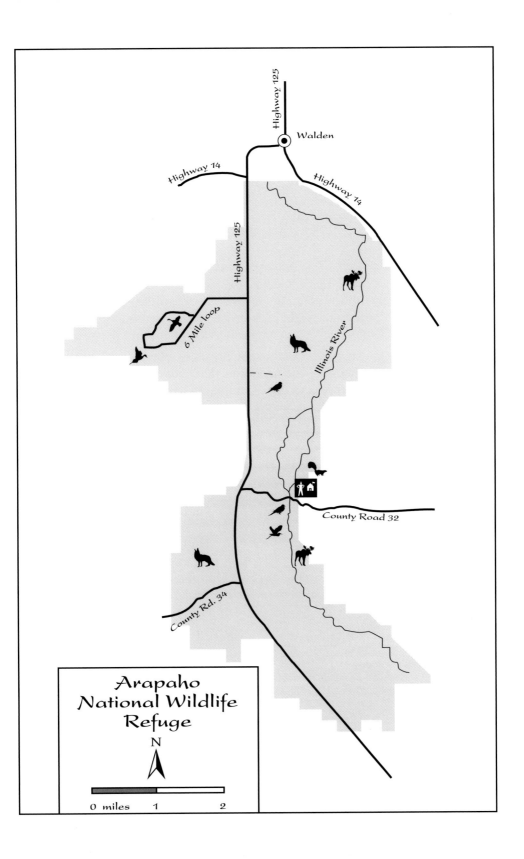

Highway 125

Walden

Highway 14

Highway 14

Highway 125

6 Mile loop

Illinois River

County Road 32

County Rd. 34

Arapaho
National Wildlife
Refuge

N

0 miles   1   2

MOUNT EVANS, COLORADO

One of the most photogenic locations in Colorado, Mount Evans has it all: wild flowers, mountain scenics, 2,000-year-old gnarled bristlecone pines, pikas, yellow-bellied marmots, bighorn sheep, and mountain goats.

LOCATION – 10 miles south of Idaho Springs

OPEN – Memorial Day to Labor Day

BEST TIME TO VISIT – Spring through fall

ECOSYSTEMS – Alpine tundra

ADMINISTRATION – U.S. Forest Service

KEY SPECIES – Mountain goat, bighorn sheep

After passing the Mount Goliath Natural Area (marked with interpretive signs), the road opens onto the tundra. Begin looking for white specks among the rocky slopes ahead and to the right of the road. These turn into mountain goats as you get closer. Goats can be anywhere between here and the summit.

In the summer, bighorn sheep and mountain goats often greet visitors along the road in this area, begging for handouts. After leaving Summit Lake, continue as if you were driving to the summit. Just before reaching the first switchback, stop and park. Look down the hillside to the left. Mountain goats often frequent this area. It is also a good location for photographing pika and yellow-bellied marmots.

Wildflowers bloom along the slopes of Mount Evans.

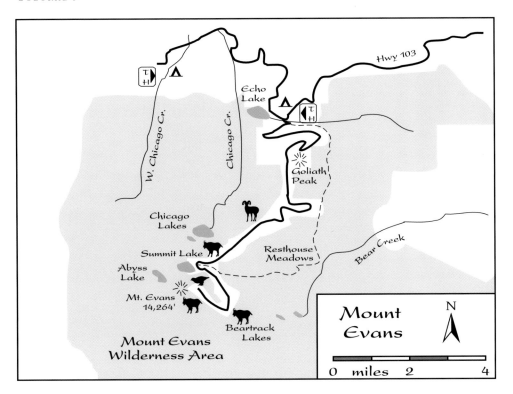

Due to heavy winter snows, the road past Echo Lake is only open from Memorial Day to Labor Day. To reach Mount Evans from Idaho Springs, take State Highway 103. Just past Echo Lake, turn right onto State Highway 5, the highest paved road in the United States. This takes you to the summit.

For additional information or a weather update, contact the U.S. Forest Service in Idaho Springs (303-567-2901).

ROCKY MOUNTAIN NATIONAL PARK

Rocky Mountain National Park, one-third of which is above timberline, encompasses many worlds. From verdant alpine valleys to glistening lakes and streams, the park holds many surprises for its visitors. The park is unsurpassed for photo opportunities for bugling wapiti, mature mule deer bucks, and full-curl bighorn rams, plus a relatively new reintroduction, the moose.

LOCATION – 65 miles northwest of Denver

OPEN – All year

BEST TIME TO VISIT – All Year

ECOSYSTEMS – Ponderosa, spruce-fir, alpine tundra

ADMINISTRATION – National Park Service

KEY SPECIES – Mule deer, wapiti, moose, bighorn sheep, pika, small mammals, birds

Hallet Peak

The time to photograph bugling wapiti is September, from Labor Day until the end of the month. During the rut, wapiti can be photographed on the east side of the park in Horseshoe and Moraine Parks, Upper Beaver Meadows, and occasionally in Hollowell Park and Sprague Lake. On the west side, wapiti sometimes gather in open clearings along the first 5 miles of park road.

The best photo location is along the Cub Lake Trail in Moraine Park. During the wapiti rut, off-trail travel is prohibited in this area, as well as in Horseshoe Park and Upper Beaver Meadows, between the hours of 5 p.m. and 7 a.m. This should not present any problems for photographers, because wapiti are often on the trail.

The best place to photograph mule deer is along Beaver Creek and the south side of Deer Mountain. To photograph deer along Beaver Creek, enter the park at the Beaver Meadows Entrance Station. After going 0.25 mile, turn left onto Bear Lake Road. Park at the first pull-off. The creek runs from west to east. Hike east, parallel to the creek. After hiking about a mile, you will see several park service buildings. If you have not located deer by now, go back and look for deer along the road between the park headquarters and Deer Ridge Junction. Another good location is along Bear Lake Road, between U.S. 36 and the Moraine Park Museum.

For moose, search the willows along U.S. 34 on the west side of the park, between the Timber Creek Campground and the Onahu Creek Trailhead.

Beginning in late May and continuing through the summer, bighorn ewes can be photographed as they lead their newborn lambs daily into Horseshoe Park to graze and to obtain minerals by eating soil. In early November, rams make their appearance along the Fall River Road, just outside the Fall River Entrance Station. This area is privately owned. Although photographs must be taken from the road, the photographic opportunities are excellent.

The best summer location in Colorado to photograph White-tailed Ptarmigan is along Trail Ridge Road. A multiple-car pull-off lies 2.3 miles west of Rainbow Curve. Across the road, on the north side, you will find the ptarmigan. They may be along the top of the ridge to the left, down by the willows on the right, near the base of the mountain about a mile to the north, or anywhere between.

Another location to search for ptarmigan is west of the Alpine Visitor Center.

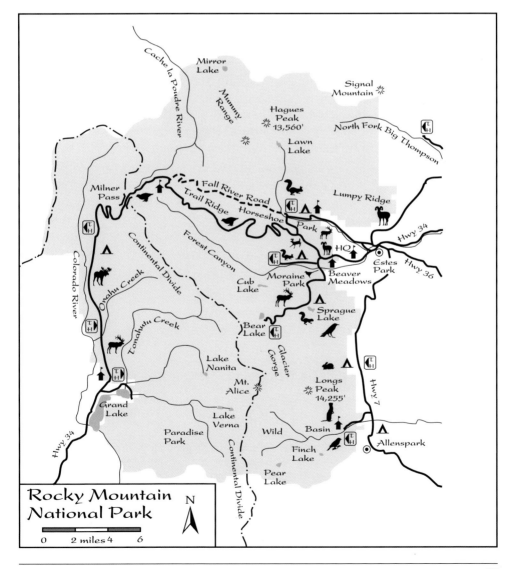

Rocky Mountain
National Park

N

0   2 miles 4   6

Search the tundra along both sides of Trail Ridge Road between Medicine Bow Curve and where the road enters treeline on its way to Milner Pass. Please treat the tundra with respect. One careless footstep can destroy what took nature a century to grow.

Pika and yellow-bellied marmots also may be photographed in the tundra along Trail Ridge Road. One of the better locations for photographing pika is one mile west of the Rock Cut. Park in the pull-off along the north side of the road. Pika can be photographed in the talus slopes extending down the mountain south of the road. Pull-offs at Many Parks Curve, Rainbow Curve, and Farview Curve are great locations to photograph Steller's Jays, Gray Jays, Clark's Nutcrackers, golden-mantled ground squirrels, and chipmunks, where they beg for visitor handouts.

Several bird species can be photographed in the Endovalley Picnic Area, including Evening Grosbeaks, Cassin's Finches, and Downey and Hairy Woodpeckers. Abert's squirrels often frequent the picnic tables near the Lawn Lake Trailhead, looking for handouts. During May and June the aspen groves across the road from this picnic area are alive with cavity nesters, including Mountain Bluebirds, House Wrens, Red-naped Sapsuckers, Tree Swallows and Violet-green Swallows. Walk the trail around Sprague Lake and you are sure to find opportunities to photograph red squirrels.

Only an hour and a half from Denver, Rocky Mountain National Park can be reached by traveling north along Interstate 25 to U.S. 36 westbound. Take U.S. 36 through Boulder and Lyons to Estes Park, the eastern gateway to the park. Reach the west end of the park by taking U.S. 34 through Grand Lake; this road becomes Trail Ridge Road in the park. Trail Ridge Road is usually open from Memorial Day until mid-October.

If your trip to Rocky takes you through the town of Lyons, be sure to stop at the Sunrise Cafe. Their breakfasts are mouth-watering, including my favorite — biscuits and gravy.

For additional information, contact Rocky Mountain National Park (970-586-1399

TELEPHONE TRAIL, UNCOMPAHGRE NATIONAL FOREST

Cavity nesters flock to the old-growth aspen and ponderosa pine forests along the Telephone Trail, a 3-mile trail beginning at the Carson Hole Picnic Area.

LOCATION — 30 miles south of Grand Junction

OPEN — All year

BEST TIME TO VISIT — May through July

ECOSYSTEMS — Aspen, ponderosa

ADMINISTRATION — U.S. Forest Service

KEY SPECIES — Cavity-nesting bird

View from canyon rim along Telephone Trail

Species using this area include Western Bluebirds, Mountain Chickadees, White-breasted and Pygmy Nuthatches, Northern Flickers, Hairy Woodpeckers, Flammulated Owls, Violet-green Swallows, Williamson's Sapsuckers, and Red-naped Sapsuckers.

Beaver ponds are located along La Fair Creek.

To reach this area from Grand Junction drive south on U.S. 50. At Whitewater, turn right and follow State Highway 141 to Forest Road 402. Turn left and go 10 miles to the Carson Hole Picnic Area.

For additional information, contact the U.S. Forest Service (970-242-8211).

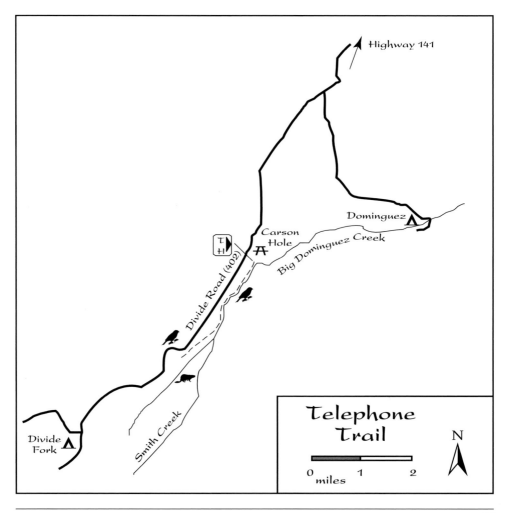

Bosque marsh lands.

NEW MEXICO

BOSQUE DEL APACHE NATIONAL WILDLIFE REFUGE

Bosque del Apache National Wildlife Refuge, embracing over 57,000 acres of marsh, grasslands, and desert uplands, straddles the Rio Grande in the shadow of the Magdalena Mountains of south-central New Mexico. The refuge is a bird photographer's paradise.

LOCATION — 95 miles south of Albuquerque

OPEN — All year (one hour before sunrise to one hour after sunet)

BEST TIME TO VISIT — November through February

ECOSYSTEMS — Desert uplands, wetlands, cottonwood

ADMINISTRATION — U.S. Fish & Wildlife Service

KEY SPECIES — Sandhill Crane, Whooping Crane, Snow Goose

Bosque del Apache is best known for opportunities to photograph Sandhill Cranes and large concentrations of waterfowl (Snow, Canada, and Ross' Geese, Mallard, Northern Pintail, Redhead, etc.) from late November through February. These birds' numbers reach a peak during mid-December.

Many other bird species can be photographed at various times throughout the year, including American Avocets, Common Yellowthroats, Mountain

Chickadees, Great Blue Herons, Turkeys, Gambel's Quail, Roadrunners, and Red-tailed Hawks. Late spring and early summer are the best times to photograph these species.

In the winter, up to a dozen Bald Eagles can often be observed in the cottonwood trees along the river. Mule deer, porcupines, and beaver often provide the patient photographer with images.

Most species of birds are best photographed from your car along the 15-mile

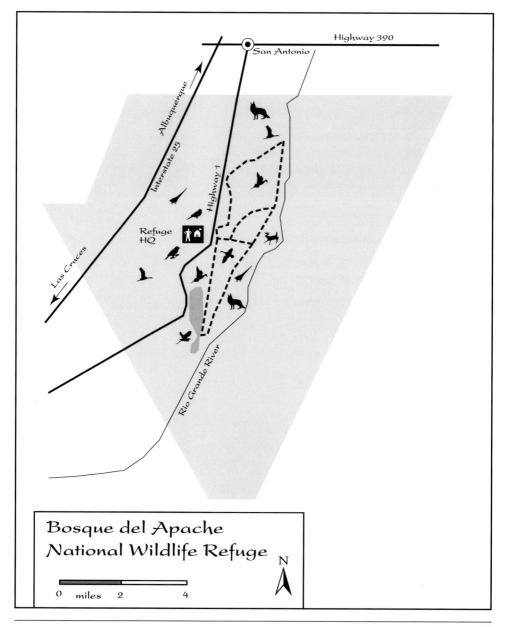

Auto Tour. It is best if you stay in your car while on the loop. If you get out, you may ruin your photo opportunities, as well as those of everyone near you. Sandhill cranes are best photographed at dawn and sunset. With a permit, you will be allowed to set up a portable blind in the backcountry. Take advantage of this — it will pay dividends.

Upon arriving at the refuge, stop by headquarters, introduce yourself, and share your intentions. Refuge personnel will assist you in any way possible.

CAUTION: The refuge is home to the western diamondback rattlesnake. Watch where you place your feet.

To reach the refuge from Albuquerque, drive 90 miles south on Interstate 25. Take Exit 139 at San Antonio, then go east along U.S. 380 for 0.5 mile. Turn right and go south along State Highway 1 for 8 miles to the refuge. For additional information, call 505-835-1828.

MAXWELL NATIONAL WILDLIFE REFUGE

Maxwell National Wildlife Refuge, established in 1966 on the open prairies and farmlands of northeastern New Mexico, manages three water-storage impoundments that help attract more than 20,000 migrating ducks and geese each year.

LOCATION — 27 miles south of Raton

OPEN — All year (24 hours)

BEST TIME TO VISIT — December through May

ECOSYSTEMS — Prairie, lake

ADMINISTRATION — U.S. Fish & Wildlife Service

KEY SPECIES — Waterfowl, shore birds, Burrowing Owls, black-tailed prairie dogs

Northern vista from Lake 13.

On the refuge, burrowing owls nest in holes excavated by black-tailed prairie dogs in a 50-acre prairie dog town. American Avocets, Black-billed Magpies, Swainson's Hawks, Northern Harriers, and Ring-necked Pheasants also find the 3,600-acre refuge suitable for rearing their young. Golden Eagles are year-round residents. Over a dozen species of waterfowl migrate through the area in the fall, including Mallards, Northern Pintails, and Redheads.

Between November and March, some 60 Bald Eagles can be observed. Red-tailed Hawks, Great Blue Herons, and Mountain Bluebirds can be found in season. Coyotes are always on the prowl, as are long-tailed weasels. In the winter, more than 10,000 Canada Geese are attracted to the refuge.

Seven miles of roads provide easy access to various parts of the refuge. Stop at headquarters to get acquainted and inform the staff of your intentions. They will help you in any way possible. If your plans include erecting a portable blind, permission to do so is granted on a case-by-case basis.

From the town of Maxwell, go northwest 0.8 miles along State Highway 445 from its intersection with Interstate 25. Turn west and follow State Highway 505 to the refuge, a distance of 2.5 miles. For additional information, call 505-375-2331.

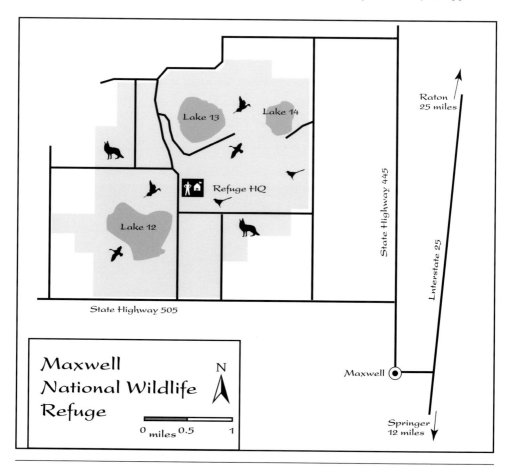

UTAH

ARCHES AND CANYONLANDS NATIONAL PARKS

Island in the Sky District, Canyonlands National Park.

Dark Angel! Fiery Furnace! Devils Garden! Arches National Park has unwelcome names, but the landscape continues to draw individuals into its grasp — at least those with a spirit of adventure. Arches National Park is Edward Abbey country.

Canyonlands National Park is an immense wilderness of rock mesas, fins, spires, arches, and hundreds of colorful canyons.

LOCATION – *Arches:* 5.1 miles north of Moab
Canyonlands: 15 miles southwest of Moab

OPEN – All year

BEST TIME TO VISIT – September through December

ECOSYSTEMS – Pinon-juniper forests, desert

ADMINISTRATION – National Park Service

KEY SPECIES – Desert bighorn, reptiles

Many species of wildlife are at home in the high-desert habitat of these parks. These are two of the few places where desert bighorn sheep can be photographed with some degree of certainty. Desert bighorns concentrate on the remote White Rim in Canyonlands National Park's Island In The Sky District, during the "rut" in October and November. A more accessible location for fall

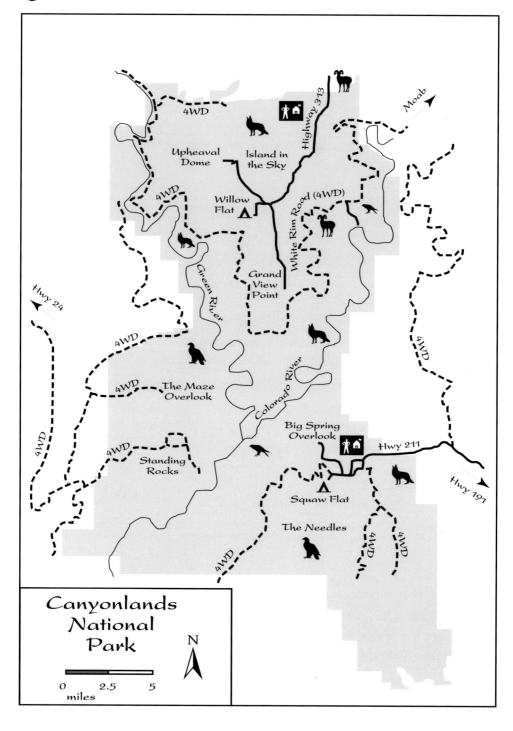

Moab

4WD

Highway 313

Upheaval
Dome

Island in
the Sky

Hwy 24

4WD

Willow
Flat

White Rim Road (4WD)

Green River

Grand
View
Point

4WD

4WD

4WD

The Maze
Overlook

Colorado River

4WD

4WD

Big Spring
Overlook

Hwy 211

4WD

4WD

Standing
Rocks

Squaw Flat

Hwy 191

The Needles

4WD

4WD

4WD

Canyonlands National Park

N

0   2.5   5
miles

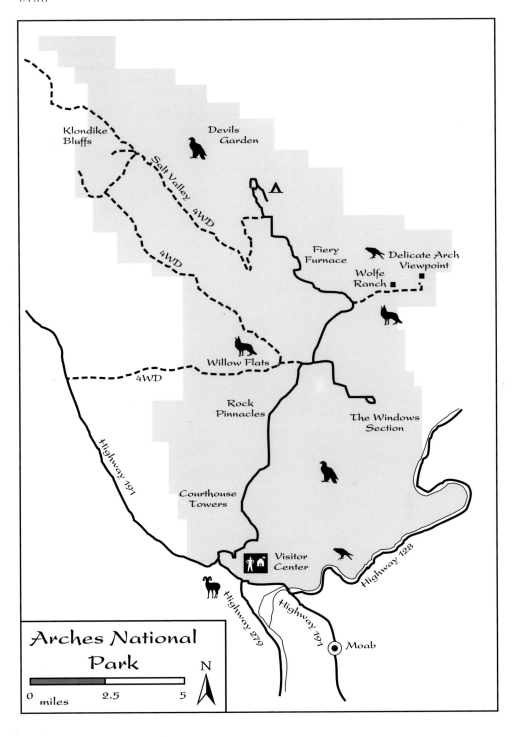

Klondike
Bluffs

Devils
Garden

Salt Valley 4WD

4WD

Fiery
Furnace

Delicate Arch
Viewpoint

Wolfe
Ranch

Willow Flats

4WD

Rock
Pinnacles

The Windows
Section

Courthouse
Towers

Highway 191

Visitor
Center

Highway 128

Highway 279

Highway 191

Moab

Arches National
Park

N

0   miles   2.5   5

View of the La Sal Mountains from Delicate Arch, Arches National Park.

bighorn photography is along U.S. 191, near its junction with State Highway 313, about 9 miles north of Moab, and along State Highway 279, which intersects U.S. 191 about 3 miles north of Moab.

Sheep sometimes frequent the rocks along U.S. 191 near the entrance to Arches National Park between September and December. Another fall location is along State Highway 128, between Moab and Cisco. Look for sheep among the rocks along the north side of the Colorado River.

Summers in this area provide opportunities to photograph an amazing variety of reptiles: eastern fence lizard, western whiptail, collared lizard, short-horned lizard, western gopher snake, corn snake, milksnake, and the poisonous midget-faded rattlesnake.

Other species found in the area include mule deer, bobcat, coyote, kit fox, ringtail, packrats, kangaroo rats, Pinyon Jays, Mountain Bluebirds, Red-tailed Hawks, and Golden Eagles.

Two great rivers, the Colorado and the Green, have carved the Canyonlands National Park into three diverse regions: the Maze, the Needles, and Island in the Sky. Island in the Sky can be reached via State Highway 313, which leaves U.S. 191 about 12 miles north of Moab. To reach the Maze, take the two- and four-wheel drive roads from State Highway 24 or 95. The Needles can be reached via State Highway 211, which leaves U.S. 191 about 44 miles south of Moab.

Arches National Park can be reached from Moab by going north along U.S. 191 for 6 miles to the park entrance.

For more information, contact Arches National Park (801-259-8161) or Canyonlands National Park (801-259-7164).

MANTI-LA SAL NATIONAL FOREST

The La Sal Loop, a scenic 37-mile road traversing desert, juniper, aspen, riparian, and mountain habitats, offers the opportunity to photograph a variety of birds, mammals, and reptiles.

LOCATION — 8 miles south of Moab

OPEN — All year

BEST TIME TO VISIT — Spring through fall (road occasionally closed in winter)

ECOSYSTEMS — Desert shrub, juniper, aspen, spruce-fir

ADMINISTRATION — U.S. Forest Service

KEY SPECIES — Lizards, pika

To reach the loop from Moab, go south 7 miles on U.S. 191, then turn left. Go 0.5 miles to the La Sal Loop road, turn right, and begin the loop.

Your first stop should be the Brumley Creek area, at the Manti-La Sal National

Brumley Creek lizard viewing area.

Forest boundary. After driving 1.5 miles on the loop road, turn left onto the Kens Lake Road. Go 2.5 miles to the Brumley Creek area. Photograph short-horned, northern side-blotched, and collared lizards along the rock face of Brumley Ridge. Although nocturnal and very secretive, ringtails inhabit the area along Brumley Creek.

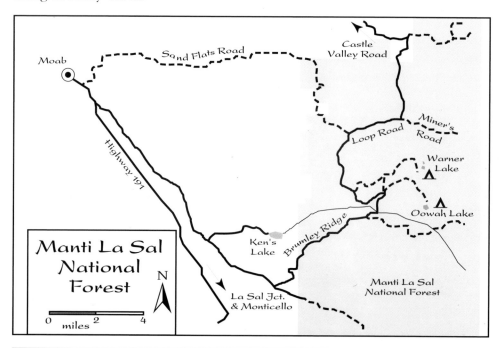

To reach a pika viewing site, turn right approximately 15 miles after beginning the loop onto Forest Road 063 (Warner Lake road). Go 5.4 miles to the Warner Campground. Take either the Burro Pass Trail (located at the Picnic & Day Use Area) or the Miner's Basin Trail (accessed from the campground check-in area) to a rock slide. Look and listen for pikas.

Mule deer are likely to be observed in many places along the loop, which comes to an end at its junction with State Highway 128.

CAUTION: This area is home to the midget faded rattlesnake. During summer this snake is nocturnal.

For additional information, contact the Moab Ranger District of the Manti-La Sal National Forest (801-259-7155).

BIG FLAT, FISHLAKE NATIONAL FOREST

Big Flat, a large mountain meadow encircled by fir, aspen, and Englemann spruce, is situated in the Tushar Mountains in the Fishlake National Forest. This is the best summer location in Utah for photographing mule deer bucks.

LOCATION – 23 miles east of Beaver

OPEN – June through October

BEST TIME TO VISIT – June through August

ECOSYSTEMS – Spruce-fir, aspen

ADMINISTRATION – U.S. Forest Service

KEY SPECIES – Mule deer

Big Flat, Fishlake National Forest.

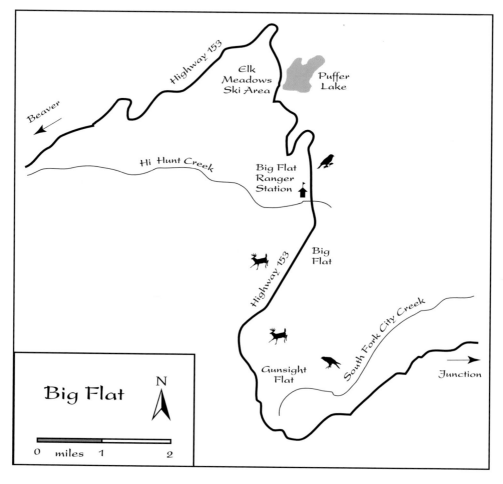

Although they are wild, most of the deer are relatively tame, making photography easy. Other species here include coyotes, wapiti, various hawks, Western Meadowlarks, Horned Larks, Mountain Bluebirds, and Golden Eagles.

To reach Big Flat, drive east from Beaver along State Road 153 for approximately 20 miles. A few miles past Puffer Lake, the forest gives way to a large meadow. A portion of the meadow is enclosed by a split-rail fence. This is the beginning of Big Flat, which continues about 4 miles to Gunsight Flat.

Stop at the U.S. Forest Service station near the split-rail-fenced meadow. The staff can advise you of any significant sightings, such as newborn fawns. For additional information, call the Beaver Ranger District of Fishlake National Forest (801-438-2436).

Central Rocky Mountains

Included within this region is Yellowstone National Park, one of the top wildlife photography locations in North America. The Central Rockies encompass the area from the Wasatch Mountains of northern Utah to the Beartooth Mountains of southern Montana. For the purpose of this book, the Wyoming Basin — including parts of central Wyoming and northwestern Colorado — is also included, as is the Platte River Valley.

NEBRASKA

PLATTE RIVER VALLEY

Each spring, 80 percent of the world's Sandhill Crane population — approximately 500,000 birds — congregates along the Platte River Valley before continuing the northward migration.

LOCATION – Platte Valley (between Lexington and Grand Island)

OPEN – All year

BEST TIME TO VISIT – March through early April for cranes; early March is best for waterfowl

ECOSYSTEMS – Agricultural, marshes, river bottom

ADMINISTRATION – Various agencies

KEY SPECIES – Sandhill Crane, waterfowl

Sunset along the Platte River.

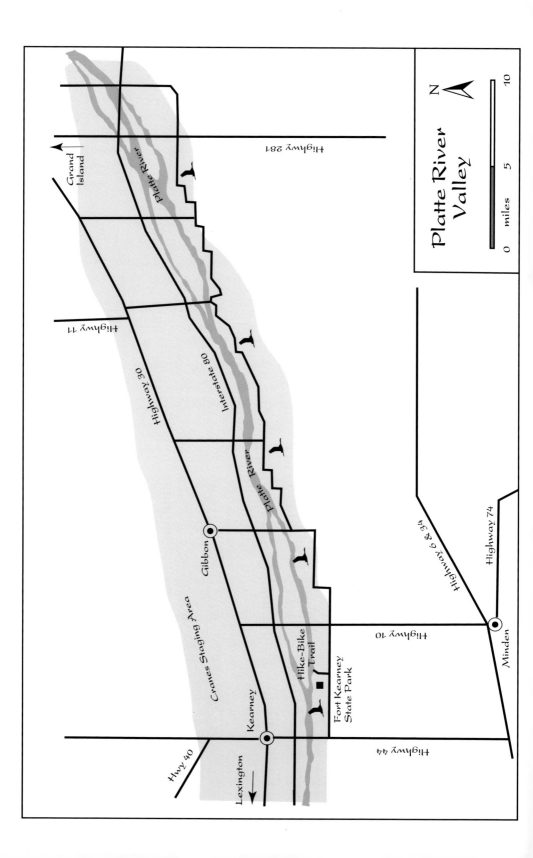

Platte River
Valley

N

0   miles   5   10

In addition, more than 300 species of migratory birds, including 9 million ducks and geese, use the area for migratory resting, over-wintering, nesting, or permanent residence. This includes the entire mid-continent flock of greater White-fronted Geese, as well as six federally endangered or threatened species: the Bald Eagle, Peregrine Falcon, Whooping Crane, Piping Plover, Eskimo Curlew, and Least Tern.

The largest concentrations of Sandhill Cranes occur between Lexington and Grand Island. Most land where Sandhill Cranes are observed is privately owned. Obtain permission from the landowner before erecting any type of photo blind.

Large numbers of Snow, White-fronted, and Canada Geese, can be photographed at several Waterfowl Production Areas (WPA) in the area. One that I recommend is Funk Lagoon WPA. It is located 1 mile east and 3 miles north of the community of Funk.

Fort Kearney State Historical Park, south of Kearney, has been designated the Crane Watch Headquarters. Observation blinds — great for observation, but not ideally suited for photography — are operated by the National Audubon Society and the Platte River Whooping Crane Trust. Both the Kearney and Grand Island visitors' bureaus can supply information on lodging, restaurants, and local points of interest. (See Appendix I.)

WYOMING

GRAND TETON NATIONAL PARK

The Teton skyline, towering almost a mile and a half above Jackson Hole, is one of the most impressive mountain panoramas in North America.

LOCATION – Western Wyoming

OPEN – All Year

BEST TIME TO VISIT – All Year

ECOSYSTEMS – Sagebrush, montane, alpine

ADMINISTRATION – National Park Service

KEY SPECIES – Moose

The Snake River and it tributaries, which flow through this area, provide some of the most consistent opportunities for photographing large bull moose south of the Canadian Border.

Pika can be photographed among the talus slopes along Paintbrush Canyon and Cascade Canyon Trails. Cascade Canyon is on the west side of Jenny Lake. You can either hike from the South Jenny Lake Trailhead or take a shuttle boat across the lake. Paintbrush Canyon can be accessed from the String Lake Trailhead, between Jenny Lake and Leigh Lake.

Oxbow Bend, which lies along the Snake River a little over 4 miles west of

View of the Tetons from Jenny Lake.

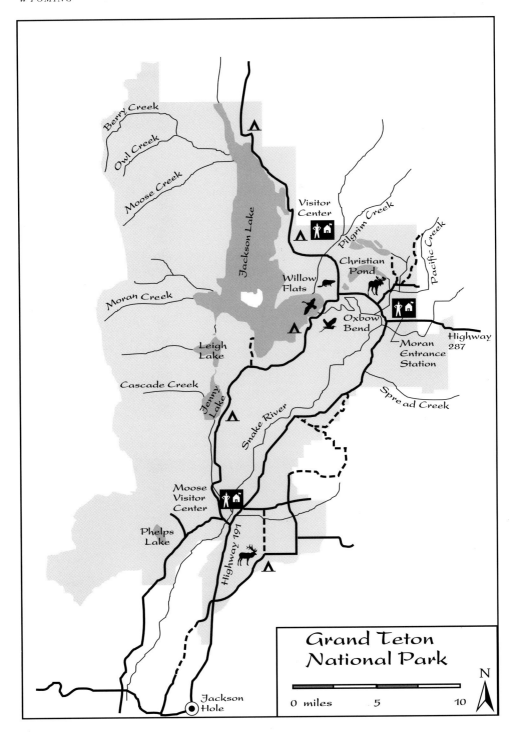

Berry Creek

Owl Creek

Moose Creek

Jackson Lake

Visitor Center

Pilgrim Creek

Pacific Creek

Christian Pond

Willow Flats

Moran Creek

Oxbow Bend

Highway 287

Moran Entrance Station

Leigh Lake

Cascade Creek

Jenny Lake

Spread Creek

Snake River

Moose Visitor Center

Phelps Lake

Highway 191

Grand Teton National Park

0 miles   5   10

N

Jackson Hole

Moran Junction, provides wildlife photographers with many photo opportunities. Beaver are active in the early morning hours, and again late in the day. Bald Eagles and Osprey are sometimes seen fishing in the slow-moving waters. Great Blue Herons nest in tall cottonwoods along the bend.

Some 3,000 wapiti spend the summer in the park, as does a small herd of bison. Beaver ponds provide habitat for Canada Geese, Cinnamon Teal, and Trumpeter Swans.

Grizzlies and black bear are present, though seldom observed.

Grand Teton National Park is in western Wyoming, just north of the town of Jackson. For more information, contact the Grand Teton National Park (307-733-2880).

NATIONAL ELK REFUGE

The National Elk Refuge, bordering the town of Jackson, Wyoming, is situated in the shadows of the Teton Range. Established in 1912, the refuge originally contained 2,760 acres. Today it covers almost 25,000 acres.

LOCATION – Jackson

OPEN – All year (daylight hours)

BEST TIME TO VISIT – Mid-November to January for American elk photography

ECOSYSTEMS – Open meadows, marshes, conifer forests

ADMINISTRATION – U.S. Fish and Wildlife Service

KEY SPECIES – Wapiti (American elk)

View of the Tetons from National Elk Refuge.

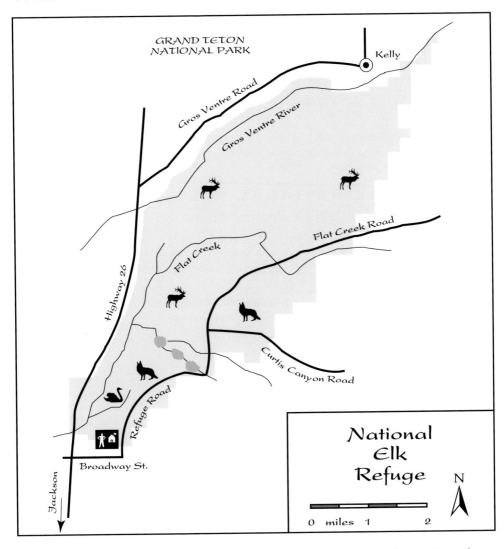

Wapiti begin arriving in late October and winter up to six months on the refuge. By December, upwards of 10,000 wapiti have gathered here. For sheer numbers of these huge mammals, the National Elk Refuge is without equal.

However, wildlife viewing is not limited to wapiti. Trumpeter Swans and other species of waterfowl can be photographed in the Flat Creek Marsh during October and November. The marsh can be viewed from several pull-offs along U.S. 89, north of Jackson. A photo blind is available on a first-come, first-serve basis, and can be reserved through the refuge office.

Moose can be photographed along the Gros Ventre River, paralleling the refuge's northern border. This area can be accessed from the Gros Ventre Road, between its junction with U.S. 89, about 7 miles north of Jackson, and the town of Kelly.

Bald Eagles and coyotes are often seen feeding on wapiti carcasses in the refuge.

Most of the refuge roads are closed between December 1 and April 30. Nevertheless, wapiti can often be photographed from the pull-offs along U.S. 89 during November and December. Horse-drawn sleighs provide access to the refuge from December through March. The sleigh rides allow you to get unbelievably close to the wapiti.

The refuge headquarters and visitor center are located near the east end of Broadway in Jackson. For more information, call the National Elk Refuge (307-733-9212).

SEEDSKADEE NATIONAL WILDLIFE REFUGE

Seedskadee National Wildlife Refuge, straddling 37 miles of the Green River in southwestern Wyoming, embraces over 14,000 acres of sagebrush uplands, along with cattail marshes, willow thickets, and cottonwoods along the river bottom. With several access roads on both sides of the river, plus on-foot access to the entire refuge (except for a small area around headquarters buildings), the refuge is highly user-friendly for wildlife photographers.

LOCATION – 38 miles north of Green River

OPEN – All year (24 hours)

BEST TIME TO VISIT – Spring, fall

ECOSYSTEMS – Sagebrush, marshes, cottonwood river bottoms

ADMINISTRATION – U.S. Fish and Wildlife Service

KEY SPECIES – Mountain Bluebird, Burrowing Owl, Red-tailed Hawk, moose, mule deer, red fox, porcupine, white-tailed prairie dog

---

Along the banks of the Green River.

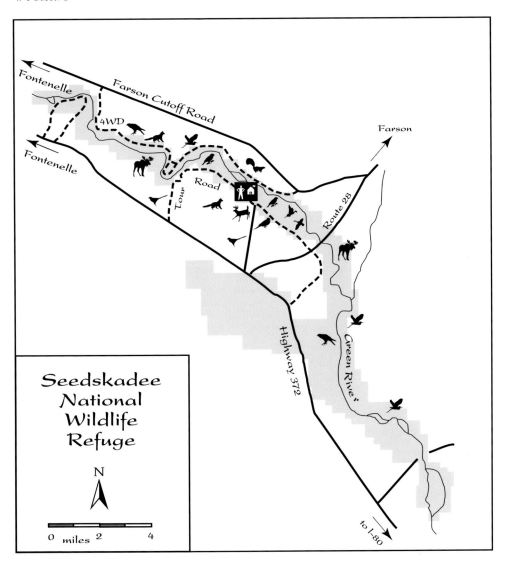

Seedskadee
National
Wildlife
Refuge

N

0 miles 2   4

The refuge is home to large numbers of Sage Grouse, and was named in their honor — Seedskadee is a Shoshone word meaning "River of the Prairie Hen."

A variety of ducks nest on the refuge, including Cinnamon Teal, Ruddies, Redheads, and the Northern Pintail. Canada Geese can be photographed along the river, where they have nested for centuries. Red-tailed Hawks inhabit the cottonwoods. Mountain Bluebirds, Mountain Plover, and White-faced Ibis are common residents. The refuge is home to five nesting colonies of Great Blue Herons. During winter, Rosy Finches can be photographed at the bird feeders near the headquarters building.

Mule deer, numbering close to 300, are common refuge residents. Large bucks are frequently observed near refuge headquarters. Several hundred moose inhabit the refuge, and can be photographed in the fall as they feed among the willows. Large numbers of white-tailed prairie dogs provide homes for nesting Burrowing Owls, and food for a large badger population. Pronghorn grazing in the sagebrush flats are easily photographed during early spring and summer. The refuge is home to several active beaver colonies. Red fox and porcupines are common, and are frequently observed.

Waterfowl impoundments may be closed for short periods in spring and fall to minimize disturbances to birds; some of these areas are still visible from roads. Permission to enter closed areas may be obtained on a case-by-case basis.

CAUTION: Except for the main entrance road and the headquarters-area tour route, all access roads are unimproved and may be passable only by four-wheel-drive or high-clearance vehicles. Check with the refuge personnel for current road conditions.

Stop at refuge headquarters, introduce yourself, and inform the personnel of your intentions. They can be very helpful. If you want to erect a temporary blind, you will need to obtain a permit, which is granted on a case-by-case basis.

To reach the refuge, go west from the town of Green River along Interstate 80 for 6 miles, then north on State Highway 372 for 30 miles. At the refuge sign, turn right and go east 2 miles to the refuge headquarters. For additional information, contact the Seedskadee National Wildlife Refuge (307-875-2187).

YELLOWSTONE NATIONAL PARK

Yellowstone National Park is the premier North American wildlife photography location south of the Canadian border. With scenic wonders as varied as Mammoth Hot Springs and the Grand Canyon of the Yellowstone, with habitats ranging from near desert to subalpine meadows and forests, and with an incredible diversity and abundance of wildlife, there is little wonder Yellowstone now carries the title International Biosphere Reserve and World Heritage Site.

LOCATION – Northwestern Wyoming

OPEN – All year

BEST TIME TO VISIT – Fall, winter

ECOSYSTEMS – Mountain lakes, montane forests, subalpine meadows

ADMINISTRATION – National Park Service

KEY SPECIES – Trumpeter Swan, wapiti, bison, pronghorn, bighorn sheep, coyote, grizzly bear

Yellowstone provides some of the best opportunities for photographing coyotes, pronghorn, bison, bighorn, moose, wapiti, and Trumpeter Swans. It is one of the few places where grizzlies can be photographed in the Lower Forty-eight. Steller's Jays, Clark's Nutcrackers, Gray Jays, the Common Raven, chipmunks, and golden-mantled ground squirrels are common throughout the park. Quite often, photographers are provided opportunities to photograph river

Mountain vista from Hayden Valley.

otters and Great Gray Owls. And now, with the reintroduction of gray wolves in March 1995, another species is added to the list.

Hayden Valley draws large numbers of bison. Cascade Meadows consistently provides opportunities for photographing coyotes. Trumpeter Swans are synonymous with Seven Mile Bridge. Herds of bighorns congregate on Mount Washburn and Mount Everts. The Gardiner entrance has no equal when it comes to photographing pronghorn. Wapiti walk the streets of Mammoth every fall.

Yellowstone becomes a magical wonderland in winter. Snow-encrusted bison and wapiti wander among steaming hot springs and geysers near Mammoth Hot Springs and Old Faithful. February is the best time to experience the park in its winter glory. At this time, Old Faithful is accessible only by snowmobile or snow coach from Flagg Ranch, near the south entrance, or from West Yellowstone. Mammoth has the only winter accommodations accessible by automobile. Regardless of where you decide to stay, rent a snowmobile. For lodging and snow-coach reservations, call TW Recreational Services Inc. (307-344-7311).

While you're in West Yellowstone, be sure to have breakfast at the Running Bear Pancake House. If your adventures don't lead you to West Yellowstone, go there anyway. Unlike Diogenes, my search has finally ended. Without question, Running Bear makes the world's best buttermilk pancakes. Hot pancakes, fresh butter, and plenty of maple syrup ... UUMMMM! Pack your bags, load your cameras with fresh film, and let's go.

Yellowstone National Park is in the extreme northwestern corner of Wyoming, with segments spilling over into Montana and Idaho. For more information, call the park (307-344-7381).

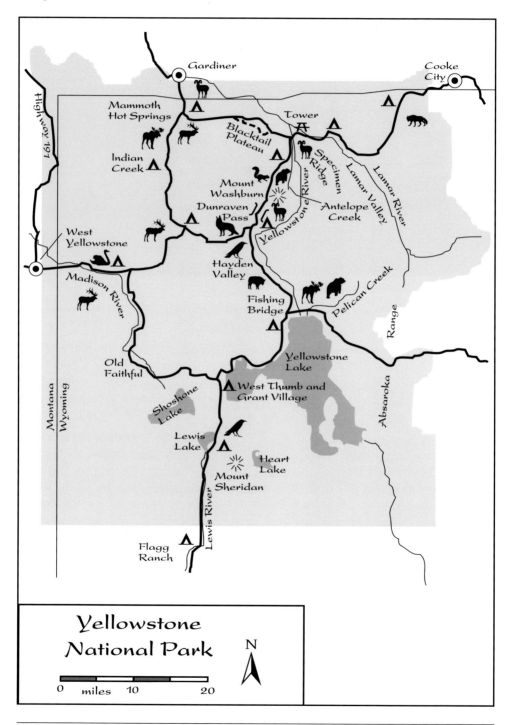

Yellowstone
National Park

N

0   miles   10   20

Northern Rocky Mountains

The Northern Rockies encompass some of the most rugged, awe-inspiring landscapes in North America, including the Bob Marshall Wilderness, the Bitterroot Mountains, and Glacier National Park. This section of the Rockies extends northward from the Sawtooth Mountains of central Idaho all the way to the Canadian border.

IDAHO

CAMAS NATIONAL WILDLIFE REFUGE

Camas National Wildlife Refuge, located in southeastern Idaho, is a blend of ponds, cattail marshes, sagebrush, and open meadows. The Leemhi Mountains are visible in the west and the Tetons in the east, providing a majestic backdrop for the 10,000-acre refuge.

LOCATION – 40 miles north of Idaho Falls

OPEN – All year (daylight hours)

BEST TIME TO VISIT – Spring, fall

ECOSYSTEMS – Marshes, sagebrush, grasslands

ADMINISTRATION – U.S. Fish and Wildlife Service

KEY SPECIES – Moose, mule deer, coyote, fox, skunk, Ring-necked Pheasant, Great Horned Owl, waterfowl, wading birds, shore birds

Refuge marsh lands.

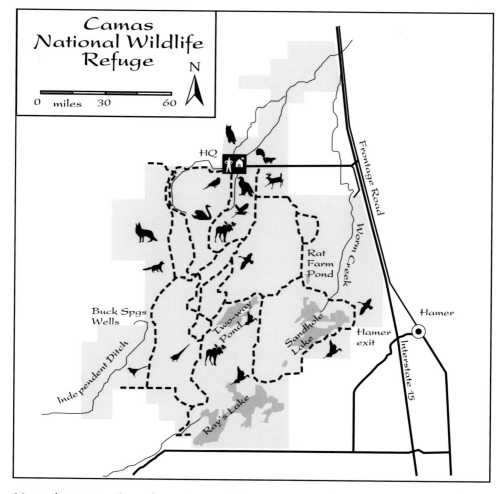

More than 30 miles of roads provide easy access into most sections of the refuge. In several areas, roads parallel canals, allowing you to photograph waterfowl from your car window.

Large numbers of Redheads, Mallards, Gadwall, and Northern Pintails nest in the wetlands. Snowy Egrets, White-faced Ibis, Great Blue Herons, Black-crowned Night Herons, and Double-crested Cormorants share a nesting colony. Sandhill Cranes and the endangered Trumpeter Swan raise their young on the refuge. During February and March, several dozen Bald Eagles roost in the cottonwoods near the refuge buildings. Ring-necked Pheasants, Long-billed Curlews, and Sage Grouse nest in the uplands along the refuge's western boundary. Great Horned Owls can be found in the trees near the canal.

More than 100 mule deer crowd the fields near headquarters each fall. Moose seek food and shelter among the willows lining Camas Creek as it winds its way eight miles through the refuge. Pronghorn, coyotes, and beaver are frequently sighted.

Off-road travel is prohibited between February 1 and July 15 without special permission, which is granted on a case-by-case basis. Permission is also required to erect a portable blind.

To reach the refuge, go north 32 miles from Idaho Falls along Interstate 15. At the Hamer exit, follow signs to the refuge, going north another 3 miles along the frontage road to an overpass. Cross the interstate and go 2 miles to refuge headquarters. For additional information, contact the Camas National Wildlife Refuge (208-662-5423).

KOOTENAI NATIONAL WILDLIFE REFUGE

Kootenai National Wildlife Refuge, situated in the Idaho panhandle only 20 miles from Canada, is bounded by the Kootenai River on the east and the Selkirk Mountains on the west. The refuge contains a diversity of habitats, from the meadows and cattail marshes by the river to the forested slopes of the mountains.

LOCATION – 5 miles west of Bonners Ferry

OPEN – All year (daylight hours)

BEST TIME TO VISIT – Spring through fall

ECOSYSTEMS – Marshes, meadows, conifer forests

ADMINISTRATION – U.S. Fish and Wildlife Service

KEY SPECIES – Moose, Wood Duck, Red-naped Sapsucker, Common Yellowthroat, Great Horned Owl, Red-tailed Hawk

During summer, upwards of 2,000 ducks, including the colorful Wood Duck, can be observed. A pair of Bald Eagles nest on the refuge. Canada Geese lead their young goslings throughout the wetlands. Common Yellowthroats, Killdeer, Juncos, Tree Swallows, Steller's Jays, Clark's Nutcrackers, and Red-naped Sapsuckers are regularly observed in suitable habitat. Red-tailed Hawks and Great Horned Owls raise their young in the cottonwoods along the river. American Dippers nest under the bridges along Myrtle Creek.

Mule deer and white-tailed deer are common. Moose are occasionally observed in the willow thickets. Coyotes can be seen prowling throughout the refuge's boundaries.

A 4.5 mile, one-way auto tour, beginning at the refuge office, provides a good overview of the refuge. Several trails, ranging from 300 yards to 2.2 miles in length, take visitors into the heart of the refuge. The Cottonwood Trail provides the closest approach to the marshes, while the Forest Trail takes hikers to the base of the Selkirks.

Three observation blinds are provided, at South Pond, Myrtle Pond, and Moose Overlook at Cascade Pond.

After you've finished a hard day of standing behind your camera, I've got the

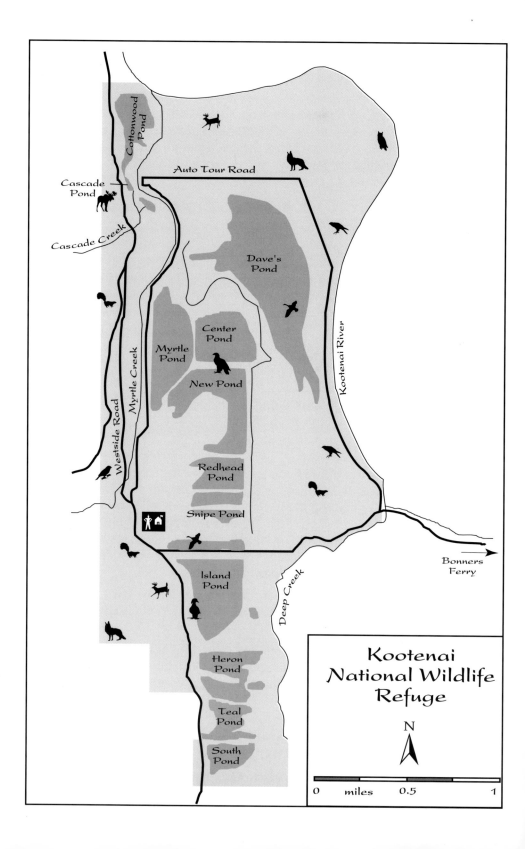

Cottonwood Pond

Auto Tour Road

Cascade Pond

Cascade Creek

Dave's Pond

Center Pond

Myrtle Pond

Kootenai River

New Pond

Westside Road

Myrtle Creek

Redhead Pond

Snipe Pond

Bonners Ferry

Island Pond

Deep Creek

Heron Pond

Teal Pond

South Pond

Kootenai
National Wildlife
Refuge

N

0   miles   0.5   1

Myrtle Creek and Selkirk Mountains' foothills.

perfect place for you. For old-fashioned, down home cooking, Maier's Family Dining in Canon Ferry is hard to beat.

To reach the refuge from Bonners Ferry, look for a sign along U.S. 95 directing visitors to turn west onto Riverside Road. Follow this road 5 miles to the refuge. For additional information, contact the Kootenai National Wildlife Refuge (208-267-3888).

SNAKE RIVER BIRDS OF PREY AREA

The Snake River Birds of Prey Area, consisting of desert-like habitat bordering vertical cliffs that tower 700 feet above the Snake River, supports North America's densest concentration of nesting raptors.

LOCATION – 17 miles southwest of Boise

OPEN – All year

BEST TIME TO VISIT – Mid-March to mid-June

ECOSYSTEMS – Semi-desert, river bottom

ADMINISTRATION – Bureau of Land Management

KEY SPECIES – Prairie Falcon, Red-tailed Hawk, Northern Harrier, Golden Eagle, badger, Townsend's ground squirrel

Fourteen bird-of-prey species regularly breed along the 81 miles of the Snake River Canyon: Northern Harriers, American Kestrels, Prairie Falcons, Red-tailed Hawks, Swainson's Hawks, Ferruginous Hawks, Golden Eagles, Western Screech Owls, Burrowing Owls, Short-eared Owls, Long-eared Owls, Common

Barn Owls, Great Horned Owls, and Turkey Vultures.

Embracing almost 500,000 acres, it is no wonder that this area hosts the country's largest badger population, along with a dense population of Townsend's ground squirrels.

Dedication Point, an impressive canyon overlook with interpretive displays, is located between Kuna and the Swan Falls Dam. This will provide you with an overview of the area. One of the signs reads, "Highest number of Prairie Falcons in the world nest in these cliffs. Estimated 5% of the world's population of Prairie Falcons nest in this area."

During the heat of summer, the majority of raptors leave this area. Spring is the best time to be here.

Stop at the Bureau of Land Management office, 3830 American Terrace, Boise, Idaho; 208-384-3000. Advise the personnel of your plans. They can provide a wealth of information, including a map of the area and the right people to contact about specific species.

To reach the area from Boise, go west along Interstate 84. At Exit 44, 4 miles west of Boise, turn south. Follow the signs for 8 miles to Kuna. From Kuna, go south along the Swan Falls Road. Follow the signs to the SRBOPA, beginning 5 miles south of Kuna. From Swan Falls Dam, located 18 miles south of Kuna, a dirt road provides access to several miles of river bottom.

The southeastern areas can be accessed from either Grand View or Bruneau. Hiking or boating is required to reach significant viewing areas. The BLM Cove Recreation Site and the Bruneau Dunes State Park are located in this section of the SRBOPA.

Snake River canyon.

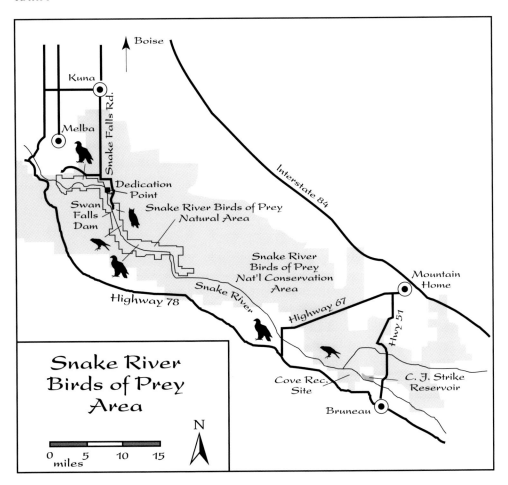

Boise

Kuna

Melba

Snake Falls Rd.

Dedication
Point

Swan
Falls
Dam

Snake River Birds of Prey
Natural Area

Snake River
Birds of Prey
Nat'l Conservation
Area

Interstate 84

Mountain
Home

Highway 78

Snake River

Highway 67

Hwy 51

Cove Rec.
Site

C. J. Strike
Reservoir

Bruneau

Snake River Birds of Prey Area

N

0   5   10   15
miles

While you're in Boise, make time for another stop: the World Center For Birds of Prey. This center is heavily involved with research and a captive breeding program for a number of endangered species, including the California Condor. The center has some very impressive and informative displays. It is open to the public Tuesday through Sunday, from 9 a.m. to 5 p.m. in summer. From November through February, the hours are 10 a.m. to 4 p.m.

To reach the World Center for Birds of Prey, take Exit 50 off Interstate 84 in Boise. Follow the signs to South Cole Road. Continue south on Cole Road about 6 miles to the center.

MONTANA

BENTON LAKE NATIONAL WILDLIFE REFUGE

Benton Lake National Wildlife Refuge, a 12,000-acre refuge featuring shallow prairie marshlands, is situated along the western edge of the famed Prairie Pothole Region. The "potholes," or wetlands, serve as a nursery for the majority of the nation's waterfowl.

LOCATION – 12 miles north of Great Falls

OPEN – All year (dawn to dusk)

BEST TIME TO VISIT – Spring through fall

ECOSYSTEMS – Marshes, prairie

ADMINISTRATION – U.S. Fish and Wildlife Service

KEY SPECIES – Waterfowl, wading birds

Among the species nesting on the refuge are Northern Pintails, Northern Shovelers, Gadwall, American Wigeon, Lesser Scaup, plus Green-winged, Blue-winged, and Cinnamon Teal.

Sharp-tailed Grouse can be photographed from a refuge blind as they perform their courtship rituals during the month of April.

Colonial nesting birds like Franklin's Gulls and Eared Grebes are abundant throughout the refuge. Barn swallows construct their nests on light fixtures on

View from the Prairie Marsh Drive.

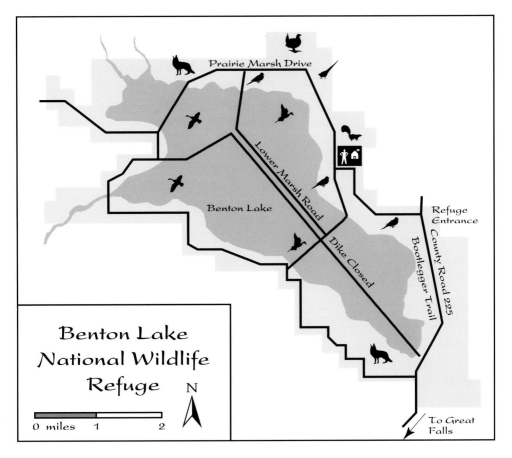

Benton Lake
National Wildlife
Refuge

N

0 miles 1 2

the refuge headquarters building. Each fall, several thousand Tundra Swans make their appearance during migration.

Other common nesting birds include Eared Grebes, Canada Geese, Northern Harriers, Soras, American Coots, Killdeer, American Avocets, Wilson's Phalaropea, California Gulls, Mourning Doves, Short-eared Owls, Horned Larks, Chestnut-collared Longspurs, and, last but not least, both Red-winged and Yellow-headed Blackbirds.

The refuge is a fawning ground for pronghorn. Mule deer, coyotes, and badger are common residents.

In addition to its hiking trails, the refuge can be accessed from the Prairie Marsh Trail Boardwalk and the 9-mile Prairie Marsh Wildlife Drive.

The thing that makes Benton Lake so special is not just the diversity of its wildlife, but also the refuge personnel. They are great people who are more than willing to assist conscientious photographers in any way possible. Before erecting a blind, stop by refuge headquarters for permission.

To reach the refuge from Great Falls, exit U.S. 87 onto County Road 225, known locally as the Bootlegger Trail. Go north 12 miles to the refuge, following the signs to refuge headquarters. For additional information, contact Benton Lake National Wildlife Refuge (406-727-7400).

GLACIER NATIONAL PARK

Glacier National Park, characterized by towering, jagged peaks, was carved by ancient glaciers. In addition to the ease with which many species can be photographed, the park provides some of the most dramatic backdrops to be found anywhere.

LOCATION – Northwestern Montana

OPEN – All year

BEST TIME TO VISIT – All year

ECOSYSTEMS – Montane forests, alpine tundra

ADMINISTRATION – National Park Service

KEY SPECIES – Bighorn sheep, mountain goat, white-tailed deer, mule deer, grizzly bear, cavity-nesting birds

Although wolf sightings are rare, their howls are occasionally heard in the Big Prairie area. During winter large numbers of wapiti congregate at this location.

Hidden Lake Trail, beginning at the Logan Pass Visitor Center and ending at Hidden Lake Overlook, provides opportunities for viewing White-tailed Ptarmigan, Rosy Finches, Townsend's Solitaires, and hoary marmots. Mountain goats often congregate near the overlook. Grizzlies are sometimes observed

Mountain vista from Mcdonald Creek.

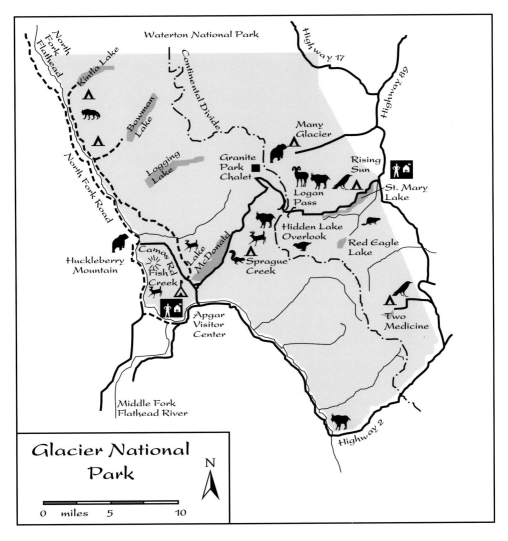

Glacier National Park

N

0 miles 5 10

along the lower slopes in search of food.

The open slopes above the Many Glacier area are probably the most productive locations in the park for grizzly photography. The Highline Trail, beginning at the Logan Pass Visitor Center, is frequented by goats and bighorn sheep.

Walton Goat Lick, situated along the park's southern boundary, attracts large numbers of goats during spring and early summer.

Two Dog Flats attracts large numbers of wapiti during fall and winter. During spring, with flowers in bloom, large numbers of songbirds can be heard, including the White-crowned Sparrow.

Red-naped Sapsuckers, Three-toed Woodpeckers, and Tree Swallows can be photographed along the Red Eagle Trail. Beaver are active in ponds along the trail.

White-tailed deer and mule deer are common in many areas of the park, as are Pileated Woodpeckers.

Glacier National Park is located in northwestern Montana. For additional information, contact the park (406-888-5790).

KELLY ISLAND

Kelly Island, surrounded by the waters of the Clark Fork River, is a prime example of good urban wildlife habitat. More than 600 acres of tranquil meadows, bordered by stands of cottonwoods, backwater sloughs, and ponderosa woodlands, provide ideal habitat for a variety of birds and mammals.

LOCATION — Missoula

OPEN — All year

BEST TIME TO VISIT — Spring through fall

ECOSYSTEMS — River bottom, woodland meadows, cottonwood and ponderosa woodlands

ADMINISTRATION — Montana Department of Fish, Wildlife and Parks

KEY SPECIES — White-tailed deer, beaver, red fox, Wood Duck, Great Blue Heron, Canada Goose

Wood Ducks incubate their eggs in artificial nest boxes along the sloughs. Lewis' Woodpeckers and Great Horned Owls nest on the island, as do Red-tailed Hawks. Great Blue Herons have established a rookery in the cottonwoods.

One of Kelly Island's many backwater sloughs.

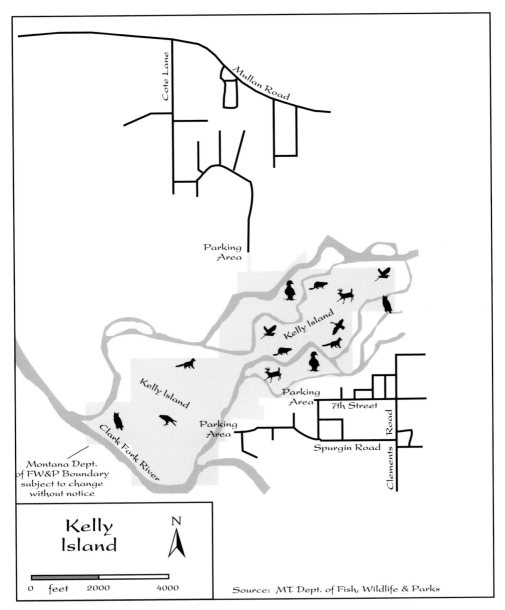

Source: MT Dept. of Fish, Wildlife & Parks

To access the north side of Kelly Island from Missoula: On the west side of town, from the intersection of Reserve and Mullan, go 3.4 miles on Mullan to Cote Lane. Look for a sign that says "Fishing Access." Turn left and follow the signs 2 miles to the trailhead. To access the south side of the island from Missoula, go south on Reserve, then turn west along 3rd Street W. After 1.9 miles, 3rd Street W turns left and becomes Clements Road. Continue south on Clements to Spurgin Road. Turn west on Spurgin Road, and follow the signs.

For additional information, contact Montana Department of Fish, Wildlife and Parks (406-444-1276).

NATIONAL BISON RANGE

The National Bison Range was established in 1908 to maintain a representative bison herd, thus preserving the species from extinction. Today, the range is home to a variety of birds and mammals, and has become a mecca for wildlife photographers.

LOCATION — 10 miles northwest of Ravalli

OPEN — All year (daylight hours)

BEST TIME TO VISIT — Spring through fall

ECOSYSTEMS — Prairies, montane forest

ADMINISTRATION — U.S. Fish and Wildlife Service

KEY SPECIES — Bison, wapiti, mule deer, white-tailed deer, bighorn sheep, pronghorn, Columbian ground squirrel

Columbian ground squirrels provide easy photo subjects, as well as prey for the local coyote and badger populations. Colonies of Bank Swallows can be photographed along Mission Creek, while white-tailed deer seek cover along its banks. Blue Grouse can be photographed along the Bitterroot Trail, as they perform their annual courtship ritual each May. Bighorn sheep gather along Red Sleep Mountain Drive, between the Bitterroot Trailhead and the High Point turnoff.

The range maintains a herd of 300 to 500 bison, with calving beginning during mid-April. Pronghorn gather on the grassy hillsides near the range's northern

Red Sleep Mountain.

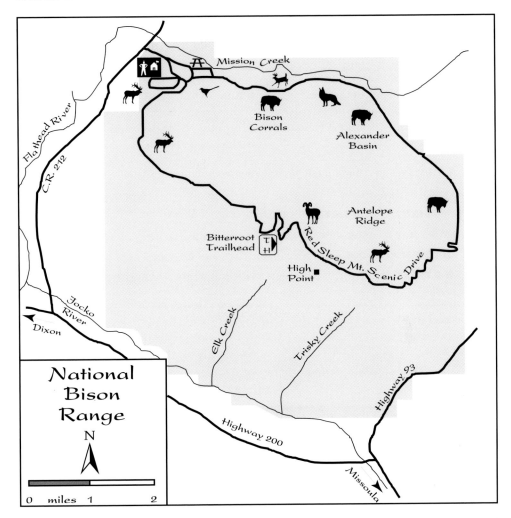

boundary. Wapiti, mule deer, yellow-bellied marmots, Mountain Bluebirds, and Black-billed Magpies all provide ready photo subjects.

The 19-mile Red Sleep Mountain Scenic Drive, traversing grassy prairies and montane forests, is open from mid-May until late October. During the remainder of the year, only a 5-mile section of the loop is open. However, a smaller loop, taking a half-hour to drive, is open all year. Refuge personnel suggest taking two hours to drive the 19-mile loop.

Visitors must remain on the road and near their car at all times. Stop at the visitor center and obtain a map of the area.

From the town of Ravalli in western Montana, go west along State Highway 200 for 6 miles to the town of Dixon. Turn right onto County Road 212, and go 4 miles to range headquarters. For additional information, contact the National Bison Range (406-644-2211).

RED ROCK LAKES NATIONAL WILDLIFE REFUGE

Red Rock Lakes National Wildlife Refuge, embracing more than 44,000 acres, is located in the Centennial Valley of southwestern Montana. Lakes and ponds account for 9,000 acres of the refuge. That leaves more than 35,000 acres for everything from shallow marshes and stabilized sand dunes to aspen groves and montane forests reaching into the subalpine zone, at close to 10,000 feet.

LOCATION — 50 miles east of Yellowstone National Park

OPEN — All year (24 hours)

BEST TIME TO VISIT — Spring through fall

ECOSYSTEMS — Marshes, grasslands, montane forests

ADMINISTRATION — U.S. Fish and Wildlife Service

KEY SPECIES — Trumpeter Swan, Sandhill Crane, waterfowl, shore birds, warblers, raptors

---

Established in 1935 to protect the Trumpeter Swan, the refuge now hosts the largest breeding population south of the Canadian border — close to 500 swans. Shambo and Culver Ponds, along with the western end of Lower Red Rock Lake, provide some of the best opportunities for photographing trumpeters.

Vista along Red Rock Pass Road.

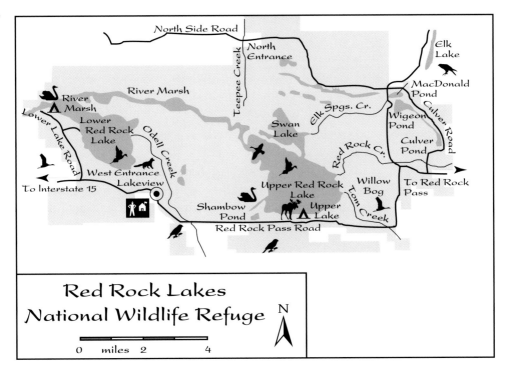

Red Rock Lakes National Wildlife Refuge

N

0   miles   2   4

More than 50,000 ducks and geese make quite a picture as they come through the refuge during migration. Common nesting species include the Canada Goose, Mallard, Northern Pintail, Gadwall, American Wigeon, Northern Shoveler, Redhead, Canvasback, Lesser Scaup, Ruddy Duck, and the Blue-winged, Green-winged, and Cinnamon Teal.

The Centennial Valley is noted for its concentrations of Swainson's and Red-tailed Hawks. Northern Harriers are plentiful throughout the refuge, and Bald Eagles are common year-round.

Sandhill Cranes frequent the area south of Upper Red Rock Lake.

Want to go on a snipe hunt? Get out your paper bag and "clicking sticks" — Common Snipe seem to be everywhere.

The Common Yellowthroat, along with MacGillivray's, Wilson's, and Yellow Warblers, can be photographed in the wetlands. Great Horned Owls may keep you awake all night as they call out to each other.

Other common nesting birds include the Forster's Tern, Killdeer, Willet, Yellow-headed Blackbird, Great Blue Heron, Black-crowned Night Heron, American Avocet, Blue Grouse, Red-naped Sapsucker, Barn Swallow, Tree Swallow, Clark's Nutcracker, Mountain Chickadee, American Dipper, Mountain Bluebird, and White-crowned Sparrow.

Birds are not the only form of wildlife on the refuge. Moose feed among the willows near Upper Lake Campground, along the south shore of Upper Red

Rock Lake. Other species often seen include pronghorn, badger, striped skunk, porcupine, red fox, and coyote.

One way to see the refuge is by water. Take an all-day canoe trip from the lower lake to the upper lake. Also, the entire refuge is open to hiking.

CAUTION: Hazardous bogs and sinkholes are found throughout the refuge. Be careful when traveling through wet areas.

Limited camping — approximately 20 sites — is available on a first-come, first-serve basis. Campers are limited to 14 consecutive days.

The Lower Lake Road is open between May 15 and December 1. Culver Road is open from July 15 until September 30. The Idlewild Trail is open to vehicles from September 1 to December 1, and for hiking only from December 2 until August 31. The Red Rock Pass, North Side and Elk Lake Roads are open year-round.

Upon arrival, talk with the personnel at refuge headquarters, and advise them of your plans. Most refuge employees can share information that can save you many hours in the field. Also, if you plan to erect a temporary blind, you must first obtain a permit.

From Interstate 15 at the community of Monida, go east along Red Rock Pass Road to the refuge, a distance of 28 miles. For additional information, contact the Red Rock Lakes National Wildlife Refuge (406-276-2536).

Canadian Rockies

The Canadian Rockies are characterized by glacier-carved peaks reflecting in the placid, turquoise waters of mountain lakes. Yoho, Kootenay, Sunwapta Falls, Bow River — these are names that conjure up visions of wilderness. The section of the Canadian Rockies included in this book begins at the Canada-U.S. border, separates the provinces of Alberta and British Columbia, and continues to the northern boundary of Jasper National Park.

ALBERTA

BANFF NATIONAL PARK

Mountains draped with glaciers, emerald forests, and the blue-green waters of mountain lakes, plus an abundance of wildlife, make Banff National Park a magnet, attracting wildlife photographers from far and wide. From beaver to grizzlies, wildlife photo opportunities abound.

LOCATION — 90 kilometers (54 miles) west of Calgary

OPEN — All year (24 hours)

BEST TIME TO VISIT — All year

ECOSYSTEMS — Lakes, rivers, coniferous forests, glaciers, alpine meadows

ADMINISTRATION — Parks Canada

KEY SPECIES — Wood bison, wapiti, mule deer, beaver, moose, Columbian ground squirrel, black bear, grizzly bear

Mount Rundle reflected in the waters of the Vermilion Lakes.

Speaking of beaver, they can be photographed at the beaver ponds near Johnson Lake and near the west end of the third Vermilion Lake.

The park features two locations where grizzlies are occasionally spotted: Bow Summit and Sunwapta Pass. Probably the best location to photograph black bear is along the Icefields Parkway, between Saskatchewan Crossing and Mount Cirrus. However, they also are frequently observed along Highway 1A between Banff and Lake Louise.

Lake Minnewanka is home to a herd of bighorn sheep.

Photographing bison is easy. Simply go to the "bison paddock" near Banff Townsite. While you are at the paddock, spend some time at the Columbian ground squirrel display, photographing these lovable critters.

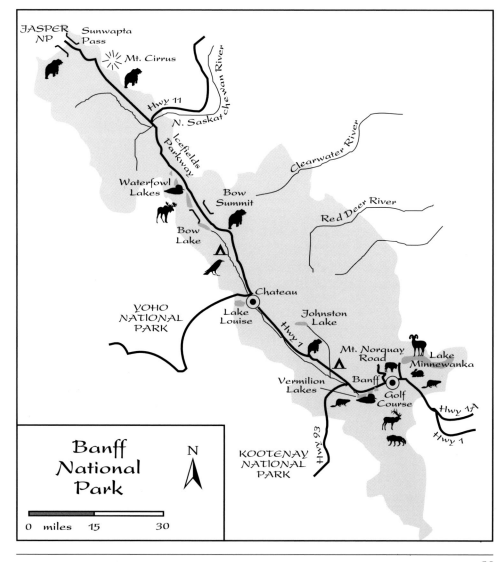

The Cephren Lake Trail is frequented by porcupines. During the rut, wapiti congregate at the Banff Townsite ballpark. They also gather at the golf course and along the east end of the Vermilion Lakes.

Hooded Mergansers can be photographed from the Marsh Trail photo blind, overlooking the Vermilion Lakes. During late summer and fall, these cocky little black-and-white birds are frequently observed at Waterfowl Lakes.

Moose feed among the willows along Fenland Trail, the area between Bow Lake and Waterfowl Lakes, and in the shallow waters of the Vermilion Lakes. Pika can be photographed among the talus slopes near the viewpoint along the Lake Louise Trail. Snowshoe Hares are often observed in the area surrounding Johnson Lake. Gray wolves are present in the lower valleys near the park's southern boundary.

Banff National Park is situated along Alberta's western border. From Calgary, travel west 117 kilometers (70 miles) along Highway 1, the TransCanada Highway, to Banff Townsite. For additional information, contact Banff National Park (403-762-1550).

JASPER NATIONAL PARK

Jasper National Park, where grizzlies roam as freely as they have for thousands of years, is a true untamed wilderness. Although many areas of the park can be observed from the Icefields Parkway, most of the park can only be reached by back packing or by pack train. Jasper is larger than Banff, Kootenay, and Yoho National Parks combined.

LOCATION – 320 kilometers (192 miles) west of Edmonton

OPEN – All year

BEST TIME TO VISIT – All year

ECOSYSTEMS – Lakes, rivers, conifer forests, glaciers, alpine meadows

ADMINISTRATION – Parks Canada

KEY SPECIES – Grizzly bear, black bear, moose, mule deer, wapiti, bighorn sheep, mountain goat, beaver, snowshoe hare, Columbian ground squirrel, pika, Canada Goose, White-tailed Ptarmigan

Grizzlies are frequently observed along the Maligne Lake Road and along Highway 16 West, between Jasper Townsite and the park's western boundary. Jonas Creek is popular with black bear, as is the area around Pyramid Lake. Blacks are also observed along Highway 93A north of Athabasca Falls, and along Highway 16 west of Jasper Townsite.

Beaver inhabit many areas of the park. Four locations are well-known for beaver activity: the Valley of Five Lakes, the Miette River and its sloughs, Cottonwood Creek north of Jasper Townsite, and Talbot Lake.

Tangle Hill, Cinquefoil Ridge, and Syncline Ridge are frequented by bighorn sheep. Columbian ground squirrels can be photographed at the Icefield Campground. Whistler Campground is the place to photograph wapiti.

Mountain goats are often observed along the Icefields Parkway north of the Mount Christie picnic area. They also frequent a couple of natural mineral licks: one along Highway 16A, just north of Athabasca Falls, and the other along Highway 16 East north of Jasper Townsite.

Mule deer can be photographed along the Maligne Lake Road, Highway 93A, Highway 16 East and West, and the area surrounding Pyramid Lake. They also are frequently sighted in Jasper Townsite.

Moose are attracted to two tarns along Highway 93A, north of Athabasca Falls. Other locations where moose are often seen are the Maligne Lake Road, Highway 16 West, Snaring River Road, and Sunwapta Falls. Snowshoe hares are frequently observed around the Icefield Campground.

Canada Geese inhabit several locations within the park. The Miette River and its sloughs, along with Talbot Lake, usually provide excellent photo opportunities. Mount Edith Cavell is probably the best location in the park for photographing pika. Both Whistlers Mountain and Signal Mountain are great locations to observe the White-tailed Ptarmigan.

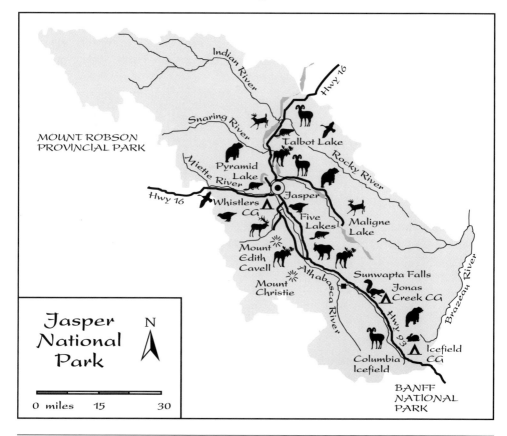

Vista along Icefields Parkway near the Columbia Icefields.

Jasper National Park lies immediately north of Banff National Park. It can be reached by traveling north from Lake Louise along the Icefields Parkway. For additional information, contact Jasper National Park (403-852-6176).

WATERTON LAKES NATIONAL PARK

Waterton Lakes National Park is the Canadian section of the Waterton/Glacier International Peace Park, designated to commemorate the long history of peace and friendship between our two nations. This park, where prairies meet mountains, holds many pleasant surprises for wildlife photographers visiting for their first time.

LOCATION – 121 kilometers (73 miles) southwest of Lethbridge

OPEN – All year

BEST TIME TO VISIT – All year

ECOSYSTEMS – Prairie, lakes, montane forests, alpine meadows

ADMINISTRATION – Parks Canada

KEY SPECIES – Columbian ground squirrel, pika, beaver, badger, bighorn sheep, mule deer, bison, wapiti, Osprey, White-tailed Ptarmigan, songbirds

Columbian ground squirrels are abundant in grasslands throughout the park. Those in the bison paddock are just waiting to have their picture made. An active beaver lodge and pond is located along Red Rock Parkway. Pika are

Southern vista of Upper Waterton Lake near Waterton Townsite.

found in several locations within the park. One of the more accessible areas is near lower Rowe Lake, where snowshoe hares also are frequently observed.

Badgers are common in the grasslands and open prairies on the park's east side, including the grassy hill between Lower and Middle Waterton Lakes. The Blakiston Falls area supports an active badger population.

A number of semi-tame bighorn sheep can be photographed at Red Rock Canyon. During fall and winter, several bighorns hang out in downtown Waterton. Mule deer are often present along Red Rock Parkway. Also, Waterton Townsite typically holds a "tame" population of mule deer. A small herd of bison can be photographed at the bison paddock.

Dark-eyed Juncos are usually present along the trail at Cameron Lake. Black-billed Magpies are common in most areas of the park. They often clean up after dinner at the picnic tables near Lower and Middle Waterton Lakes.

Clark's Nutcrackers can be photographed along the Goat Lake Trail. White-tailed Ptarmigan can be photographed along one of the trails near the park's western boundary. Red-naped Sapsuckers nest in the aspen groves near the Bertha Trailhead. Steller's Jays are common along the trails near Cameron Lake. White-crowned Sparrows can be photographed near Linnet Lake, along the entrance road across from the visitor information center. The aspen grove near the Bertha Trailhead provides nesting cavities for several Tree Swallows.

Other wildlife species common to the park include the coyote, wapiti, black bear, Spotted Sandpiper, Osprey, Ruffed Grouse, Belted Kingfisher, Northern

Flicker, Western Wood Pewee, Cliff Swallow, Red-breasted Nuthatch, Ruby-crowned Kinglet, Varied Thrush, Yellow-rumped Warbler, Yellow Warbler, Wilson's Warbler, Savannah Sparrow, Red-winged Blackbird, and Pine Siskin.

Situated in the extreme southwest corner of Alberta, the park is located 121 kilometers (73 miles) southwest of Lethbridge, and can be reached by traveling southwest along Highway 5. The visitor center in Waterton Townsite is a very good source for information. For additional information, contact Waterton Lakes National Park (403-859-2224).

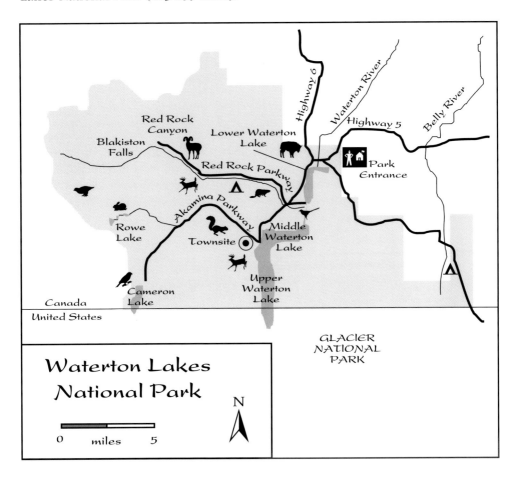

BRITISH COLUMBIA

KOOTENAY NATIONAL PARK

In Kootenay National Park, precipitous mountains, roaring rivers, and plummeting waterfalls combine to produce some of the most breathtaking vistas in North America. The lush valleys and dense forests provide the ideal environment for black bear, mountain goats, and many other species.

LOCATION – Southeastern British Columbia

OPEN – All year

BEST TIME TO VISIT – All year

ECOSYSTEMS – Coniferous forests, alpine meadows

ADMINISTRATION – Parks Canada

KEY SPECIES – Black bear, gray wolf, mountain goat, mule deer, wapiti, jays

---

Gray wolves still roam the Kootenay Valley, howling at night for all to hear. Mule deer, wapiti, and moose frequent the natural mineral lick located south of the Wardle Picnic Area. Columbian ground squirrels have colonized a section of the McLeod Meadows Picnic Area. Mountain goats are occasionally observed along the slopes of Mount Wardle.

Each fall, wapiti can be seen grazing near the Dolly Varden Picnic Area, along

Cloud-filled Kootenay Valley.

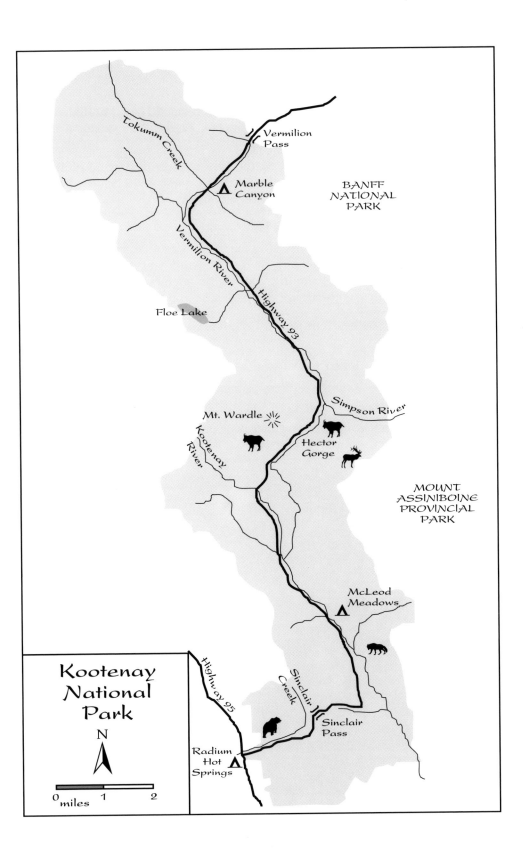

Vermilion
Pass

Tokumm Creek

Marble
Canyon

Vermilion River

Highway 93

BANFF
NATIONAL
PARK

Floe Lake

Simpson River

Mt. Wardle

Kootenay River

Hector
Gorge

MOUNT
ASSINIBOINE
PROVINCIAL
PARK

McLeod
Meadows

Highway 95

Sinclair Creek

Sinclair
Pass

Kootenay
National
Park

N

Radium
Hot
Springs

0 miles 1 2

the Banff-Windermere Parkway. Black bear can be spotted along Sinclair Creek, near the Sinclair Creek picnic area.

Species of birds common to the park include Red-tailed Hawk, Ruffed Grouse, Spotted Sandpiper, Northern Flicker, Gray Jay, Clark's Nutcracker, Common Raven, American Dipper, and Pine Siskin.

Kootenay National Park, situated along the eastern edge of British Columbia, is 230 kilometers (138 miles) north of the Canada/United States border. For additional information, contact the park (604-347-9615).

YOHO NATIONAL PARK

Yoho National Park, British Columbia's gem of the Canadian Rockies, is named after the Cree word "yoho," meaning awe or astonishment. With roaring rivers, thundering waterfalls, and towering, glacier-carved mountains supplying the landscape, there can be little doubt the park was aptly named.

LOCATION — Southeastern British Columbia

OPEN — All year

BEST TIME TO VISIT — All year

ECOSYSTEMS — Coniferous forests, alpine meadows

ADMINISTRATION — Parks Canada

KEY SPECIES — Grizzly bear, black bear, moose, bighorn sheep, mountain goat, lynx, Osprey

Glacier carved mountains of Yoho.

The park also features abundant and diverse wildlife. Clark's Nutcrackers frequently solicit handouts from park visitors at Takakkaw Falls. Leanchoil Marsh and the Beaver Dam Nature Trail marsh attract Great Blue Herons. Great Horned Owls are also common to these locations.

Other birds common to the park include Ospreys, Red-tailed Hawks, Killdeer,

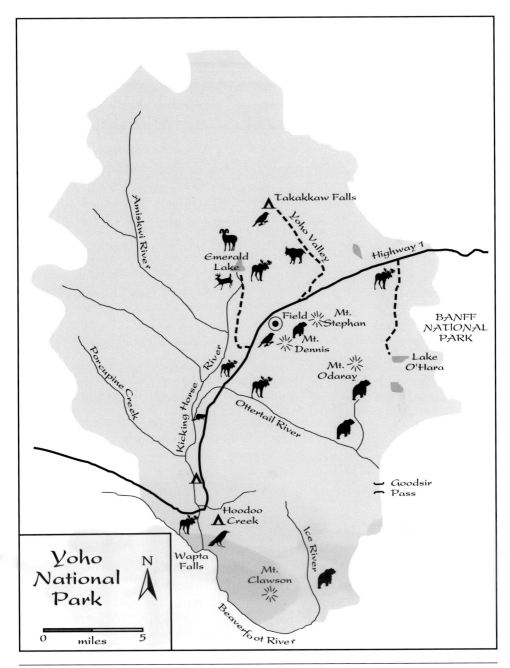

Spotted Sandpipers, Common Snipe, Rufous Hummingbirds, Northern Flickers, Violet-green Swallows, Cliff Swallows, Gray Jays, Common Ravens, Boreal Chickadees, Red-breasted Nuthatches, Orange-crowned Warblers, Townsend's Warblers, Common Yellowthroats, White-crowned Sparrows, and Dark-eyed Juncos.

Beavers are active in the Lower Kicking Horse River Valley, along Ottertail Flats. Canada lynx have been observed throughout the park, from valley bottoms to treeline. Prominent locations include the Amiskwi burn and the deciduous habitats along the lower Kicking Horse, Porcupine and Beaverfoot Valleys. The Kicking Horse Corridor hosts the park's largest black bear population.

The Ice River area, according to a study completed in 1978, contained some of the best grizzly habitat in the park, embracing slide paths and important alpine habitat. Ground squirrels are an important food source for grizzlies, and their abundance in both Rockwall and Goodsir Pass contributes to the importance of these areas.

Mountain goats are often observed along the Yoho Valley Road to Takakkaw Falls. They also congregate near the intersection of Highway 1A and the Trans Canada Highway, near the park's east entrance. Bighorn sheep also gather at this intersection.

Bighorn sheep, mule deer, and moose are frequently observed from the trail along Emerald Lake's shore. Moose can be photographed among the sloughs and fens throughout the park. Of particular note is the area near the lake along the Ice River Road as you approach the park's western boundary. Other locations attracting moose are the Beaverfoot River and the Otterhead and Porcupine Valley fire roads. A couple of natural mineral licks should provide plenty of photo opportunities: the Wapta Falls lick and the Ottertail lick.

Yoho National Park is west of Lake Louise and is bounded by Banff National Park on the east and Kootenay National Park on the south. For additional information, contact Yoho National Park (604-343-6324).

Chapter 4

SPECIES

Pika

DESCRIPTION — Brown to gray; short, rounded ears; short tail (not visible); guinea-pig sized.

SCIENTIFIC NAME — *Ochotona princeps*

FAMILY — Pika (Ochotonidae)

BREEDING SEASON — April through June

GESTATION PERIOD — 30 days

NUMBER OF YOUNG — 2 to 4 (usually 3)

Pikas range throughout the Rocky Mountains, from northern New Mexico into Alberta and British Columbia. They live among huge rock piles known as talus slopes, often adjacent to open meadows in spruce-fir forests, to high above timberline. The open meadows are important as a food source.

Pika spend the summer cutting, gathering, and drying their harvest of grasses and leaves, known as "hay piles." These piles, spread out on rocks to dry, are a dead giveaway that pika are nearby. In Rocky Mountain National Park, this activity usually begins in mid-July.

Your first indication that pika are present likely will be their metallic-sounding, nasal bark, which probably function as alarm call. Also look for chalky white to brownish white stains on rocks, produced by the highly concentrated pika urine.

Pika are diurnal — busy from dawn to dusk.

PHOTOGRAPHIC TECHNIQUES

Pikas are small — very small. You will need a high-powered telephoto lens (500 mm to 600 mm). I have not found it necessary to use a blind. Simply set up your tripod in a good location and wait ... and wait ... and wait. Your patience will reward you.

TIME OF YEAR

Pikas are most easily located and photographed between July and September.

PHOTOGRAPHIC HOT SPOTS

ROCKY MOUNTAIN NATIONAL PARK, COLORADO

My favorite location for photographing pika is along Trail Ridge Road, near Rock Cut. From the Rock Cut, go west 1 mile. Park in the pull-off along the north side of the road. Pika live among the talus slopes immediately south of the road.

For additional information, see Chapter 3.

WHITE PINE LAKE, WASATCH-CACHE NATIONAL FOREST, UTAH

White Pine Lake, located 10,000 feet above sea level, provides a picturesque backdrop as you photograph pikas on the nearby talus slopes. The lake is a 3-mile hike from the trailhead. Look for "hay piles" and pika among the talus slopes south and west of the lake.

From Salt Lake City, drive south along U.S. 89 for 10 miles. Go east on State Highway 209 to Granite. From Granite, continue east on State Highway 210 to Little Cottonwood Canyon. The White Pine Lake trailhead is 0.75 mile east of Tanners Flat Campground.

For additional information, contact the U.S. Forest Service (801-524-5042).

BANFF NATIONAL PARK, ALBERTA

In Lake Louise, exit Highway 1 and follow the signs to the lake and the Chateau Lake Louise parking lot. Follow the hiking trail along the north side of the lake approximately 4 kilometers (2.5 miles) to a viewpoint. Listen for pika among the rocks and boulders in this area.

For additional information, see Chapter 3.

JASPER NATIONAL PARK, ALBERTA

Mount Edith Cavell hosts one of the most accessible locations for pika photography in Jasper National Park. Go south from Jasper Townsite on Provincial Highway 93A approximately 5 miles. Turn right (west) to Mount Edith Cavell and follow the road to the trailhead. Pika will be found among the rocks along the trail, about a 10-minute hike from the parking area.

For additional information, see Chapter 3.

WATERTON LAKES NATIONAL PARK, ALBERTA

Pika are found in several locations within the park. One of the more accessible areas is near lower Rowe Lake. To reach the area, take the Akamina Parkway from Waterton Townsite. After traveling approximately 9 kilometers (5.4 miles), you will come to a trailhead on your right. Follow the trail 3.9 kilometers (2.3 miles) to the lower Rowe Lake area. Search the talus slopes for pika, listening for their calls.

For additional information, see Chapter 3.

Snowshoe hare, winter pelage

Snowshoe hare, summer pelage

Snowshoe Hare

DESCRIPTION—
Summer: grayish brown; tail black on top, white below.
Winter: white all over with black-tipped ears.

Larger than cottontails, smaller than white-tailed jack rabbits; large feet.

SCIENTIFIC NAME – *Lepus americanus*

FAMILY – Rabbit (Leporidae)

BREEDING SEASON – March to August

GESTATION PERIOD – 38 days

NUMBER OF YOUNG – 1 to 7 (average 3)

The snowshoe hare — grayish brown in summer and white in winter — demonstrates nature's camouflage at its best. The hare's transformation into its winter pelage (coat) commences in September and is completed by late November or early December. This is known as the autumnal molt. The pre-vernal molt begins in early April. Early or late snowfalls, which may catch hares with the wrong color of fur, place them at great risk from predators.

Snowshoe hares are commonly found in dense boreal forests containing an abundance of shrub understory. In Colorado, suitable habitat often exists between 8,000 feet and 11,000 feet. Farther north, in Canada, these hares are found in valley bottoms near 6,000 feet.

Forest fires benefit the snowshoe hare because shrubs soon colonize land that has been decimated by fire. These areas provide ideal habitat.

Snowshoe hares are often called "rabbits." However, they are true hares. Newborn hares are precocial, meaning they come into the world fully furred and able to move about soon after birth. Rabbits' offspring are altricial — they are born blind, naked, and completely helpless. Young hares are called "leverets" during their first year.

The snowshoe hare is primarily nocturnal. It retires to depressions under brush or shrubs during the day. These unlined depressions are called "forms."

Over time, snowshoe hares literally eat themselves out of house and home. As a result, their numbers are subject to great fluctuations. Population crashes occur about every 10 years.

PHOTOGRAPHIC TECHNIQUES

First, locate your subject. Search dense forests containing areas of thick undergrowth. Willow thickets often provide suitable cover. Look for signs such as scat (droppings) or tunnels through brush and undergrowth. In winter, look for tracks in the snow. During this time of year, snowshoe hares eat the bark from young trees, so look for saplings with bark stripped away at the base.

Take advantage of early or late snowfalls. An early-spring thaw is just as good. A white hare really stands out in a forest without snow, as does a gray hare during a late snowfall.

If your subject is in the open when you first spot it, it will probably run. Don't worry. Most likely, it will not go very far. Moving slowly, renew your search beneath nearby logs and brush piles. After you've located the subject; again, continue moving slowly. The hare will remain motionless, probably thinking you have not seen it. Now, you can take your pictures.

Another technique for locating snowshoe hares is to drive rural roads early in the morning. Hares can sometimes be observed feeding along the roadside.

Most of my snowshoe hare images have been taken using an 80-200 mm, f2.8 lens. However, it would have been easier with my 200-400 mm, f4.

Don't forget to make the necessary corrections to your meter reading when metering off white subjects. (See Exposure, Chapter 2.)

TIME OF YEAR

Photograph snowshoe hares when you find them. I have had the most success during early and late snowfalls. Snowshoe hares sport their white winter pelage from December through March; they wear a brownish gray coat from April into November.

PHOTOGRAPHIC HOT SPOTS

Snowshoe hares are common in most regions covered by this book. When photographing in parks or wildlife refuges, check with park personnel for recent snowshoe hare sightings and locations.

Rocky Mountain National Park, Colorado

One of the most accessible locations in the park for photographing snowshoe hares is the Longs Peak Trail. I have observed a number of hares in this area. To reach the Longs Peak trailhead, go south from Estes Park on Colorado Highway 7 approximately 7 miles. Turn right (west) at the Longs Peak Trail sign, and drive to the parking area. Search the coniferous woodlands along the trail, from trailhead to treeline.

For additional information, see Chapter 3.

Heyburn State Park, Idaho

Heyburn State Park, along the shore of Lake Chatcolet, is comprised of shallow lakes, extensive marshes, and verdant forests. Six trails meander among 400-year-old ponderosas.

Almost 8,000 acres of mature forest in Heyburn State Park, much of it containing dense undergrowth, provide suitable habitat for the snowshoe hare. Search areas of dense cover along the trails. Early morning is the best time.

From Coeur d'Alene, drive 35 miles south along U.S. 95 to Plummer. Go east 5 miles on State Highway 5 to the park entrance. For additional information, contact Heyburn State Park (208-686-1308). During winter, the park headquarters is closed on weekends.

Banff National Park, Alberta

Near Banff Townsite, exit the Trans Canada Highway at take the Lake Minnewanka exit. Go north, following Lake Minnewanka Road until it dead-ends at Johnson Lake. Snowshoe hares are often observed in the area surrounding the lake.

For additional information, see Chapter 3.

Jasper National Park, Alberta

Snowshoe hares are frequently observed around the Icefield Campground. May seems to be the best month for photography. The campground is located 109 kilometers (65 miles) south of Jasper Townsite, along the Icefields Parkway.

For additional information, see Chapter 3.

Waterton Lakes National Park, Alberta

Snowshoe hares are found in several areas within the park. One of the more accessible locations is near lower Rowe Lake. To reach this area, take the Akamina Parkway from Waterton Townsite. After traveling approximately 9 kilometers (5.4 miles), you will come to a trailhead on your right. Follow the trail 2 or 3 kilometers (1.2 to 1.8 miles) in search of your subjects.

For additional information, see Chapter 3.

Porcupine

DESCRIPTION – Yellowish black color; 18 to 22 inches long; 7- to 9-inch tail; 10 to 28 pounds.

SCIENTIFIC NAME – *Erethizon dorsatum*

FAMILY – New World Porcupines (Erethizontidae)

BREEDING SEASON – September and October

GESTATION PERIOD – 205 to 217 days

NUMBER OF YOUNG – Single kit (rarely twins)

Porcupines are often observed along roadsides early in the morning and again at dusk, waddling along with their unmistakable, pigeon-toed gait.

Mostly nocturnal, a porcupine will take shelter under a rocky overhang, in a hollow log, or in a stream-side willow thicket during the day. These frequently used shelters are easily recognized by their musty odor and the presence of crescent-shaped scat.

With their armor of some 30,000 quills, it is no wonder porcupines are solitary animals. However, in extremely cold weather, several porcupines may share a den. Males and females obviously get together sometime — females bear a single kit in April or May.

Porcupines are precocial. The kit is a miniature version of its parents, with eyes open at birth and soft quills that harden within a half-hour of being exposed to air.

Porcupines are known for stripping the bark from aspen and ponderosa trees in search of their preferred fare, the succulent inner bark known as the cambium layer. This, however, is their winter diet. During spring and summer, they seem to prefer herbs and forbs, along with seeds and tender buds.

These animals are common in open pine woodlands throughout the Rockies. But their range of habitats is large, from broadleaf woodland streams to willow thickets above treeline. In northwestern Colorado, I have observed porcupines among stands of Gambel oak adjacent to sagebrush-covered hillsides.

When abundant, their presence is obvious — large branches will be stripped of bark. It is not uncommon for porcupines to kill the tops of trees. Scat, along with small pieces of bark at the base, will identify a tree selected by porcupines; small teeth marks may also be evident. Not all bark stripping is the result of porcupine activity, however. Small branches that have been stripped are often the work of red squirrels.

PHOTOGRAPHIC TECHNIQUES

Find 'em and photograph 'em! Unfortunately, finding them is not always easy.

Begin by looking for porcupine activity, such as branches and tree trunks stripped of bark, along with dead tree tops. Network with park personnel. Once you have pinpointed an area supporting an active porcupine population, begin a systematic search. Check rocky overhangs and hollow logs. Search among willows in the area. Drive the roads before sunrise and again at dusk.

Once you've located your subject, you normally will be able to get fairly close to it. An 80-200 mm lens should be ideal. And, since porcupines almost always seek areas where light levels are low, I recommend using a flash.

TIME OF YEAR

Locating and photographing porcupines may be somewhat easier during winter, because their foraging area is a fraction of what it is during summer. Young porcupines may be photographed, tagging along behind their mother, in late April and May. Otherwise, since porcupines are active all year, I recommend photographing them whenever you find them.

PHOTOGRAPHIC HOT SPOTS

ARAPAHO NATIONAL WILDLIFE REFUGE, COLORADO

I recommend beginning your search from a convenient overlook on the hill immediately south of refuge headquarters. From this location, using your binoculars, you can scan the willows along the Illinois River for evidence of porcupine activity. If this proves unproductive, move south along the hill and repeat your search. Early in the morning, you may actually see porcupines feeding in the trees.

For directions and additional information, see Chapter 3.

OURAY NATIONAL WILDLIFE REFUGE, UTAH

Ouray National Wildlife Refuge, encompassing almost 12,000 acres along the banks of the Green River, features miles of hiking trails and a 10-mile auto tour. The refuge's habitat diversity — desert shrub to cattail marshes, grasslands to cottonwood bottoms — contributes to a wide assortment of wildlife species.

Porcupines are fairly common in the refuge. Early morning is the best time to look. Spend most of your time searching among the willows.

From Vernal, drive southwest along U.S. 40 for 14 miles. Turn left onto State Highway 88, and follow this 15 miles to the refuge. For additional information, contact the U.S. Fish and Wildlife Service (801-789-0351).

SEEDSKADEE NATIONAL WILDLIFE REFUGE, WYOMING

Porcupines are common in the refuge. Carefully search the willows in the Green River bottomlands for their presence. Using binoculars, you can observe a section of river bottom along the west side of the river from the road. On the east side of the river, another road provides access. Early mornings are best.

For additional information, see Chapter 3.

SILVER CREEK PRESERVE, IDAHO

Silver Creek Preserve is comprised of 2,800 acres of aspen groves and willows along spring-fed Silver Creek, surrounded by sagebrush desert. The preserve is owned and operated by The Nature Conservancy.

Be sure to stop at the preserve headquarters. Sign in and advise the staff of your plans. In addition to furnishing a preserve map, they can be very helpful in locating porcupines.

To reach the preserve, go west from the town of Picabo along U.S. 20. After a bit more than 3 miles, you will pass a highway on your right, going toward Gannett. Just past this junction, turn left and follow a road 2 miles to Silver Creek Preserve headquarters.

For additional information, contact The Nature Conservancy (208-726-3007).

RED ROCK LAKES NATIONAL WILDLIFE REFUGE, MONTANA

Porcupines are common throughout the wooded areas in the refuge. Search the willows near the lakes. Also, inquire among the people living in nearby Lakeview. Porcupines make occasional visits to the residents in search of items to gnaw upon, such as axe handles, saddles, harnesses, barn doors, and the like. Be at one of these locations early in the morning, and you've got your picture.

For additional information, see Chapter 3.

BANFF NATIONAL PARK, ALBERTA

The area along the Cephren Lake Trail is frequented by porcupines. To reach the trail, go northwest from Lake Louise approximately 120 kilometers (72 miles) along the Icefields Parkway. The trail can be accessed from the Waterfowl Lakes Campground, located on the west side of the highway.

Beaver

DESCRIPTION — Brown fur; scaly, flattened, paddle-shaped tail; 25 to 30 inches long; 9- to 10-inch tail; 35 to 60 pounds (some reported over 100 pounds).

SCIENTIFIC NAME — *Castor canadensis*

FAMILY — Beaver (Castoridae)

BREEDING SEASON — Late January to late February

GESTATION PERIOD — 120 days

NUMBER OF YOUNG — 1 to 6 (usually 4 or 5)

Beavers are nature's hydrological engineers. They create their own habitat through dam construction, then manipulate the changed ecosystem to suit their needs. Primarily nocturnal, beavers are common in small ponds, lakes, and slow-moving rivers throughout the Rockies.

Once a suitable dam location has been selected along a stream, the work begins. (Hence the adage, "busy as a beaver.") Trees are felled and sectioned. Bark is stripped. Branches and tree sections are dragged by mouth to the construction site, placed across the water, woven together, and held in place with mud. The work is continued until the water level rises to suit the beavers' needs. The finished dam may be 5 or 6 feet high and 100 feet across. According to author David M. Armstrong, the record beaver dam is 14 feet high and 3,000 feet long.

Once the dam has been constructed, a lodge is built. The lodge has at least two underwater passages, with living quarters above water. Canals are often dug to expedite the movement of logs to the lodge. It is not uncommon for a beaver lodge to extend 6 feet above water and to be 12 feet or more in diameter.

Beavers do not always build lodges. Along rivers, and sometimes in large lakes, they simply dig a home into the bank. These earthen dwellings are known as dens.

Beavers devour large quantities of willow and aspen, their main food sources throughout the Rockies. These trees' availability determines how long beavers will be active in one place.

A lodge is usually occupied by two adults, their kits, and offspring from the past two years. As many as 12 beavers have been observed in a single dwelling. Upon reaching their second birthday, the young leave the lodge in search of virgin territory, where they will construct new dams and lodges.

As a warning of the presence of intruders, beavers often slap their tails sharply on the water before diving. A highly adapted respiratory and circulatory system allows them to remain submerged up to five minutes.

Beavers do not hibernate in winter. In autumn, as the mountains become clothed in golden aspen leaves, they stockpile an underwater food cache of green limbs and logs before their lake freezes over. All of the members of the colony work together on this activity.

PHOTOGRAPHIC TECHNIQUES

Patience is the key for obtaining beaver photographs. First, locate an active beaver colony. Fresh wood chips, sectioned logs, and gnawed stumps near a stream or slow-moving river are dead giveaways of an active beaver lodge.

A good blind is helpful in areas where beavers are not accustomed to people. Beavers almost always wear a path from the water to the place where they are cutting trees. Locate your blind in this area. After you work with a colony for several days, the beavers usually will accept your presence, and a blind will no longer be necessary.

An ISO 400 film will allow you to shoot photographs when beavers are active, in the low-light conditions of early morning and dusk.

A beaver is a very dark subject. When metering, remember to compensate by one-half stop (see Exposure, Chapter 2).

TIME OF YEAR

Fortunately, beavers are not always nocturnal. Occasionally, they are active at dawn or dusk. From mid-September through mid-October, they are often active during daylight hours, so this is the best time of the year to photograph them.

PHOTOGRAPHIC HOT SPOTS

TWO MOON PARK, MONTANA

Two Moon County Park, an urban park in the northeast section of Billings, features cottonwood river bottoms, dense underbrush, and cattail-lined sloughs along the Yellowstone River.

The park supports an active beaver colony. Quietly make your way through dense cover to the park's north side. You should have no problem photographing beavers in the slough as they carry out their daily chores. Stop by the caretakers' house and inform them of your intentions.

In Billings, go north on Main Street, then east onto Bench Boulevard. Follow Bench approximately 5 miles, turn right onto a gravel road, and go to the parking area at the bottom of the hill.

For additional information, contact Yellowstone County (406-256-2703).

BANFF NATIONAL PARK, ALBERTA

Two areas near Banff Townsite are worthy of your inspection: Johnson Lake and Vermilion Lakes.

Johnson Lake is near Lake Minnewanka. As you approach Banff Townsite from the east along Highway 1, take the Lake Minnewanka exit to the north. Follow Lake Minnewanka Road until its end at Johnson Lake. Beaver ponds are located on the northeast side of the lake. A trail from the parking area leads to the ponds.

The Vermilion Lakes are only a few minutes west of Banff Townsite. From town, take the Mount Norquay Road as if you were heading to the Trans Canada Highway. However, just before reaching the highway, turn left onto Vermilion Lakes Drive. Continue approximately 2 miles until reaching the third Vermilion Lake. You will see an area where a number of trees have been felled by beavers. This is my favorite location for beaver photography. I have found beavers to be active here during daylight hours, not only in the fall but also in spring and summer.

For additional information, see Chapter 3.

JASPER NATIONAL PARK, ALBERTA

The park abounds with opportunities for photographing beavers. Four locations are a "must."

The first is the Valley of Five Lakes, located less than 10 kilometers (6 miles) south of Jasper Townsite. To reach the area, go south from town on the Icefields Parkway. Approximately 8 kilometers (5 miles) from town, the highway crosses the Athabasca River. One and a half kilometers (0.9 mile) after crossing the river, you will come to the Valley of Five Lakes trailhead on the east side of the highway. From the trailhead to the lakes is just over 1.5 kilometers (0.9 mile).

The Miette River and its sloughs comprise the second noteworthy location for photographing beavers. Immediately south of town, Highway 16 crosses the Icefields Parkway. Going west from this intersection, Highway 16 parallels the river all the way to the border with British Columbia border. Along its first 5 kilometers (3 miles), the north side of the highway is an active beaver habitat.

Cottonwood Creek is the next location. It can be reached by taking the Pyramid Lake Road from Jasper Townsite. This road crosses Cottonwood Creek 2.5 kilometers (1.5 miles) north of town. Search the area west of the road for beaver activity.

Talbot Lake is the fourth location worthy of your consideration. Located 26 kilometers (16 miles) north of town, the lake is situated along the east side of Highway 16. A beaver lodge is located near the east end of the lake.

For additional information, see Chapter 3.

WATERTON LAKES NATIONAL PARK, ALBERTA

An active beaver lodge and pond are located along Red Rock Parkway. From Waterton Townsite, go northeast approximately 3.5 kilometers (2 miles) to Red Rock Parkway. Turn left and go 3 kilometers (1.8 miles). The beaver pond is located south of the parkway.

For additional information, see Chapter 3.

YOHO NATIONAL PARK, BRITISH COLUMBIA

Beavers are found in several areas within the park. However, some locations, such as the upper Ice River Valley, are accessible only to Paul Bunyan types. One area with reasonable access is the Lower Kicking Horse River Valley, along Ottertail Flats. This is along the west side of the Trans Canada Highway, between 9 and 13 kilometers (5.4 and 7.8 miles) south of Field.

For additional information, see Chapter 3.

Yellow-bellied Marmot

DESCRIPTION — Brownish above; yellowish below; 14 to 20 inches long; 5 to 10 pounds.

SCIENTIFIC NAME — *Marmota flaviventris*

FAMILY — Squirrel (Sciuridae)

BREEDING SEASON — Within two weeks after emergence from hibernation (usually March or April)

GESTATION PERIOD — 28 to 35 days

NUMBER OF YOUNG — 3 to 6 (average of 5)

Marmots are most often observed sunbathing atop large boulders after their morning feast of lush grasses. From these rocky perches, they often sound a series of high-pitched chirps to warn of approaching danger.

In the Rockies, yellow-bellied marmots occupy suitable habitat from northern New Mexico to central Montana. Marmots can be found anywhere from pastures along the foothills to alpine tundra; they prefer talus slopes and boulder-strewn areas, which provide protection from predators.

Marmots dig extensive underground burrows, usually locating the entrance under a boulder. However, they are not restricted to rocky areas. Marmots occasionally take up residence under cabins or other human structures. They also require nearby areas containing lush forage.

Yellow-bellied marmots form colonies containing as many as several dozen individuals. A colony consists of a single adult male, his "harem" of several females, and numerous litters of young, along with yearlings born up to two years before.

Breeding occurs within the first two weeks after marmots emerge from hibernation in March or April. Three to six naked, blind babies are born in late April or May. A month later, the babies emerge from the den, ready to explore the world. By the end of August, they will be fully grown.

A day in the life of a marmot begins at sunrise, with feasting on lush, green plants. After all this "hard work," a mid-morning nap is required. Around noon the sun must get a little too hot, for the marmot retires to an underground burrow. After the proper amount of much-needed rest, the marmot reappears in mid-afternoon from its burrow. Serious foraging now begins. Of course, this is interspersed with occasional naps. After a full day of such activities, the marmot returns to the burrow to get a full night's sleep, so its arduous tasks can begin once more the next morning.

Around mid-July, yellow-bellied marmots sometimes escape the increasing summer heat by going into estivation, a form of dormancy or torpor, where body activity and metabolism decreases. In September or October, hibernation begins. Body temperatures during hibernation may drop as low as 36 degrees Fahrenheit.

PHOTOGRAPHIC TECHNIQUES

I have found the early morning hours to be best for photographing marmots. The light is better, and the marmots tend to be more active.

When an unannounced intruder (photographer) approaches an active marmot colony, a series of high-pitched warning calls is usually given as the residents disappear into their burrows. When this happens, find a comfortable location within photographic range and wait. After determining that you present no threat, the marmots usually will resume their activity, allowing you many photographic opportunities.

Avoid sudden movements when photographing marmots. Allow them to come to you. A 400 mm lens will allow a comfortable working distance while providing enough magnification to produce desirable images.

TIME OF YEAR

Marmots can be photographed from March or April until the following fall, when hibernation begins again. I have found marmots very approachable along Trail Ridge Road in Rocky Mountain National Park soon after it opens on Memorial Day.

PHOTOGRAPHIC HOT SPOTS

MOUNT EVANS, COLORADO

Mount Evans, only a few hours from Denver, has a paved road to its 14,264-foot summit, providing some of the most spectacular vistas in Colorado, plus opportunities for photographing several wildlife species, including yellow-bellied marmots.

Once above treeline, you're likely to see marmots anywhere. One of my favorite locations is the first switchback past Summit Lake, on your way to the summit. There is room to park along the south side of the road at the switchback. At this point, an old road once continued straight ahead. You should have no problem locating marmots along this trail.

For additional information, see Chapter 3.

ROCKY MOUNTAIN NATIONAL PARK, COLORADO

Marmots are habituated to the presence of people at Forest Canyon Overlook and the Rock Cut, two stops along Trail Ridge Road. Search the rocks and boulders along the paths for bundles of brown fur scampering about.

For additional information, see Chapter 3.

YELLOWSTONE NATIONAL PARK, WYOMING

The yellow-bellied marmot is common throughout the park. Those at Mount Washburn generally prove to be easy photographic subjects. Two different trails take you to the summit. To reach the area, take the road from Canyon Village toward Tower Junction. After driving approximately 5 miles you will see a parking area on the right. A sign designates this as Dunraven Pass. The parking lot is also the trailhead for a 3.6-mile hike to the summit of Mount Washburn. It is a moderately easy hike to the summit. However, you will gain almost 1,400 feet in elevation.

Another approach is to continue past Dunraven Pass another 4 miles. You will see a road on the right and a sign proclaiming "Mt. Washburn." Don't get too excited. The road leads to the Chittenden parking area. It is still a 3-mile hike to the summit.

For additional information, see Chapter 3.

Yellow-bellied marmot near his rocky den

Abert's Squirrel

DESCRIPTION – Three color phases: gray with white underparts; black; and dark brown. Conspicuous ear tassels; 12 inches long; 9-inch tail.

SCIENTIFIC NAME – *Sciurus aberti*

FAMILY – Squirrel (Sciuridae)

BREEDING SEASON – Late March to May

GESTATION PERIOD – 42 days

NUMBER OF YOUNG – 2 to 5

Abert's squirrels inhabit ponderosa woodlands in the southern Rockies, the Colorado Plateau, and the Sierra Madre. In the regions covered by this book, they can be found between 5,600 feet and 9,000 feet along the east slope of the southern Rockies, from northern New Mexico to southern Wyoming.

Born between May and early July, young Abert's squirrels begin venturing from their nests in ponderosa trees when they are seven weeks old. They do not hibernate.

Abert's squirrels are most easily spotted early in the morning, as they go from ponderosa to ponderosa to feed on young, staminate (male) cones, buds, and the inner bark of small twigs. Though these squirrels are occasionally found in spruce-fir forests, they will not be far from a ponderosa woodland.

A sure sign of Abert's squirrel activity is a forest floor littered with ponderosa needles and peeled twigs, beneath a tree adorned with stripped branches.

PHOTOGRAPHIC TECHNIQUES

Photographing Abert's squirrels is a matter of being at the right place at the right time. The right time is usually early in the morning. Although the right place is ponderosa woodlands, I have found it more productive to search picnic areas and campgrounds in or adjacent to ponderosa woodlands than to look in the woods themselves. The squirrels are most accustomed to human activity in these areas, where they are attracted to the food left behind.

TIME OF YEAR

Since more people are picnicking and camping between May and September, these months are best for locating and photographing Abert's squirrels.

PHOTOGRAPHIC HOT SPOTS

Rocky Mountain National Park, Colorado

My favorite location for photographing Abert's squirrels is the picnic area near the alluvial fan (rock slide) in Endovalley. From the Sheep Lakes parking area in Horseshoe Park, go west along the park road, taking the first right onto Fall River Road. The picnic tables will be on your right, near the alluvial fan.

Do not overlook the Moraine Park Campground. The campground is situated in the middle of a ponderosa woodland — prime Abert's squirrel habitat. From the Beaver Meadows entrance kiosk, take the first left onto Bear Lake Road. Turn right opposite the entrance road into the Moraine Park Museum. Follow the signs to the campground.

For additional information, see Chapter 3.

Abert's squirrel resting on branch

Fox Squirrel

DESCRIPTION — Brownish gray body; bushy tail; 10 to 15 inches long; 9- to 14-inch tail; 1.25 to 3 pounds.

SCIENTIFIC NAME — *Sciurus niger*

FAMILY — Squirrel (Sciuridae)

BREEDING SEASON — January and February (primary period); May and June (secondary period)

GESTATION PERIOD — 44 days

NUMBER OF YOUNG — 2 to 4

Fox squirrels, common in most city parks and many neighborhoods throughout the Rocky Mountains, are often the first squirrel that many people see.

Initially, fox squirrels were found only in the eastern and central United States. However, they are capable of adapting to a wide range of habitats, and they have extended their range westward, primarily along river corridors. This westward expansion was hastened when some people introduced squirrels into new areas.

Breeding occurs during two principal periods: January and February, the primary season, and again in May and June. These times often vary in northern areas of the Rockies.

Preferred den sites are hollow tree cavities. If these are unavailable, a leaf nest is often constructed, sometimes from scratch. More often than not, however, an abandoned magpie nest is converted. Squirrel nests made with leaves are easy to distinguish from bird nests, which are constructed from sticks and twigs. A typical leaf nest is 12 to 20 inches in diameter.

After a gestation period of 44 days, two to four altricial (blind, naked, and helpless) young are born. Development of the young squirrels is slow. Their eyes do not open until the fifth week, and they are almost two months old before they venture forth and begin exploring their nest tree. It's usually another two weeks before they set foot on the ground.

Sexual maturity is reached in just under a year. Yearling females tend to produce only one litter their first year, while older females usually breed twice a year.

Fox squirrels spend a good deal of time on the ground in search of their favorite foods: fungi, seeds, nuts, and, when available, acorns.

PHOTOGRAPHIC TECHNIQUES

City parks and zoos are the easiest places to locate and photograph fox squirrels. At such locations, they are unafraid of people. Avoid sudden, jerky movements, and allow them to come to you — they often will. A 400 mm telephoto is sufficient. On one occasion, I used my 135 mm lens, obtaining excellent results.

TIME OF YEAR

Spring and summer are good times to photograph this likable squirrel, because many people are in the parks at those times and squirrels often hang around, waiting for scraps. However, don't overlook the opportunities for colorful backgrounds provided by autumn leaves.

PHOTOGRAPHIC HOT SPOTS

CENTRAL PARK, BOULDER, COLORADO

I once heard a radio announcer describe Boulder as "halfway between Aspen (Colorado) and reality." It's true, many "squirrels" inhabit Boulder's Central Park — including fox squirrels.

Feasting on Boulder's typically healthy handouts of tofu, hummus, and vegetarian chili, the squirrels have become quiet tame and easy to photograph. However, the park is not without its obstacles to photography. Harsh shadows and mixed lighting are problems on bright and sunny days. I recommend the use of a fill flash to eliminate these harmful effects.

Straddling over a mile of Boulder Creek, Central Park is between Canyon Boulevard and Arapahoe Avenue near downtown.

While you're in Boulder, make a point to have breakfast at Lucile's. This is one of the few places west of the Mississippi where you can order grits with your breakfast. If you don't like grits (and I find that hard to comprehend), you can substitute hash browns. Lucile's Cajun breakfasts are awesome.

DENVER ZOO, DENVER, COLORADO

The Denver Zoo, home to more than 1,300 exotic animals, provides many photographic opportunities. The zoo is also home to many free-roaming fox squirrels.

Squirrels can be photographed in the trees lining the zoo's walkways, and at park benches, begging peanuts from visitors. Just about anywhere you go in the zoo, you'll find fox squirrels waiting to be photographed.

The main zoo entrance and parking area are on 23rd Avenue, between York Street and Colorado Boulevard, east of downtown Denver. For additional information, contact the Denver Zoo (303-331-4100).

GREENBELT, FORT COLLINS, COLORADO

The Fort Collins Greenbelt features a paved trail beginning at Colorado State University's Environmental Learning Center. This follows the Cache la Poudre River through Fort Collins, ending at Taft Hill Road, a distance of 8.2 miles.

Fox squirrels can be heard chattering in the cottonwoods along the entire length of the trail. Simply choose a location, get your equipment ready, and enjoy the day photographing fox squirrels.

To reach the Environmental Learning Center, go south on Drake Road. Continue 1 mile past Timberline Road and look for a water-treatment plant on your left. Immediately south of the plant you will cross a water canal. Turn left. The learning center and trailhead are at the end of this road.

For additional information, contact the city of Fort Collins (970-491-1661).

GREENWAY, PUEBLO, COLORADO

The Greenway, situated along the banks of the Arkansas River, is home to many species of songbirds, wading birds, and waterfowl. The fox squirrel also makes its home here.

Photograph fox squirrels among the cottonwoods lining the 3-mile hiking and biking trail. The trail begins at the nature center on West 11th Street, just west of State Highway 45, and ends at Pueblo Reservoir. For additional information, contact the city of Pueblo's Parks Division (719-545-9114).

Golden-mantled Ground Squirrel

DESCRIPTION — Tan to reddish brown upper; whitish beneath; black stripe along body (not extending into face or tail); 6 to 8 inches long; 2- to 5-inch tail

SCIENTIFIC NAME — *Spermophilus lateralis*

FAMILY — Squirrel (Sciuridae)

BREEDING SEASON — March to June

GESTATION PERIOD — 28 to 30 days

NUMBER OF YOUNG — 2 to 8 (usually 5)

Golden-mantled ground squirrels, typically the first animals to greet visitors in many national parks, make up nature's self-appointed welcoming committee.

These inquisitive "beggars" of the squirrel family can be found throughout the Rocky Mountains, from northern New Mexico to central Alberta and British Columbia. They occupy a variety of life zones, ranging from pinon-juniper habitats to alpine tundra. They make their home in burrows under rocks, bushes, or other suitable cover.

Often mistaken for chipmunks, golden-mantled ground squirrels are larger and lack black stripes on their heads.

Upon the first snow in late September or October, this little ground-dwelling squirrel disappears into its burrow, where it remains throughout the winter in a deep sleep.

In late March or April, the males reappear in breeding condition. Two weeks later, the females come into estrus and breeding takes place. In areas where winter persists, this may not occur until May.

PHOTOGRAPHIC TECHNIQUES

Golden-mantled ground squirrels are easy to photograph. First, find a suitable location. Then get out your camera and wait. These squirrels are very curious, and once they accept your presence, they usually will approach you. In fact, you often can obtain frame-filling images with a 200 mm lens.

TIME OF YEAR

The golden-mantled ground squirrel is inactive during the winter and most of the fall. Therefore, April through September are usually the best months.

PHOTOGRAPHIC HOT SPOTS

Golden-mantled ground squirrels are "people friendly." Wherever people congregate, the golden-mantled ground squirrel begs for handouts. Campgrounds, picnic areas, scenic overlooks, and visitor centers are all good places to photograph these curious ground squirrels.

ROCKY MOUNTAIN NATIONAL PARK, COLORADO

Golden-mantled ground squirrels are abundant throughout the park. However, I have two favorite locations: Many Parks Curve and Farview Curve. Both overlooks are situated along Trail Ridge Road. Many Parks is on the east side of the Continental Divide, while Farview Curve is located on the west.

For additional information, see Chapter 3.

YELLOWSTONE NATIONAL PARK, WYOMING

Everything that I have said about chipmunks in Yellowstone also applies to the golden-mantled ground squirrel. After all, this plump, little squirrel is nothing more than a chipmunk with an eating problem. The overlooks at Canyon Village and Tower Falls should provide ample photo opportunities. For additional information, see Chapter 3.

GLACIER NATIONAL PARK, MONTANA

Golden-mantled ground squirrels are frequently observed along Glacier's roadside pull-offs and overlooks, as well as picnic areas. I recommend investigating the Rising Sun Picnic Area, across from St. Mary Lake. In fact, it would be worth your time to explore the entire area across from Lake Mary. For additional information, see Chapter 3.

Jasper National Park, Alberta

Wherever you find people, you'll find the gregarious golden-mantled ground squirrel. All campgrounds, picnic areas, and scenic overlooks usually support populations. One good place to find them is the Icefield Campground, just north of the park's southern boundary, along the east side of the Icefields Parkway. For additional information, see Chapter 3.

Waterton Lakes National Park, Alberta

Golden-mantled ground squirrels are numerous along the Bear's Hump Trail, a 1.4 kilometer (0.8 mile) trail immediately south of the visitor information center in Waterton Townsite. Another location worth investigating is the picnic area and the area around the interpretive display at Blakiston Falls. To reach this area, go 3 kilometers (1.8 miles) northeast of Waterton Townsite to Red Rock Parkway. Turn left onto the parkway and go to the end.

For additional information, see Chapter 3.

Yoho National Park, British Columbia

Like chipmunks, golden-mantled ground squirrels are everywhere in Yoho — at least it seems that way. You should be able to photograph these lovable little rodents at picnic areas and viewpoints and along hiking trails. For directions and additional information, see Chapter 3.

Alert golden-mantled ground squirrel

Columbian Ground Squirrel

DESCRIPTION — Dappled, grayish upper parts; reddish brown legs and feet; 10 to 12 inches long; 3- to 5-inch tail.

SCIENTIFIC NAME — *Spermophilus columbianus*

FAMILY — Squirrel (Sciuridae)

BREEDING SEASON — Mid-April to late May

GESTATION PERIOD — 24 days

NUMBER OF YOUNG — 1 to 8 (usually 3 or 4)

A shrill chirp from a lone sentry, sending other members of the colony scampering to their burrows, is usually the first indication that one has come upon a community of Columbian ground squirrels.

East of the Continental Divide, Columbian ground squirrels can be found from Dillon, Montana, northward into the Willmore Wilderness, north of Jasper, Alberta. West of the Divide, their range extends from central Idaho and eastern Washington northward into eastern British Columbia.

In Montana, the Columbian ground squirrel is generally believed to live only west of the Divide. However, during the past 30 to 40 years this has changed. One possible explanation for the eastward migration is the large number of sprinkler irrigation systems installed on farms.

These squirrels' burrows are typically located in open clearings in wooded areas, meadows, or prairies. A bare dirt mound at the entrance serves as a lookout post.

These ground squirrels disappear below ground in late summer, spending the next eight months hibernating in their winter dens. In Canada, this can occur as early as late July, while in Glacier National Park hibernation begins in late September.

The squirrels emerge from their dens in late March in warmer climates and early May in colder environments. Breeding takes place within the first week of emergence. Males are the first to emerge. Approximately three weeks after the female emerges, she is often observed carrying nest materials — straw and grasses — in her mouth, as she prepares the den for the birth of her young.

After a gestation period of 24 days, three to four young ground squirrels are born. Within 25 days of birth, the young are weaned and appear above ground for the first time.

According to Jan Murie of the University of Alberta, 80 percent of the second-year males disperse to nearby colonies, while some occasionally form new colonies. This behavior is rarely exhibited by females.

Among ground squirrels, Columbians are relatively long-lived, with the average age running between five and seven years. However, shorter life spans do occur at higher altitudes. The maximum known age is 14 years.

PHOTOGRAPHIC TECHNIQUES

Jan Murie suggests photographing the following Columbian ground squirrel behaviors:

1.) Females collecting nest materials in spring.

2.) Squirrels kicking their hind feet in the air while entering small burrow openings.

3.) Juveniles playing in the first few weeks after appearing above ground.

4.) Play among yearlings in spring.

As with most ground squirrels, I recommend using a 400 mm or larger lens. However, the image illustrating this section was taken from my car window with a 135 mm lens.

Columbian ground squirrels usually are quick to resume activity once you settle down in their area. Simply find a suitable location and wait patiently for them to re-emerge from their burrows. In a very short time, your patience will be rewarded.

TIME OF YEAR

Since the Columbian ground squirrel hibernates eight months out of the year, your only photo opportunities will be from April through July. However, if juveniles are your quarry, your best bet will be from late May through mid-June.

PHOTOGRAPHIC HOT SPOTS

NATIONAL BISON RANGE, MONTANA

Many species of wildlife can be photographed in the range, including the diminutive Columbian ground squirrel. One location that's accessible and easy to find is the picnic area east of the entrance. From the town of Ravalli in western Montana, go west along State Highway 200 for 6 miles to the town of Dixon. Turn right onto County Road 212, and go 4 miles to range headquarters.

For additional information, see Chapter 3.

BANFF NATIONAL PARK, ALBERTA

The Buffalo Paddock north of town provides excellent opportunities for photographing Columbian ground squirrels. Go northeast along Banff Avenue. A sign at the end of town will direct you to turn left to the Buffalo Paddock. Cross Highway 1 and follow the signs. Just inside the fenced paddock, you will find a Columbian ground squirrel colony, with an interpretive display and viewing platform. For additional information, see Chapter 3.

JASPER NATIONAL PARK, ALBERTA

Icefield Campground is a good place to photograph the Columbian ground squirrel. The campground is located just north of the park's southern boundary, across from the Columbia Icefield along the Icefields Parkway. For directions and additional information, see Chapter 3.

WATERTON LAKES NATIONAL PARK, ALBERTA

Columbian ground squirrels are abundant in grasslands throughout the park. I have found them to be approachable in the "bison paddock." The paddock entrance is along Highway 6, 2 kilometers (1.2 miles) northwest of the park entrance station.

For directions and additional information, see Chapter 3.

Black-tailed prairie dog

White-tailed prairie dog

Black-tailed Prairie Dog/ White-tailed Prairie Dog

DESCRIPTION — Brownish yellow above; whitish below; small ears; 11 to 12 inches long; 3- to 4-inch tail; 2 to 3 pounds.

Black-tailed: black-tipped tail

White-tailed: white-tipped tail.

SCIENTIFIC NAME — *Cynomys ludovicianus (black-tailed)*
Cynomys leucurus (white-tailed)

FAMILY — Squirrel (Sciuridae)

BREEDING SEASON — March

GESTATION PERIOD — 28 to 33 days

NUMBER OF YOUNG — 3 to 6

Destroyers of range land — that's the charge. However, research has found the prairie dog to be beneficial to grasslands, by fertilizing and aerating the soil.

The endangered black-footed ferret depends almost entirely on the prairie dog as a food source. These ferrets also use prairie dog burrows for den sites. And the ferret is not the only species dependent on prairie dogs. Burrowing owls find protection from predators, nest, and raise their young in prairie dog burrows. As prairie dog populations have declined, so have these species.

The black-tailed prairie dog is the most widely distributed; they can be found in towns and prairies at lower elevations to the east. The white-tailed prairie dog, making its home at higher elevations, seeks open country between the mountain ranges.

White-tailed prairie dogs are less colonial than black-tails; their "town" populations hardly ever exceed 200 individuals. It is not uncommon for town populations of the black-tailed prairie dogs to reach into the thousands. In Texas, one black-tail town contained an estimated 400 million prairie dogs and covered 25,000 square miles.

Prairie dog towns are easily identified by numerous mounds of bare earth, 3 to 6 feet in diameter and a foot or two high. Each mound contains an entrance leading into an intricate series of underground tunnels.

Prairie dogs are active during the day, with one or two sentinels usually standing guard. Unwelcome visitors are greeted by a series of high-pitched, nasal barks, warning others of the intruder's arrival.

The black-tailed prairie dog is active all year. However, during periods of snowfall or extremely cold weather, it may remain underground.

White-tailed prairie dogs hibernate during the winter months. It is not uncommon for them to enter estivation, a time of dormancy, sometime in late July. Certain animals estivate in order to escape summer heat. During estivation, neither body temperature nor metabolism is reduced to the same extent as in hibernation.

PHOTOGRAPHIC TECHNIQUES

Unless you select a location where prairie dogs are conditioned to human presence, a blind may be necessary. If so, it will require time for them to adjust to the blind's presence. Set up the day before you plan to take pictures. The morning of the shoot, get situated in the blind while the sky is still dark.

In some areas I've been able to use my car as a blind. This is where a good window mount comes in handy. Position your camera and window mount ahead of time. Drive slowly until you spot activity. Stop your car, and begin taking pictures.

At a couple of locations, I've found prairie dogs so accustomed to people that I've been able to get out of my car, walk around and take pictures. Once, at Arapaho National Wildlife Refuge in Colorado, I had to wait for one prairie dog to retreat — he was too close for me to take pictures with a 135 mm lens.

As you can see, it's difficult to say what lens is best for photographing prairie dogs. In some areas you may get by with an 80-200 mm zoom lens, while other areas may require the use of a 500 mm telephoto. Most of the time you'll be better off with something in the 500 mm range.

TIME OF YEAR

White-tailed prairie dogs often estivate in July, prior to entering hibernation. Therefore, it is best to plan your photography for April, May, or June.

The black-tailed prairie dog can be photographed year-round, except during snowstorms and extremely cold weather.

Young prairie dogs usually emerge from their burrows sometime in May. This is the best time to photograph them.

PHOTOGRAPHIC HOT SPOTS

MAXWELL NATIONAL WILDLIFE REFUGE, NEW MEXICO

Black-tailed prairie dogs find ample space to excavate their burrows on this 3,600-acre refuge. Seven miles of roads provide easy access. Stop at refuge headquarters to get acquainted, and inform officials of your intentions. If your plans include erecting a portable blind, you'll need permission to do so.

For additional information, see Chapter 3.

ARAPAHO NATIONAL WILDLIFE REFUGE, COLORADO

The white-tailed prairie dog, standing at attention with curiosity piqued, welcomes all visitors to the refuge. While photographing these little guys from the window of my Cherokee, I've had them scamper over, sit on their hind legs, and attempt to look through the window.

The Self-Guided Auto Tour, a six-mile loop, is the best place to photograph these charming rodents. You do not have to worry about finding them — they will find you. The tour loop begins 3 miles south of Walden on the west side of State Highway 125. Follow the signs.

For additional information, see Chapter 3.

OURAY NATIONAL WILDLIFE REFUGE, UTAH

Ouray National Wildlife Refuge, encompassing almost 12,000 acres along the banks of the Green River, features miles of hiking trails and a 10-mile auto tour. The refuge's habitat diversity — desert shrub to cattail marshes, grasslands to cottonwood bottoms — contributes to a wide assortment of wildlife species.

White-tailed prairie dogs inhabit many areas of the refuge. As you enter the refuge you'll pass two small colonies. Before visiting, stop by the refuge headquarters in Vernal. (See Appendix I for the address.) If you want to erect a portable blind you need to obtain a permit.

From Vernal, drive southwest along U.S. 40 for 14 miles. Turn left onto State Highway 88 and follow this 15 miles to the refuge. For additional information, contact the U.S. Fish and Wildlife Service (801-789-0351).

SEEDSKADEE NATIONAL WILDLIFE REFUGE, WYOMING

With several access roads on both sides of the Green River, plus on-foot access to almost the entire refuge, Seedskadee is "user friendly" for wildlife photographers. White-tailed prairie dogs inhabit almost 2,000 acres of the refuge. Scout the area west of State Highway 372. It will be necessary to examine the area closely when searching for white-tails. They form much smaller colonies than their black-tailed cousins do.

For additional information, see Chapter 3.

GREYCLIFF PRAIRIE DOG TOWN STATE PARK, MONTANA

This is probably the best location in North America for photographing black-tailed prairie dogs. They show practically no fear of humans and readily adjust to the presence of a photographer in their midst. Needless to say, photo opportunities are excellent. The prairie dogs are most active between mid-March and October.

Greycliff Prairie Dog Town State Park is 60 miles east of Bozeman and 69 miles west of Billings, along Interstate 90. Take the Greycliff exit, Exit 377, and follow the signs to the prairie dog town, immediately south and east of the exit. For additional information, (406-252-4654).

Prairie dogs at entrance to burrow

Coyote

DESCRIPTION – Grayish brown body; reddish brown markings on head and legs; tail tipped with black; 32 to 40 inches long; 14-inch tail; 30 to 50 pounds (usually closer to 30 pounds).

SCIENTIFIC NAME – *Canis latrans*

FAMILY – Dog (Canidae)

BREEDING SEASON – January to March

GESTATION PERIOD – 60 to 63 days

NUMBER OF YOUNG – 4 to 10 (usually 5 to 7)

According to Native American traditions, the world in which man lives is a dream of the coyote. When coyote awakes, man will be gone. The name coyote comes from the Aztec word coyotl, which means "barking dog."

In the face of extensive persecution, coyotes not only have managed to survive but also have extended their range.

Coyotes mate between the months of January and March, with courtship behavior beginning two to three months earlier. It is uncommon for coyotes to mate for life. However, a mated pair usually remains together for several years.

The female often prepares a number of den sites, usually in remodeled badger burrows, before giving birth. The den may be a simple hole in the ground or an intricate network of tunnels containing several entrances. Dens typically are located near water. If the family is disturbed, the female will move the pups to one of the alternate locations.

After a gestation of 60 to 63 days, the female gives birth to six or seven hairless pups. Their eyes remain closed for nine to fourteen days. At about three weeks of age, they emerge from the den. When the pups are between eight and ten weeks of age, the family abandons the den.

The male coyote provides food for the female and pups as long as they remain at the den. Coyotes' diet is varied. Small mammals, birds, insects, and even berries are sometimes the fare of the day. During winter, when deep snow inhibits the movement of hoofed mammals, it is not uncommon for coyotes to take down a deer or even an elk. Coyotes are most active around sunrise and sunset.

The coyote may live alone, in pairs, or in packs. However, their basic social unit is the mated pair and their young. By October or November, most of the young coyotes leave the family structure.

Coyotes are frequently identified incorrectly as either foxes or wolves. A running fox extends its tail straight out, while the coyote commonly carries its tail between its legs. Also, the tail of a red fox has a white tip, while the coyote has a black-tipped tail. The muzzle of the coyote is decidedly pointed, while the head of the wolf is flat and more massive.

Coyotes follow a very specific hunting routine, using the same path over and over. This route may consist of trails made by deer or elk, stock paths, and even man-made footpaths or roadways. These hunting trails may extend up to 10 miles, and, as long as prey remains accessible, will be used throughout the life of the animal. Coyotes often will follow a flight of ravens or magpies in search of a carcass.

Coyotes communicate with each other through an assortment of vocalizations, including barking (a series of "yips"), the trailing howl, and the group serenade, comprised of a series of "yips" followed by howling.

PHOTOGRAPHIC TECHNIQUES

It's difficult to say which lens is best to use when photographing coyotes. I've had opportunities to photograph coyotes along Trail Ridge Road in Rocky Mountain National Park using a 50 mm lens. In Yellowstone National Park, I've actually been able to photograph coyotes begging for food at picnic tables. However, most of the time it will be necessary to use a 500 mm to 600 mm telephoto lens.

In the national parks, coyotes often become habituated to people. In these areas, scout locations frequented by the coyotes. After locating a subject, remain in your vehicle, using it as a blind. This is where a solid window mount comes in handy.

Another way to photograph coyotes is to lure them into range using a predator call. (See Calling Wildlife, Chapter 2.) An injured-rabbit call usually works best. Use either a mouth-blown call or an electronic caller.

Erect your blind in an open meadow or along a trail intersection with good visibility. Set up your camera with the wind at your back. If you are using an electronic caller with a separate speaker, locate the speaker under brush or in high grass, as far upwind from you as possible. Coyotes invariably circle downwind before making their final approach. The coyote's attention will be focused on where the sound is coming from, rather than on where you are located.

CAUTION: Avoid calling too loudly. Call at a volume lower than the animal you are imitating would use. As your subject approaches the speaker, reduce the volume. It is not uncommon for a coyote to take half an hour to come into photographic range.

Coyotes can be effectively called day and night. However, early morning hours will often be more productive. Since national parks prohibit visitors from calling wildlife, I recommend national wildlife refuges. I have found most refuge personnel very helpful.

TIME OF YEAR

Coyotes can be photographed year-round. However, if you plan to use a predator call, you will probably have more success during fall and winter.

PHOTOGRAPHIC HOT SPOTS

BOSQUE DEL APACHE NATIONAL WILDLIFE REFUGE, NEW MEXICO

While driving the refuge's 15-mile auto tour, coyotes are often observed. Upon arriving, stop at the refuge office, introduce yourself, and share your intentions. Refuge personnel will assist you in any way possible. If your plans include erecting a portable blind, you'll need permission to do so, and it is granted on a case-by-case basis.

CAUTION: The refuge is home to the western diamondback rattlesnake. Watch where you place your feet.

For complete directions and additional information, see Chapter 3.

ARAPAHO NATIONAL WILDLIFE REFUGE, COLORADO

The Arapaho National Wildlife Refuge is situated in North Park, in the center of a glacial basin surrounded by mountains. Numerous roads crisscross the refuge. Select a remote section, set up your blind, and begin calling. However, first obtain permission from personnel at the refuge headquarters, located along State Highway 125, 7 miles south of Walden. Turn east at the refuge entrance sign onto a gravel road and follow the signs to headquarters.

For complete directions and additional information, see Chapter 3.

YELLOWSTONE NATIONAL PARK, WYOMING

Cascade Meadows is the most consistent location in the United States for photographing wild coyotes successfully. The photo opportunities at this location are like the old saying about the weather: "If you don't like the weather, wait an hour or so, and it'll change." In other words, if the coyotes aren't around when you arrive, wait an hour or so, and they'll be there.

Cascade Meadows is situated along both sides of Norris Canyon Road, less than a mile west of Canyon Junction. Typically, more activity occurs along the north side of the road.

As you drive north from Canyon Junction, the first picnic area along the west side of the road occasionally produces good results. Accustomed to receiving handouts, the coyotes at this location are unafraid of people.

For complete directions and additional information, see Chapter 3.

CAMAS NATIONAL WILDLIFE REFUGE, IDAHO

Camas National Wildlife Refuge, located in southeastern Idaho, is a blend of ponds, cattail marshes, sagebrush, and open meadows. The Leemhi Mountains are visible to the west, and the Tetons to the east, providing a majestic backdrop for the 10,000-acre refuge.

Your first stop should be refuge headquarters, advising officials of your intentions. Initiate your quest for coyotes in the sagebrush and open meadows along the western edge of the refuge.

For complete directions and additional information, see Chapter 3.

BENTON LAKE NATIONAL WILDLIFE REFUGE, MONTANA

Coyotes are often observed out in the fields in the early morning hours, scouting their next meal. If you're lucky, you might be able to locate a den site. Before erecting a blind or attempting to call coyotes, stop by refuge headquarters and inform personnel of your intentions.

For complete directions and additional information, see Chapter 3.

Gray Wolf

DESCRIPTION — Gray, black, or white; yellow eyes; 50 to 100 pounds (115 pounds not uncommon, unconfirmed record is 227 pounds); females smaller.

SCIENTIFIC NAME — *Canis lupus*

FAMILY — Dog (Canidae)

BREEDING SEASON — Late winter to early spring

GESTATION PERIOD — 63 days

NUMBER OF YOUNG — 3 to 9 (usually 4 to 6)

The hunter's moon, peeking over the mountain, cast its magic across the meadow. A Great Horned Owl called out in the clear mountain air. In the distance, its mate answered. A lone shadow raced across the open meadow. Another followed. Then another ... and another. Then two more. They came to a halt along the creek winding its way through the aspen grove. Heads raised toward the moon, and the wolves began howling.

Wolves once were common throughout North America. Since the early 1900s however, they have been missing in most of their former range south of the Canadian border.

Wolf-recovery groups throughout the United States are involved in wolf education programs, as well as lobbying for legislative action designed to re-establish and protect wolves.

In 1987, the endangered red wolf was reintroduced into the wild at the Alligator River National Wildlife Refuge in North Carolina. During the winter of 1994-95, gray wolves from Canada were released in Idaho and Yellowstone National Park. The Colorado-based wolf-recovery group, Sinapu (the Ute word for wolves) is spearheading an effort to restore gray wolves into their former range in that state.

Many obstacles must be overcome and much work remains before the howl of the wolf will once again be common throughout the Rockies.

Two species of wolf are indigenous to North America: the red wolf (Canis rufus) and the gray wolf (Canis lupus). At one time, the red wolf occupied the southeastern United States, while the gray wolf inhabited the remainder of the continent, with the exception of the coastal areas of California. According to taxonomist E. A. Goldman, 24 subspecies of the gray wolf could be found in North America. Today, most are extinct. However, a few remain. For example, the eastern timber wolf (C. l. lycaon), the northern Rocky Mountain wolf (C. l. occidentalis), the Arctic wolf (C. l. arctos), and the Mexican wolf (C. l. baileyi) are actually subspecies of the gray wolf.

The northern Rocky Mountain wolf is the focus of this book. At one time, this wolf inhabited the Rockies from northern New Mexico through Alberta and British Columbia. Today, the only viable population exists in Canada.

Wolves prey primarily on members of the deer family, including deer, elk, moose, caribou, and, in certain locations, musk ox.

Wolves are highly social animals, living in packs. The alpha male dominates other males in the pack, while the alpha female dominates the females. It is not uncommon for alpha females to lead a pack.

Pack size appears to vary with prey size. Wolves hunting deer form smaller packs than wolves preying on moose. Most packs in the Lower Forty-eight states number between 5 and 10 wolves, while Canadian and Alaskan packs frequently contain 15 or 20 animals. One pack in Alaska was confirmed at 36 wolves.

A wolf pack customarily changes size throughout the year. During summer, the pack may split up, and wolves may hunt in pairs or individually. In late fall, the pack attains maximum size. Mortality rates, especially for young wolves, are high during the winter, at approximately 50 percent. The larger pack size increases their chance for survival, since hunting proficiency is increased through numbers. In early spring, it is customary for most of the young wolves that survived the winter to set out on their own.

Only one hunt in 10 usually is successful. The life of the wolf is a feast-or-famine existence; they commonly go three to five days without eating. After a successful hunt, each member of the pack will gorge, consuming up to 20 pounds of fresh meat. Typically, the pack will remain near the kill until the entire carcass has been consumed.

Mating occurs from late winter to early spring. Wolves inhabiting southern latitudes mate earlier than northern wolves. Only the alpha male and female are allowed to mate. Den sites are often used by generation after generation. The den may be located in a natural cave, a shelter formed by a rock slide, or a chamber dug into the ground. After a gestation period of two months, four to six pups are whelped.

Pups are altricial — born deaf and blind. After approximately three weeks, they begin exploring the outside world. At nine weeks, they begin following the pack to a "rendezvous site," a secure location where they remain in safety while the pack hunts. Like dens, these locations are used many years. Within a couple of weeks, hunting lessons begin.

Mature gray wolves average between 50 and 100 pounds. Females weigh 10 to 20 pounds less. Colder regions often produce individuals over 100 pounds. In Alaska and northern Canada, wolves weighing 175 pounds are not uncommon. David Mech, a Fish & Wildlife Service biologist, refers to an unconfirmed report of a wolf from the Yukon territories weighing 227 pounds.

Unfortunately, much misinformation concerning wolves exists. Once, in 1994, while talking to an individual concerning wolf reintroduction, I stated how wolves have very little impact on livestock. Very indignant, he informed me that he had witnessed, on several occasions, wolves killing his father's cattle in eastern Colorado. I quickly began doing a few mental calculations. He was approximately 20 years old, which would have placed his birth around 1974. Maybe in his previous life he could have witnessed the killings, but not in this life. The last wolf native to Colorado was killed in 1943, in Conejos County, along the south-central Colorado border.

In the entire history of this country, there has never been a confirmed incident of a healthy, wild wolf attacking a human. Such an attack would be entirely out of character. Wolves are exceedingly shy animals.

PHOTOGRAPHIC TECHNIQUES

Wolves are shy, secretive, and intelligent animals. Locating wild wolves can be very difficult, especially in the Rockies. Alaska is the best choice for photographing wolves in the wild. Even there, you may see them, and then again you may not!

Like mountain lions, the only guaranteed method for capturing wolf images on film is to photograph captive animals. I am aware of at least seven facilities in the Rockies where you can photograph captive wolves in natural settings, including five game farms, one animal rescue facility, and a wolf sanctuary (see Appendix I).

Game farms provide the photographer with captive raised animals. At some facilities, the animals are released into large fenced compounds, while other facilities allow the wolves to roam free. At game farms, the wolves are under the control of a handler.

Prairie Wind, the Colorado rescue facility, has a couple of wolves that can be released from holding pens and photographed in natural settings.

Mission: Wolf, a wolf sanctuary in south-central Colorado, has more than 30 wolves and wolf hybrids. The wolves are housed in very large, fenced enclosures. Several times each day, visitors are escorted into the enclosures.

Both Mission: Wolf and Prairie Wind are non-profit organizations. While their photographic opportunities may not equal those at game farms, both organizations provide a wonderful service for many unfortunate animals.

An 80-200 mm zoom lens will be all you need 95 percent of the time. However, for those extremely tight, frame-filling head shots, you will probably want something in the 400 mm range.

TIME OF YEAR

Adult wolves are most photogenic between November and March. During this time they are fully clothed in their winter coats. Wolf pups can be photographed soon after they are whelped, with April through June being the best months.

PHOTOGRAPHIC HOT SPOTS

While not exactly "hot spots," there are three areas in the Rockies where wolves are occasionally spotted. However, I would not plan a trip to these areas solely to photograph wolves.

YELLOWSTONE NATIONAL PARK, WYOMING

In March 1995, 14 gray wolves were released in the park. Within the first five months of release, close to 4,000 wolf sightings were reported. These sightings occurred in the Lamar Valley, west of Tower Junction. However, these wolves are fitted with radio collars, and they are not what you would call choice photo subjects.

For complete directions and additional information, see Chapter 3.

GLACIER NATIONAL PARK, MONTANA

While it is rare to see wolves in Glacier, the "Camas Creek pack" is occasionally observed between Camas Creek and Kintla Lake, along the park's western boundary. From Apgar, go northwest along the Camas Road, connecting with either the Inside or Outside North Fork Road.

For complete directions and additional information, see Chapter 3.

BANFF NATIONAL PARK, ALBERTA

Wolves are present between Banff's east entrance gate and the intersection of Highway 93 with the Trans Canada Highway, and south to the park boundary. I have observed wolves in the valley near the Highway 93 intersection.

For complete directions and additional information, see Chapter 3.

Red Fox

DESCRIPTION – Rufous above; white below; black lower legs and feet; bushy tail with white tip; 22 to 25 inches long, 15-inch tail; 8 to 15 pounds.

    "Silver" variation: black.

    "Cross" variation: brownish with black

SCIENTIFIC NAME – *Vulpes vulpes*

FAMILY – Dog (Canidae)

BREEDING SEASON – Late January to early February

GESTATION PERIOD – 53 days

NUMBER OF YOUNG – 1 to 11 kits (usually 4 or 5)

Old children's stories call the sly red fox Reynard, a fitting "handle" derived from the French word renard, said to mean "unconquerable through cleverness." The fox's reputation precedes him.

The red fox is found throughout most of North America, as well as in Europe and Asia. Females are called vixens; the pups are known as kits; and the males are called dogs. The males, or dogs, average 25 percent larger than vixens.

These foxes come in three colors: red, black, and brown with black markings. The black form is known as the "silver fox," and the brownish one is the "cross fox." The red, or rufous, variety is simply called a red fox. All three sport a white-tipped tail.

Red foxes prefer denning in open woodlands or meadows. Den preparation takes place in March. Water will almost always be nearby. The den entrance, 6 to 12 inches in diameter, is usually dug into the side of a bank. However, a den under a fallen log or beneath the roots of a large tree is not to be overlooked. Once, I came across a den excavated in a 20-cubic-yard sand pile deposited by a dump truck. A fox den may contain several entrances. If not disturbed, a pair of foxes, may use the same den year after year.

Breeding takes place in late January or early February. In mid-March, after a gestation period of 53 days, four or five blind, brown balls of fur are born. After 10 or 12 days, the young kits open their eyes for the first time. By late April, when they are five or six weeks old, the young kits venture into the outside world for the first time. Both adults share in the raising of the kits. Within a week or two, the kits may be moved to a new den.

Hunting lessons begin at the age of 10 weeks. By early fall — hunting lessons complete — the kits leave their family to seek territories of their own. At this time, the adults, preferring the solitary life, split up. However, once a bond is formed, they will most likely come together season after season, and they are inseparable while raising their young kits.

Red foxes are primarily night hunters, although they may venture forth at dawn and dusk. Hunting territories vary between one and five miles in diameter, depending upon food availability. Night after night, the same trail is followed. No brush pile or thicket is overlooked. Soon a noticeable pathway has been worn.

PHOTOGRAPHIC TECHNIQUES

If photographing kits at their den is your cup of tea, scout known fox habitat for the presence of an active den. The best time to do this is between late March and mid-April. Fresh dirt outside the entrance indicates the den is active. Foxes typically locate their dens along the side of an embankment. However, I photographed one fox family using an abandoned water conduit for its den, gaining entrance through a rusty opening. In early May, when the kits begin venturing outside, look for scat, bones, and feathers at the entrance.

After locating an active den, set up your blind approximately 75 to 100 feet away, taking lighting into consideration. Move it a little closer each day, until you are close enough to obtain the shots you want using a 400 mm or 500 mm lens.

Wait two or three days after erecting the blind before attempting to take pictures. Arrive at the blind while it is still dark. By mid-morning, after playing hard, the kits usually return to their den for a nap. Later in the afternoon they typically re-emerge. Do not enter or exit the blind while they are outside their den.

Foxes, like people, have individual personalities. With some it may be necessary to exercise more caution.

Activity often takes place outside the den while light levels are low. I've seen kits playing outside their den before the sun ever thought about coming up. At times like these, a fast lens (500 mm, f4) can come in handy.

To photograph a red fox coming to a call, you need a blind. Set up the blind in an open meadow with the wind at your back. Red foxes, like most predators, will make their approach from the downwind side. The "hand squeak" is very effective for calling. (See Calling Wildlife, Chapter 2.) Begin by producing six or seven squeaks. Vary the volume and duration. Be careful not to use too much volume — red foxes are extremely sensitive to excessively loud calling. Repeat every five or six minutes. When a fox appears, stop calling. If it refuses to come closer, a little coaxing may be required. Simply produce an occasional squeak at reduced volume. Remember, it's better to call too softly and less frequently than too loud and too often.

TIME OF YEAR

The best red fox photography occurs between November and March. Dressed in their winter coats, the adults are more photogenic at this time. Kits can often be photographed at their den as early as mid-April and as late as mid-June.

PHOTOGRAPHIC HOT SPOTS

WHEAT RIDGE GREENBELT, COLORADO

Urban wildlife at its best. Cottonwoods, willows, and grassy meadows characterize this major Denver-area greenbelt.

Take your time while searching for den locations. Investigate all embankments, especially those in the more inaccessible areas near the creek.

Three parks — Prospect, Wheatridge, and Johnson — straddle the greenbelt. Both Prospect Park and Wheatridge Park are situated along the south side of 44th Avenue; Prospect is between Youngfield and Kipling streets, and Wheatridge is between Kipling and Wadsworth Boulevard. Johnson Park is immediately south of the intersection of Wadsworth and Interstate 70.

To reach the area, go west from Interstate 25 along Interstate 70. Take either the Wadsworth or Kipling exit and go south.

For additional information, contact the city of Wheat Ridge (303-423-2626).

SEEDSKADEE NATIONAL WILDLIFE REFUGE, WYOMING

Red foxes are often observed along the refuge roads. Search the embankments and hillsides along the northern end of the auto-tour road.

For complete directions and additional information, see Chapter 3.

CAMAS NATIONAL WILDLIFE REFUGE, IDAHO

Camas National Wildlife Refuge, in southeastern Idaho, is a blend of ponds, cattail marshes, sagebrush, and open meadows. Initiate your quest for red foxes in the western sections of the refuge, searching embankments for the presence of dens.

For complete directions and additional information, see Chapter 3.

FREEZEOUT LAKE WILDLIFE MANAGEMENT AREA, MONTANA

Freezeout Lake was once a huge swamp, and only alkali flats were left when it dried up during drought years. Since the completion of an irrigation project that diverts mountain run-off, water now remains year-round in Freezeout Lake.

Freezeout is known for its large concentrations of waterfowl during migration times. However, the area's plentiful population of prey also contributes to a healthy red fox population.

Roads throughout the area provide easy access in your quest for the elusive red fox. Even during hunting season (October to December), when certain locations are closed, much of the area remains open.

Your first stop should be the Freezeout Lake headquarters. Stop in and say hello, advise the officials of your intentions, and pick up a map of the area.

From Great Falls, drive northwest 12 miles along Interstate 15. Turn left onto U.S. 89. Go northwest 30 miles to the wildlife management area. For additional information, contact the Montana Department of Fish, Wildlife and Parks (406-467-2646).

RED ROCK LAKES NATIONAL WILDLIFE REFUGE, MONTANA

Red foxes are often observed near marshy areas in the refuge. I recommend investigating the fields adjacent to Lower Red Rock Lake, and, especially, the area along Odell Creek.

CAUTION: Hazardous bogs and sinkholes are found throughout the refuge. Caution is advised when traveling through wet areas.

For complete directions and additional information, see Chapter 3.

Black Bear

DESCRIPTION—Black, brown, cinnamon, cream, or gray; tan muzzle; males 600 pounds, females 350 pounds.

SCIENTIFIC NAME—*Ursus americanus*

FAMILY—Bear (Ursidae)

BREEDING SEASON—June and July

GESTATION PERIOD—6 to 8 weeks (delayed implantation)

NUMBER OF YOUNG—1 to 4 (usually 2)

Seldom seen, the black bear is nevertheless common throughout forested areas of the Rocky Mountains. Black bears usually are found in areas producing tasty forbs and grasses during spring and summer, followed by abundant fall crops of nuts and berries.

Each fall, two or three months prior to denning, black bears begin feeding with added urgency. Actual denning begins in late October or early November. Dens are located in some type of natural cavity, such as a hollow tree, under a log, or in a cave.

Black bears do not hibernate. Instead, they enter a period of deep sleep, or dormancy. During this time, body temperature and metabolism remain near normal. It is not uncommon for them to briefly leave their dens during periods of warm weather. In fact, in the southern United States, where food is available year-round, black bears normally avoid denning altogether.

Cubs are born in January or February, while the female, or sow, is still in a state of dormancy. Sows giving birth the first time usually produce a single cub. Thereafter, twins are common.

In April, the sow emerges from the den with her cubs. Young cubs stay with their mother for a year and a half. During this time the sow will not mate. Breeding takes place every two years, between late May and July. Egg implantation is delayed until November, when embryonic development begins.

Black bears tend to be more active at night. However, during their fall feeding forays, they are often observed during the day. The home range of the black bear will vary in size, depending upon available food supplies, from as small as 20 square miles to almost 200 square miles. Claw marks on tree trucks identify an area as bear territory.

PHOTOGRAPHIC TECHNIQUES

When photographing bears, caution should always be observed. Three vital rules apply: 1) Never get between a sow and her cubs; 2) Never get between a bear and its food; and 3) Never startle a bear. It's also good to avoid a direct approach to a bear, and never get too close. It's better to be safe than "dinner."

A 400 mm or 500 mm telephoto lens will provide the power you need, allowing a safe working distance when photographing black bears.

Unless you take certain steps, your black bear photos will look like "black blob" photos. Exposure compensation is necessary if the subject fills a major portion of the viewfinder (see Exposure, Chapter 2). Also, catch-light is critical. Shooting from a low angle will assist in picking up catch-light in your subject's eyes. Shooting from a low angle also will lend more importance and excitement to your images.

IN CASE OF ATTACK: If, after observing all safety precautions, a bear attack occurs, lie on the ground and play dead, coiling up into a fetal position with your hands clasped behind your head. This procedure has saved the lives of numbers of individuals involved in bear attacks.

FOR THEIR SAKE, do not feed bears. This causes them to associate food with people. Eventually, someone becomes frightened by a bear's behavior or a bear injures someone. The end result usually is that the bear is shot and killed.

TIME OF YEAR

Spring and fall are the best times for photographing black bears, simply because they are most often seen during these times. In April, bears emerge from their winter dens with feeding on their minds. Many bear observations are made between this time and early June. During September and October, they are often active during daytime.

PHOTOGRAPHIC HOT SPOTS

BANFF NATIONAL PARK, ALBERTA

A few kilometers north of Banff Townsite, Highway 1A intersects the Trans Canada Highway. Black bears are occasionally observed along Highway 1A, between this intersection and Lake Louise Village. Most sightings occur along the first 25 kilometers (15 miles) of the highway.

Another area frequented by blacks is the Icefields Parkway, between Highway 11 at Saskatchewan Crossing and Mount Cirrus, a distance of approximately 28 kilometers (17 miles). This is probably the best location in the park for finding and photographing black bears.

For complete directions and additional information, see Chapter 3.

JASPER NATIONAL PARK, ALBERTA

Black bears are abundant in Jasper National Park. They generally avoid contact with humans; nevertheless, this park is one of the best locations remaining in North America for photographing blacks bears. Several locations are worth investigation, including Jonas Creek, Maligne Lake Road, Pyramid Lake, Highway 93A, and Highway 16 west of Jasper Townsite.

Jonas Creek crosses the Icefields Parkway near the Jonas Creek Campground, 77 kilometers (46 miles) south of Jasper Townsite.

To access the Maligne Lake Road, go north on Highway 16 approximately 2 kilometers (1.2 miles) from the intersection of Connaught Drive and Highway 16, on the north side of Jasper Townsite. Turn right as if you were going to the Jasper Park Lodge. However, after crossing the Athabasca River, turn left on Lodge Road instead of going right to the lodge. After 2 kilometers (1.2 miles), Lodge Road turns to the right and becomes Maligne Lake Road. Follow it to Maligne Lake, searching for bears along the way.

Pyramid Lake can be reached from Jasper Townsite by going northwest on Pine Avenue. Pine eventually turns into Pyramid Lake Road. Follow it until you arrive at Pyramid Lake. Before reaching the lake, you will pass riding stables adjacent to Patricia Lake. Inquire at the stables concerning recent bear sightings in the area.

Highway 93A, beginning 7 kilometers (4.2 miles) south of town, follows the old highway a distance of 23 miles, ending near Athabasca Falls. Several side roads going west leave the main highway. Take them all as you scout the area for black bears.

Highway 16 West, crossing the Icefields Parkway south of Jasper Townsite, provides access to British Columbia to the west, a distance of only 25 kilometers (15 miles). The highway parallels the Miette River along the way. Black bears often are sighted along this stretch of highway.

For complete directions and additional information, see Chapter 3.

KOOTENAY NATIONAL PARK, BRITISH COLUMBIA

Despite a healthy black bear population in the park, bears are seldom observed. Bears along Sinclair Creek may be the exception. After descending Sinclair Pass, the Banff-Windermere Parkway (Highway 93) follows Sinclair Creek for some distance. Black bears frequent this area — particularly the Sinclair Creek picnic area. This is a few kilometers east of Radium Hot Springs, near the park's western boundary.

For complete directions and additional information, see Chapter 3.

YOHO NATIONAL PARK, BRITISH COLUMBIA

The Kicking Horse Corridor hosts the park's largest black bear population. Scout the area along the Trans Canada Highway, between Field and the park's western boundary.

For complete directions and additional information, see Chapter 3.

Black bear moving through underbrush

Grizzly Bear

DESCRIPTION – Brown, black, or blond; silver-tipped guard hairs; males 300 to 600 pounds, females 200 to 400 pounds.

SCIENTIFIC NAME – *Ursus arctos*

FAMILY – Bear (Ursidae)

BREEDING SEASON – May to July

GESTATION PERIOD – 6 to 8 weeks (delayed implantation)

NUMBER OF YOUNG – 1 to 4 (usually 2)

Respected by Native Americans, grizzlies were seen as an obstacle to be eliminated by whites as they brought "civilization" to the American West. A bear of open country, the grizzly is found in sagebrush steppes, mountain meadows, riparian areas, rock slides, and forest edges.

The grizzly's long, silvery or white guard hairs, the outer hairs of its coat, produce the bear's grizzled appearance, giving rise to its name and nickname, "the silvertip."

The grizzly is crepuscular, tending to be most active at dawn and dusk. Extremely fast, they are capable of outrunning a horse.

Mating occurs between May and July. As with the black bear, the grizzly's egg implantation is delayed until autumn. The young are born during January or February while the sow is in her den. Between one and four cubs (usually two) are born. The young cubs and their mother emerge from the den sometime in April or May.

Dens are usually dug on a north-facing slope. However, the bears may take advantage of a natural cavity. Grizzlies typically enter their den during an early-winter snowstorm in November. Like other members of the bear family, grizzlies do not actually hibernate. Instead, they enter a period of dormancy or deep sleep.

Grizzlies are "digging machines." Tremendous amounts of soil are excavated and large boulders seemingly moved with ease as they search for a meal no larger than a ground squirrel. Carcasses of large mammals are hidden under sticks and other debris for feeding on later. The "owner" will not be far away. These signs, along with tracks and scat, proclaim the presence of a grizzly.

When you're in grizzly country, an ounce of prevention is worth ... your life! Only those with a death wish should approach a grizzly in the wild. I like the advice of my good friends Cathy and Gordon Illg, in their book Rocky Mountain Safari. They say not to approach a grizzly "...without first making out your last will and testament."

Until the late 1800s, grizzlies could be found throughout most of the American West. Today, only Alaska and Canada host viable grizzly populations. Less than 1,000 grizzlies cling to existence in the Lower Forty-eight. Stephen Torbit, in his book *Large Mammals Of The Central Rockies*, writes, "If all the grizzlies are gone, I believe that we're all much poorer, so poor that the debt can never be erased. If all the grizzlies are gone ... the mountains are only mountains, their most distinctive wilderness element has been eradicated, they are a wilderness in name only."

If we, in our thirst for material wealth, destroy that which is wild, then we destroy ourselves. The grizzly is a symbol of all that is wild.

PHOTOGRAPHIC TECHNIQUES

Three important safety rules apply: 1) Never get between a sow and her cubs; 2) Never get between a grizzly and its food; and 3) Never startle a grizzly. Also, avoid a direct approach to your subject, and maintain a safe working distance. This is where a 600 mm telephoto comes in handy.

IN CASE OF ATTACK: Coil up into a fetal position and play dead, with your hands clasped behind your head.

When your subject has been located, make an educated guess as to its direction of travel. Do not approach. Instead, move ahead parallel to the bear's anticipated route to a point a safe distance from where it will likely pass. Set up your equipment and wait. It is safer to allow your subject to come to you than to take a chance on approaching your subject.

If you happen to locate a cached food supply, it might be possible to set up your equipment a safe distance away and wait for the grizzly to return. In all likelihood, the bear will be nearby, ready to protect its food from all challengers, including you. DO NOT STAY IN THE VICINITY.

TIME OF YEAR

Like black bears, grizzlies are most often observed and photographed in April and May, after emerging from their den, and during September and October, just prior to entering the den for the winter.

PHOTOGRAPHIC HOT SPOTS

YELLOWSTONE NATIONAL PARK, WYOMING

Yellowstone probably provides the best photo opportunities for grizzlies in the Lower Forty-eight. September and October are typically the best months to shoot.

Two locations are noted for grizzly activity: Antelope Creek and Fishing Bridge Campground. Antelope Creek is east of the road between Tower Falls and Dunraven Pass. Some of the better viewing areas are 3 to 4 miles south of Tower Falls. Fishing Bridge Campground is along the north shore of Yellowstone Lake. Each fall, grizzlies feed on spawning trout near the campground.

Other areas worth mentioning are Willow Park, Dunraven Pass, and Hayden Valley. Willow Park is near Indian Creek Campground, between Mammoth and Norris. Dunraven Pass is near the Mount Washburn Trailhead. Hayden Valley needs no introduction.

For complete directions and additional information, see Chapter 3.

GLACIER NATIONAL PARK, MONTANA

Glacier is one of the few places where grizzlies can still be observed south of the Canadian border. The Many Glacier area is among the best locations in the park. Scout the treeless slopes up to Iceberg Lake. Also try the open grasslands along the Cracker Lake Trail. The trailhead is at the Many Glacier Hotel parking area.

Two other good locations for finding grizzlies are Hidden Lake Overlook and Granite Peak Chalet. July and August is when you are most likely to see the bears.

The Hidden Lake Overlook is reached from the Logan Pass Visitor Center by following the 1.5-mile boardwalk to its end. The Granite Peak Chalet, reached from Logan Pass, is at the end of the 7.5-mile Highline Trail. At both locations, you are often too far away from the bears for decent photos.

Fortunately, there are other locations. Huckleberry Mountain can be very productive. Drive north from Apgar along the Camas Road. You will come to the Camas Mountain Nature Trail at the end of the paved road. Huckleberry Mountain lies to the south. Grizzlies are often observed in this area in spring and fall.

For complete directions and additional information, see Chapter 3.

BANFF NATIONAL PARK, ALBERTA

This park features two locations where grizzlies are occasionally spotted: Bow Summit and Sunwapta Pass.

Bow Summit is approximately 85 kilometers (51 miles) northwest of Lake Louise, along the Icefields Parkway. Sunwapta Pass, also on the Icefields Parkway, is along the boundary between Banff and Jasper National Parks, near the Columbia Icefields.

For complete directions and additional information, see Chapter 3.

JASPER NATIONAL PARK, ALBERTA

Two locations in the park are worth investigation: Maligne Lake Road and Highway 16 West. Both black bears and grizzlies are sometimes observed in these areas. However, blacks stay in the forested areas, while grizzlies prefer more open spaces.

To access the Maligne Lake Road, go north on Highway 16 approximately 2 kilometers (1.2 miles) from the intersection of Connaught Drive and Highway 16, on the north side of Jasper Townsite. Turn right as if you were going to the Jasper Park Lodge. After crossing the Athabasca River turn left on Lodge Road instead of going right to the lodge. After 2 kilometers (1.2 miles), Lodge Road turns to the right and becomes Maligne Lake Road. Follow it to Maligne Lake.

Highway 16 West, crossing the Icefields Parkway south of Jasper Townsite, provides access to British Columbia to the west, only 25 kilometers (15 miles) away. Grizzlies are often observed along this stretch of highway.

For complete directions and additional information, see Chapter 3.

YOHO NATIONAL PARK, BRITISH COLUMBIA

When searching for grizzlies in Yoho, keep in mind that they prefer open areas, whereas black bears prefer the cover of wooded thickets.

In a study conducted in 1978, two scientists compiled a list of important grizzly habitats throughout the park. This list covers four areas:

1) The Beaverfoot/Lower Kicking Horse area contains extensive slide paths and nearby alpine habitat, along Clawson Peak's west side.

2) The Ice River area embraces slide paths and important alpine habitat.

3) Ottertail Valley has good habitat on the slide paths up Float Creek and McArthur Creek during spring, along with that portion of the Ottertail Valley between these creeks.

4) The Amiskwi-Kiwetinok area burned in 1971, and this open space is superb habitat, providing choice berries.

In early spring, before plants begin leafing out, the Mount Dennis and Mount Stephen avalanche chutes are rich with hedysarum, whose roots are an important food source. Another location of hedysarum is the upper McArthur Valley chutes along the southern face of Mount Odaray.

After plants have begun sprouting and leafing out, the avalanche chutes along McArthur Creek and the Ottertail River are important for their production of grasses and cow parsnip.

During the berry season, Goodsir Flats and the Trans Canada Highway right-of-way are notable for the production of buffalo berries.

Ground squirrels are an important grizzly food source, and their abundance in both the Rockwall and Goodsir Pass areas contributes to the importance of these areas. After the berry season, Goodsir Flats continues as important grizzly habitat because of its production of hedysarum roots, as does Upper Helmet Creek and the avalanche chutes along Upper McArthur Creek.

For complete directions and additional information, see Chapter 3.

Ringtail

DESCRIPTION – Buff above; white underside; ringed tail; large eyes; prominent rounded ears; male 14 to 16 inches long; 15-inch tail; 0.5 to 2.5 pounds.

SCIENTIFIC NAME – *Bassariscus astutus*

FAMILY – Raccoon (Procyonidae)

BREEDING SEASON – February to June (peaks in March and April)

GESTATION PERIOD – 51 to 54 days

NUMBER OF YOUNG – 3 or 4

The ringtail, sometimes improperly called miner's cat, civet cat, or ringtailed cat, is not a member of the cat family at all, but instead a close relative to the raccoon. Ringtails prefer rocky terrain in shrub lands and the pinon-juniper life zone. Water is never far away.

In the Rockies, ringtails are found in New Mexico, Utah, Colorado, and southwestern Wyoming. They are at home from the lowest elevations to just above 9,000 feet.

Active almost exclusively at night, the ringtail sleeps the day away in its den among the rocks, in a hollow tree, or in an underground burrow. Den sites are frequently changed.

The ringtail is classified as a carnivore, but it eats everything from insects and small rodents to fruits and nuts.

Breeding activity is spread between the months of February and June. However, most mating occurs during March and April, with the majority of young born in May and June. Two months after birth the young begin foraging with their mother. In another month, they begin denning by themselves.

In spite of being somewhat common and active year-round, ringtails are rarely observed because of their secretive and nocturnal habits.

PHOTOGRAPHIC TECHNIQUES

Photographing ringtails in the wild is extremely challenging. First, there's the problem of locating your subject. Then, because ringtails are nocturnal, your activities must be conducted in the dark.

However, if you are intent on photographing under these circumstances, one solution may be the use of an infrared triggering device, such as the Dalebeam from Protech (see Appendix I). When your subject breaks the infrared beam of the Dalebeam, your camera and flash are fired by an electronic impulse.

Talk with refuge personnel, park rangers, and state and federal wildlife biologists to find out where ringtails are most likely to be found. Check the area for tracks. Set up your equipment and hope for the best.

The only consistent way to obtain good images is to locate a captive animal and photograph it in natural-looking surroundings. Check with game farms to see if they have ringtails available for photography (see Appendix I).

When photographing a captive ringtail, an 80-200 mm zoom lens is ideal. If the ringtail is in a tree and you're using the sky for a background, it needs to be blue. It will help to have a northern "sunny f16" sky for your background. (See Sunny f16 Sky, Chapter 2.) Front lighting is important when using blue sky for a background.

TIME OF YEAR

Ringtails can be photographed throughout the year — if you can locate them.

PHOTOGRAPHIC HOT SPOTS

There is no such thing as a hot spot where ringtails can be photographed, with the exception of photographing a captive ringtail at a game farm. However, known ringtail populations exist at the following locations.

ARCHES NATIONAL PARK, UTAH

Dark Angel! Fiery Furnace! Devils Garden! These are unwelcome names, but Arches' landscape continues to draw individuals with a spirit of adventure into its grasp. This is Edward Abbey country.

Ringtails may thrive in a dry arid country, but they need water. Search among the cottonwood and tamarisk stands dotting the washes. Wolfe Ranch is a good location to begin your search for the elusive ringtail.

For complete directions and additional information, see Chapter 3.

CANYONLANDS NATIONAL PARK, UTAH

Many species of wildlife are at home in the high-desert habitat of Canyonlands, including the ringtail. The park encompasses 527 square miles of wilderness. Its roads are mostly four-wheel-drive, and its trails are primitive. To locate a ringtail, I strongly advise talking with National Park Service biologists. They can save you untold hours of work and frustration. Contact park headquarters in Moab (see Appendix I).

For complete directions and additional information, see Chapter 3.

MANTI-LA SAL NATIONAL FOREST, UTAH

The La Sal Loop, a portion of which negotiates the Manti-La Sal National Forest, traverses desert scrub, juniper, aspen, riparian, and mountain habitats. Begin your quest for ringtails along Brumley Creek. You might try using a road-killed rodent as bait. Work among the rocks of Brumley Ridge, or locate a hollow tree or log along the creek.

CAUTION: This area is home to the midget faded rattlesnake. During summer this snake is nocturnal.

For complete directions and additional information, see Chapter 3.

Long-tailed Weasel

DESCRIPTION — Summer: rich brown above; buff below; black-tipped tail. Winter: all white, except for black tip on tail.
Males: 9 to 10.5 inches long; 4- to 6-inch tail; females are 20 percent smaller.

SCIENTIFIC NAME — *Mustela frenata*

FAMILY — Weasel (Mustelidae)

BREEDING SEASON — June to August; monestrous (delayed implantation)

GESTATION PERIOD — 27 days

NUMBER OF YOUNG — 4 to 9 (usually 6 or 7)

The long-tailed weasel hunts year-round, its unmistakable "inch-worm" gait propelling it in a never-ending search for prey. Ranging from ponderosa woodlands to alpine tundra, long-tailed weasels occupy rocky, brush-covered areas near water. One of the better places to find them is near pika colonies.

The home range of male long-tailed weasels is approximately 35 acres. However, as food supplies diminish, weasel territories can double or triple in size. Females occupy about one-third of the space required by males.

Long-tailed weasels make a complete circuit of their territory every 10 days, traveling the same route over and over. Scat dropped on rocks identifies these trails. Investigating every nook and cranny for prey, males cover between 200 and 250 yards each night, while females travel only about half that distance.

Unlike most predators, weasels are comfortable hunting day or night. In fact, available data suggest long-tailed weasels are better suited to daylight activity. The diet of long-tailed weasels includes everything from mice and voles to snowshoe hares and tree squirrels. Even small birds, insects, and vegetable matter are periodically added to the diet. Berries, in particular, seem to be relished.

Long-tailed weasels hunt mostly on the ground, but they are capable climbers and will pursue prey into trees if necessary.

After a kill, light feeding usually takes place, followed by a brief siesta. Upon waking, the meal is generally finished off, except in the case of large prey such as squirrels or rabbits.

Weasels have the reputation of being "vicious killers." This is not true. They are, quite simply, hungry. Their high metabolism rate requires them to eat between 25 percent and 35 percent of their body weight every day. This would be the equivalent of an adult male needing 50 pounds of food a day to survive.

The life of the weasel is comprised of the search for food and resting. Rest takes place in an appropriated ground squirrel or pocket gopher burrow, which the weasel frequently expands. The entrance is usually littered with scat, primarily comprised of matted hair.

Weasels have a short life expectancy of 18 months, probably a result of their high metabolic rate. Females reach sexual maturity by 10 to 12 weeks of age, and sometimes as early as six weeks. This is nature's way of compensating for their short life span.

Breeding takes places between June and August. However, because of delayed implantation, the female will not give birth until the following year. Four to nine young are born in a grass- and hair-lined nest chamber in late April or early May. The babies are born altricial — blind and helpless — with a light covering of white hairs. Their eyes open at about five weeks.

In winter, the long-tailed weasel is all white, except for a black-tipped tail. As a result, it is mistakenly called an ermine by many people. The ermine, previously named the short-tailed weasel, is smaller and is relatively rare in the central Rockies. The tail of the long-tailed weasel comprises more than half the length of its body and head, while the ermine's tail is less than half this length. Also, the ermine has light-colored feet in its summer coat, while the long-tail has dark-colored feet.

The spring molt from all-white winter pelage to a rich brown summer coat begins in March. The autumnal molt begins in October. Each molt may take two months to complete. In the southern portions of its range, the long-tailed weasel remains brown all year, while the ermine dons its winter whites throughout its range.

PHOTOGRAPHIC TECHNIQUES

Like other members of the weasel family, the long-tailed weasel requires luck to photograph. Long-tailed weasels are extremely active. However, when one has been located, it usually will show itself again and again — a trait you can count on. David Armstrong, in his book *Rocky Mountain Mammals*, describes the long-tailed weasel as neither bold nor curious: "It is simply oblivious ... the animals are preoccupied with their immediate concerns (more often mice than men)."

Whatever the reasons behind weasel behavior, take advantage of the opportunity when they appear. I once shot a 36-exposure roll of film while following a long-tailed weasel in its search for food, but obtained only two acceptable images from the entire roll. And I was using an 80-200 mm, f2.8, autofocus lens. Like I said, they are very active.

Recommending a lens is difficult. Most of the time, an 80-200 mm zoom lens works quite well. However, at other times you may want something in the 400 mm range. In either case, an autofocus lens is worth its weight in gold when photographing these highly active little critters.

When your subject first presents itself, avoid sudden movements. Distance from your subject doesn't seem to matter. I've had weasels come within five feet and check me out. If luck prevails, you'll go home with some nice images.

When photographing long-tailed weasels in snow, don't forget to correct your meter reading. (See Exposure, Chapter 2.) Otherwise, your slides will come back from the lab underexposed.

TIME OF YEAR

Long-tailed weasels are active year-round. Locating them can be easier in winter when their tracks are visible in the snow. Between April and September, they can be photographed in their rich brown summer pelage. From October through March, they sport their all-white winter coats.

PHOTOGRAPHIC HOT SPOTS

Long-tailed weasels are common throughout the regions covered by this book. National parks are a good place to look. Talk with park personnel, who often can direct you to locations where weasels are frequently observed.

ROCKY MOUNTAIN NATIONAL PARK, COLORADO

I have consistently observed weasels along the backside of the old Hidden Valley Ski Lodge, now being converted into an educational center. From Deer Ridge Junction, follow Trail Ridge Road past the beaver pond boardwalk. The entrance road into Hidden Valley will be on your right.

Another location worth investigating is the area near the Wild Basin Ranger Station. Go south from Estes Park along Highway 7 for 12 miles. Turn right at the Wild Basin sign. Follow the road to the Ranger Station and Wild Basin trailhead parking area.

For complete directions and additional information, see Chapter 3.

YELLOWSTONE NATIONAL PARK, WYOMING

Weasels frequently prey on ground squirrels and chipmunks, so if you locate these rodents you eventually may see a weasel. The picnic areas north of Canyon Junction deserve investigation.

For complete directions and additional information, see Chapter 3.

GLACIER NATIONAL PARK, MONTANA

Chipmunks and ground squirrels are commonly observed in the area along the road across from St. Mary Lake. Because these animals are a primary food source of long-tailed weasels, this location is worthy of careful scrutiny.

For complete directions and additional information, see Chapter 3.

WATERTON LAKES NATIONAL PARK, ALBERTA

Because Columbian ground squirrels are a major food source for weasels, I suggest searching the many ground squirrel colonies in the park. A good starting place is the "bison paddock," located off Highway 6, 2 kilometers (1.2 miles) northwest of the park entrance station.

For complete directions and additional information, see Chapter 3.

Badger

DESCRIPTION — Grizzled gray, black face with white markings; black feet; broad, flat back; 18 to 22 inches long; 4- to 6-inch tail; 10 to 25 pounds.

SCIENTIFIC NAME — *Taxidea taxus*

FAMILY — Weasel (Mustelidae)

BREEDING SEASON — Late summer

GESTATION PERIOD — Delayed implantation; young born March or April

NUMBER OF YOUNG — 1 to 5 (usually 4); born March or April

The somewhat distinguished title of "nature's digging machine" undeniably belongs to the badger. Powerful front legs, equipped with formidable inch-and-a-half claws, allow the badger to disappear quickly into the ground amid a cloud of flying debris.

One writer described the scene at a badger's foraging site as looking like it had been impacted by a "light explosive." Badgers in search of food may travel up to eight miles in a single evening, leaving behind a trail of destruction.

Badgers' denning burrows are much neater than their foraging excavations. Because of their large territory, badgers often utilize a different den each night.

Badger dens are highly conspicuous: roughly 10 inches across, elliptical in cross-section, and typically located upon open slopes in sandy soils. Those used for rearing young usually have large deposits of dirt at the entrance.

Food consists of ground squirrels and other small rodents, along with ground-nesting birds, reptiles, and even an occasional insect. Excess food is often stashed in an abandoned den.

Breeding takes place in late summer and fall. As with other members of the weasel family, egg implantation is delayed in female badgers. Usually, four young are born sometime between February and May. The female cares for the young. After the cubs are three to four weeks old, they emerge from the natal den and usually never return.

While predominately nocturnal, badgers also may be active during the day. Although they seek shelter from the elements and sleep during periods of extremely cold weather, badgers are generally active year-round.

Badgers have the reputation of hunting in partnership with coyotes. While the coyote aggressively goes after its meal, the badger stands by, ready to take advantage of any prey attempting to escape.

PHOTOGRAPHIC TECHNIQUES

Locate a natal den and set up a photo blind nearby. National wildlife refuge personnel can sometimes be helpful in pointing you to a den location.

Your best opportunities will be at dawn or dusk. Because light levels are low during these periods, a 200 or 400 ISO film will often come in handy, while a 400 mm or 500 mm telephoto lens will supply the necessary magnification.

Game farms afford excellent year-round opportunities to photograph badgers. An 80-200 mm zoom lens will prove invaluable for photographing game-farm badgers.

TIME OF YEAR

The best time to photograph badgers is when the young are in their natal den, sometime between the months of February and June.

PHOTOGRAPHIC HOT SPOTS

ARAPAHO NATIONAL WILDLIFE REFUGE, COLORADO

The Arapaho National Wildlife Refuge is situated in North Park, in the center of a glacial basin surrounded by mountains. Numerous gravel roads crisscross the refuge, providing easy access to various areas. I recommend going to refuge headquarters and informing officials of your intention to photograph badgers. Often, they can point you in the right direction, saving you time.

For complete directions and additional information, see Chapter 3.

SEEDSKADEE NATIONAL WILDLIFE REFUGE, WYOMING

Badgers are closely associated with prairie dog colonies. Search the section of refuge located west of State Highway 372 for badger activity.

For complete directions and additional information, see Chapter 3.

SNAKE RIVER BIRDS OF PREY AREA, IDAHO

Embracing almost 500,000 acres, it's no wonder the Snake River Birds of Prey Area hosts the country's largest badger population.

Your first stop should be the Bureau of Land Management office in Boise, 3848 Development Avenue (208-384-3000). The staff can provide a wealth of information, including the right biologists and other people to contact and a map of the area.

I recommend stopping at the parking area between Kuna and the Swan Falls Dam. There you will find interpretive exhibits and an overlook for canyon viewing. This will provide you with an overview of the area.

From Boise, go west along Interstate 84. At Exit 44, four miles west of Boise, turn south for 8 miles to Kuna. From Kuna, go south along the Swan Falls Road. Follow the signs to the SRBOPA, beginning 5 miles south of Kuna. From Swan Falls Dam, located 18 miles south of Kuna, a dirt road provides access to several miles of river bottom.

For complete directions and additional information, see Chapter 3.

BENTON LAKE NATIONAL WILDLIFE REFUGE, MONTANA

Benton Lake National Wildlife Refuge, a 12,000-acre refuge featuring shallow prairie marshlands, is one of the top locations in North America for photographing waterfowl and their young. Although wary, badgers are occasionally observed from the 9-mile Prairie Marsh Wildlife Drive.

For complete directions and additional information, see Chapter 3.

WATERTON LAKES NATIONAL PARK, ALBERTA

Badgers are common in the grasslands and open prairies on the park's east side. One such area is the grassy hill between Lower and Middle Waterton Lakes, 3 kilometers (1.8 miles) northwest of Waterton Townsite.

Another location is the area around Blakiston Falls, located at the end of Red Rock Parkway. The parkway is 3 kilometers (1.8 miles) northeast of town.

For complete directions and additional information, see Chapter 3.

Striped Skunk

DESCRIPTION – Black, with white stripe on forehead and back; 13 to 18 inches long, 7- to 10-inch tail, 6 to 14 pounds (female slightly smaller).

SCIENTIFIC NAME – *Mephitis mephitis*

FAMILY – Weasel (Mustelidae)

BREEDING SEASON – February to early April

GESTATION PERIOD – 62 to 66 days

NUMBER OF YOUNG – 2 to 10 (average of 5)

The striped skunk is the most common and widely distributed of the five skunk species found in North America. However, it is rarely observed because of its largely nocturnal lifestyle. These skunks seem to prefer open meadows and mixed woodlands, but they often live in close proximity to humans, sometimes denning beneath buildings.

Striped skunks tend to seek underground burrows during periods of colder weather. During warmer weather, they seem to be comfortable in above-ground resting spots, especially during daytime hours.

Dens are frequently located on south-facing slopes. It is not uncommon for a striped skunk to appropriate an abandoned badger or rabbit burrow. Sometimes, they'll even share the burrow with the other species, claiming a separate section where they are sure not to disturb the other animal. When such burrows are unavailable, skunks are capable of digging their own; this normally occurs in late summer or fall, just prior to winter.

Skunks do not hibernate. However, they often enter periods of torpor or dormancy — a slight slowing of the metabolism — during intervals of extreme cold. The duration varies with sex, age, and geographic location.

Skunks are best known for "spraying" uninvited intruders. However, striped skunks will do everything possible to get an intruder to leave before spraying. Avoidance is preferred — the skunk most likely will run away. If that fails, confrontation usually comes next. The skunk faces the intruder while stomping its front feet; sometimes, it simultaneously clicks its teeth. If this fails to drive the intruder away, watch out. The next step usually is spraying.

Once this decision has been made, the skunk turns so its "south end" faces the intruder, raises its tail, takes aim, and, as they say, the rest is history. The spray is accurate for a distance of approximately 10 feet. Young kits are capable of spraying as soon as their eyes open, at about three weeks.

Breeding takes place sometime between February and early April. After a two-month gestation period, an average of five blind, helpless kits are born. By early July, the young are already weaned and following their mother single-file on hunting forays.

While striped skunks may travel several miles during a single night's outing, rarely will they cover an area larger than half a square mile. Instead, the skunks wander about, checking out almost every burrow they pass.

Food consists of everything from insects and fruit to ground-nesting birds and their eggs. This varied diet is one reason skunks often live close to humans. They are not above eating garbage when it's available.

Skunks are primarily nocturnal; they rest in a protected spot during the day. Skunk scent is a good indicator of their presence in the area, as are shallow, 2-inch diameter holes made while digging in search of insect larvae.

PHOTOGRAPHIC TECHNIQUES

Baiting is almost the only way to attract and photograph wild skunks with any consistency. Establishing a bait station can sometimes take several months.

The first step is to talk with people and find out where skunks have been spotted. One hint: Skunks often feed on food left out for dogs. Once you've found a location frequented by skunks, set up a "bait station" and a nearby photo blind. If it's dog food they want, feed 'em dog food. Otherwise, go to your local butcher and ask for scraps. Allow the scraps to "age" for several days without the benefit of refrigeration.

Once skunks begin coming to your bait station, it's time to get into your blind and play the waiting game. A 400 mm telephoto lens will provide the necessary power for frame-filling images — and allow a comfortable working distance. Since skunks are primarily nocturnal, a flash unit is a necessity. Make sure baiting for photographic purposes is legal in your area.

An alternative is to photograph a captive skunk. Contact game farms (see Appendix I). Another possibility is to find an individual who owns a skunk. Descented skunks are sometimes kept as pets. Place ads in newspapers or check with local veterinary offices for owners of skunks. Check with state wildlife agencies for license holders. (In some states, a license is required to own a wild animal.) For captive skunks, which usually are descented, I find my 200-400 mm, f2.8, autofocus lens fits the bill.

TIME OF YEAR

Obviously, captive skunks can be photographed any time. Kits are best photographed in July, when they begin following their mother around single-file. There's nothing cuter.

During extremely cold weather, most skunks are inactive.

PHOTOGRAPHIC HOT SPOTS

The following locations host populations of striped skunks. Never erect a portable blind or attempt baiting at these locations without first getting permission from refuge personnel.

ARAPAHO NATIONAL WILDLIFE REFUGE, COLORADO

The Arapaho National Wildlife Refuge is surrounded by mountains — the Park Range on the west, Rabbit Ears Mountains on the south, Never Summer Range on the southeast, and the Medicine Bow Range on the northeast and east.

I recommend stopping at refuge headquarters and informing the staff of your intentions. They can often help you locate skunks. Headquarters is located along State Highway 125, 7 miles south of Walden. Turn east at the refuge entrance sign onto a gravel road and follow the signs.

For complete directions and additional information, see Chapter 3.

SEEDSKADEE NATIONAL WILDLIFE REFUGE, WYOMING

The striped skunk is a common resident of this refuge. Search among the cottonwoods in the bottomlands for their presence. Three refuge roads provide river access — two roads on the west side of the Green River, and one along its east bank.

For complete directions and additional information, see Chapter 3.

CAMAS NATIONAL WILDLIFE REFUGE, IDAHO

Camas National Wildlife Refuge, located in southeastern Idaho, is a blend of ponds, cattail marshes, sagebrush, and open meadows. The Leemhi Mountains are visible to the west, and the Tetons to the east, providing a majestic backdrop for the 10,000-acre refuge.

Investigate the areas around the refuge's old farm buildings. Also, talk with refuge personnel. They can advise where some of the more recent sighting have occurred.

For complete directions and additional information, see Chapter 3.

KOOTENAI NATIONAL WILDLIFE REFUGE, IDAHO

Situated in the Idaho panhandle, only 20 miles from Canada, this refuge is bounded by the Kootenai River on the east and the Selkirk Mountains on the west.

Striped skunks are common in many areas of the refuge. They are sometimes observed tromping among the grasses in upland areas or along brush rows, searching for the eggs of ground-nesting birds. Other times, their travels may take them into the forests along the base of the Selkirks, or foraging around refuge buildings.

For complete directions and additional information, see Chapter 3.

BENTON LAKE NATIONAL WILDLIFE REFUGE, MONTANA

Skunks are occasionally observed at dawn, sniffing around refuge structures. They also can be seen along the 9-mile Prairie Marsh Wildlife Drive in search of their morning meal of grubs or the eggs of ground-nesting birds.

For complete directions and additional information, see Chapter 3.

Mountain Lion

DESCRIPTION—Gray to reddish brown along back; buff white underside.

      Females: 90 to 140 pounds.

      Males: 150 to 210 pounds.

SCIENTIFIC NAME—*Felis concolor*

FAMILY—Cat (Felidae)

BREEDING SEASON—May breed any time of year

GESTATION PERIOD—13 or 14 weeks

NUMBER OF YOUNG—1 to 6 cubs (usually 3)

The "ghost of the mountains" is known by many names in North America — cougar, puma, panther, and mountain lion. Western mountain lions are typically found in broken country, such as pinon-juniper woodlands, shrub, and montane forest habitats. The key factor is the presence of mule deer. Lions eat an average of one mule deer per week. They also feed on an occasional elk, bighorn sheep, or even small mammals and birds.

Mountain lions are most active at night. Nevertheless, they often hunt during the day. Territories range from 10 square miles to as large as 100 square miles. The presence and abundance of prey is the determining factor. Mountain lions have been known to travel 25 miles in a single night in search of a meal.

Lions often move their kill to a secluded spot where feeding takes place. A half-hearted attempt usually is made to cover the remaining carcass using leaves, twigs, grass, and dirt. The lion then returns several times until the carcass is consumed. This practice is particularly common among females with kittens.

Mountain lion scat is deposited in a prominent location and only partially concealed; it is often used as a territorial marker. The scat is cylindrical and often segmented. Hair and bones are usually conspicuous.

Males scrape leaves or earth into a pile using their claws, and then urinate on the stack. These mounds, called "scrapes," act as territorial boundaries.

PHOTOGRAPHIC TECHNIQUES

Mountain lions are highly secretive, usually going out of their way to avoid human contact. This makes them extremely difficult to locate, let alone photograph, in the wild. Nevertheless, mountain lions have been called using mouth-blown or electronic callers that simulate the distress call of an injured rabbit.

All predators, including mountain lions, know the cry of an injured rabbit and recognize it as an easy meal. Most manufacturers of rabbit callers sell instructional records or cassette tapes. Some of these are actual recordings of a screaming rabbit. These are useful for learning how to use your mouth-blown caller.

Volume is extremely important. Most people use too high a volume. Use a volume similar to what a rabbit would actually produce or lower.

Camouflage clothing and a blind are helpful when working with these shy, secretive cats. It is best to locate your blind in an open area.

When using an electronic caller, place the speaker in brush or high grass away from your blind. Mountain lions, and other predators, circle downwind when coming to a call. Keep this in mind when positioning the blind.

I recommend using a cover scent when calling predators. Cover scents can be purchased by mail from Johnny Stewart Game Calls or Cabela's (see Appendix I), or check with your local sporting goods store.

Photo opportunities when using this method are usually brief, so be ready. If you are fortunate enough to call a lion, wait until you have the perfect pose before pressing the shutter release. Mountain lions have an amazing ability to hear even the slightest sound.

Since lions' main diet consists of deer, not rabbits, results when using this method are often limited. Over 90 percent of all published mountain lion photos are images of captive animals. A number of game farms meet the needs of photographers wanting mountain lion images, as well as other hard-to-photograph animals. In the Rocky Mountains, there are at least five such establishments. (See Appendix I.)

Game farms allow photographers to photograph these species in their natural habitat, under controlled conditions. The animal is released into a large, fenced compound and worked by a handler to provide the poses you request. Base prices range from $150 to $400, depending on the species and the time required. Some game farms offer discounts when photographing animals during certain months of the year, for photographing more than one species, or if you bring additional photographers along.

Several organizations lead workshops at these facilities. The cost of workshops usually includes photographing a number of species, lodging, and instruction. You can often spend less money by attending one of the workshops than by going to a game farm on your own — and have a lot more fun in the process.

TIME OF YEAR

When using the calling method, October through March will be most productive, especially in the early morning hours. If you plan to attend a game farm, any time of the year will work.

The background you may want to include in your images — snow, spring flowers, or fall colors — will dictate when to schedule your shoot. Or, do you want images of mountain lion kittens, along with one of their parents? If so, check with the game farm in advance to find out when they expect a new litter.

PHOTOGRAPHIC HOT SPOTS

If you want to photograph mountain lions the hard way — calling them in — your best chance is in Colorado, in the foothills along the east slope of the Rockies. Based on conversations with many individuals, I would choose the area between Boulder and Estes Park as having the highest concentration of mountain lions likely to come to a call. Mule deer are plentiful. Sightings occur regularly, often in people's yards. For a number of reasons, lions in this area have lost much of their fear of humans. This has produced a climate in which I believe lions will come to a call.

CAUTION: These lions' lack of fear also increases the danger of a photographer being attacked. In case of attack, the most important rule is: DO NOT RUN. Make yourself look as large and imposing as possible. Yell and wave your arms.

The areas around Sugarloaf Road and Magnolia Drive, west of Boulder, are worth investigating. To reach either road, go west from Boulder on Colorado Highway 119. After traveling approximately 5 miles, you will come to Magnolia Drive (County Road 132) taking off to the south. To reach Sugarloaf Road (County Road 122), continue west for one-eighth of a mile. Sugarloaf Road leaves the north side of Highway 119.

The majority of mountain lion sightings in this area have occurred along the first 6 miles of Magnolia Drive or Sugarloaf Road. One person in the Mountain Meadows subdivision reported seeing a mountain lion kill a mule deer in her back yard. The next day, the lion returned with two kittens — and continued coming back for several days until the carcass was devoured.

Another area worth trying is along U.S. Highway 36 and Colorado Highway 7, between Lyons and Estes Park. One person I talked with said he knew of 28 different lions sighted in this area within a year. Driving home late one night, I observed a mountain lion near Mile 28 in the South St. Vrain Canyon, along Highway 7.

Good luck! This method provides no guarantees. If you want a little less challenge and a guarantee, go to one of the Rockies' fine game farms where, for a modest fee, you can photograph mountain lions to your heart's content.

Mountain lion surveys the area

Canada Lynx

DESCRIPTION — Gray to yellowish gray; single black band encircling tip of short tail; long black ear tufts; long ruffs of fur hanging from cheeks; long legs with large, furred feet; 32- to 40-inch body; 20 to 35 pounds (females slightly smaller).

SCIENTIFIC NAME — *Felis canadensis*

FAMILY — Cat (Felidae)

BREEDING SEASON — February and March

GESTATION PERIOD — 60 days

NUMBER OF YOUNG — 2 to 4

The Canada lynx makes its home high in the snow-covered Rocky Mountains, among the fir and spruce trees of the boreal forest. Naturalist and writer Adolph Murie, in his book *Mammals of Denali*, writes, "How empty the woods and willow patches become with the decline of the hares and the departure of the lynx. It is like an empty stage after the actors have finished their play and departed.... But the hares will return again to dance in the moonlight, and the lynx will be back in his rich domain walking with stately and regal step."

Lynx habitat is defined by the presence of dense stands of conifers and rock outcrops. Colorado represents the southern end of this remarkable animal's range.

Breeding takes place in late winter. Afterward, the female selects a suitable den, more often than not in a rock cave. Following a 60-day gestation period, she gives birth to two to four kittens sometime during April or May. By July, the young are weaned and begin venturing forth from their den.

Lynx hunt during the night, searching dense boreal forests or the willows along streams for their favorite prey, the snowshoe hare. The size of their home territory varies greatly, influenced by factors such as age, sex, population, and time of year. The smallest territory covers barely 4 square miles, while larger hunting territories can include as much as 20 square miles.

As a result of the close relationship between the lynx and the snowshoe hare, population declines within the hare community have a direct effect upon the lynx population. As the hare population increases, their food supply gets depleted and their numbers eventually decline. This decline is hastened by an increased lynx population. Finally, the lynx population is reduced as hares disappear, and the cycle begins all over again. These cycles last 9 or 10 years.

An interesting study uncovered as this book was being written contradicts the conventional wisdom on showshoe hare population cycles. The study, conducted in Banff National Park, clearly showed that hare populations in the area neither increased nor declined. The final word has not been written on this subject.

In any case, lynx do not limit their diets to snowshoe hares. Deer mice, ruffed grouse, ptarmigan, squirrels, deer, and wapiti all sooner or later may be hunted by the Canada lynx.

PHOTOGRAPHIC TECHNIQUES

Game farms provide practically the only opportunity for photographing these beautiful animals with any degree of certainty. If you're so-inclined, you can try your hand at luring a lynx into photographic range using an electronic caller. Apply the techniques used for calling bobcats. Because of the sparse population of these animals, your chances of success are not good.

That leaves game-farm animals. I've obtained some very nice images in this manner. An 80-200 mm, f2.8, autofocus lens will be all you need to photograph the Canada lynx at any game farm. Since these animals often seek the shade of a tree, thus forcing the use of slow shutter speeds, a dedicated fill flash can often be worth its weight in gold.

TIME OF YEAR

Game-farm lynx can be photographed any season of the year. Spring is the time to obtain images of lynx among wild flowers. Lynx standing among snow-covered spruce or fir trees make wonderful photographs, as do scenes containing fall colors. July is usually best if you intend to photograph young kittens.

PHOTOGRAPHIC HOT SPOTS

Game farms provide the only true "hot spots" for photographing the elusive Canada lynx (see Appendix I).

If your heart is set on photographing wild lynx, it would be worthwhile to check out the following locations.

WHITE RIVER NATIONAL FOREST, COLORADO

Lynx are known to inhabit the White River National Forest, situated in west-central Colorado. One location you might want to investigate is the area surrounding Mount of the Holy Cross, west of U.S. 24, between Interstate 70 and the town of Leadville. For additional information, contact the U.S. Forest Service (970-328-6388).

YOHO NATIONAL PARK, BRITISH COLUMBIA

Canada lynx have been observed throughout the park, during all seasons, from valley bottoms to treeline. Prominent locations include the Amiskwi burn and the deciduous habitats along the lower Kicking Horse, Porcupine, and Beaverfoot valleys.

For complete directions and additional information, see Chapter 3.

*Canada lynx kittens
exploring*

Bobcat

DESCRIPTION — Reddish brown, tawny, or gray (some animals have spotted bodies; ears black on back side, tipped with short, black hair tufts; dark bands on top of tail; 25- to 30-inch body; 5-inch tail; 12 to 20 pounds (females slightly smaller).

SCIENTIFIC NAME — *Felis rufus*

FAMILY — Cat (Felidae)

BREEDING SEASON — January to September (peaks in March and April)

GESTATION PERIOD — 60 days

NUMBER OF YOUNG — 1 to 6 (average of 4)

Pound for pound, ounce for ounce, the bobcat is the toughest, strongest, most determined predator in North America. If a bobcat gets it in his mind to take down a deer, come hell or high water that deer is going down. Weighing no more than 20 pounds — not much bigger than a large house cat — the bobcat is capable of taking down animals five times as big as itself. When he's backed into a corner, watch out!

Found throughout the Rocky Mountains, the bobcat is at home in thick, brushy cover, as well as rocky terrain. Although bobcats prey on everything from mice to deer, their primary food source is rabbits. They love rabbit stew! As a result, they are often found in rabbit habitat, where woodlands meet meadows and in brushy thickets along stream beds.

Bobcats roam between two and four miles a day in pursuit of prey. Hunting territories may cover anywhere from half a square mile to 20 square miles. The average size is somewhere between 10 and 12 square miles.

Males tend to cover their entire territory, while females operate from a central location. For example, a female may have a favorite lookout site and regularly come and go from this location.

Females may come into estrus anytime between January and September. However, breeding peaks during March and April.

After mating, the female selects a nursery den under a brush pile, beneath a log, in a natural crevice among rocks, or even under an abandoned building. After a gestation period of approximately 60 days, three or four kittens are born, usually in May or June. The female raises the young without any assistance from the male. During this time she is very sensitive, and if disturbed she may abandon the den and move the kittens to a new location. Weaning takes place when the kittens are two months old. At this time, they begin exploring the world outside their den.

The bobcat is primarily nocturnal, although activity usually begins in late afternoon. Because of their small size, secretive nature, and nocturnal habits, they are seldom observed by humans. They are active year-round.

PHOTOGRAPHIC TECHNIQUES

If you hope to obtain bobcat images with any degree of certainty, you have only two choices: using a predator call (see Chapter 2) or photographing game-farm animals.

To call a bobcat, set up in rabbit habitat, such as brushy thickets along streams or meadow edges. Bobcats may come very quickly to a call, or they can take up to an hour. It is not at all uncommon for a bobcat to sit down 100 feet away and just wait. Once you spot it, you often wonder how long it has been sitting there.

While an injured-rabbit call often works well, the woodpecker distress call sold by Johnny Stewart Wildlife Calls seems more effective. (See Appendix I.)

Bobcats prefer to use cover when making their approach. Therefore, it is best to set up in an opening along a willow-lined creek or fence line. Bobcats are not extremely sensitive to smell, so it makes little difference if you locate your blind downwind or upwind of your call.

For this type of photography, I recommend a lens in the 500 mm range.

The all-around lens for photographing game-farm bobcats is the 80-200 mm, f2.8, autofocus lens. However, for tight shots, I prefer something in the 400 mm to 500 mm range.

TIME OF YEAR

Game-farm animals can be photographed year-round. Bobcat kittens are best photographed during July. Snow provides a good winter backdrop, as do wildflowers in spring and fall colors in the autumn.

Predator calling for bobcats is best accomplished in the months of December through March.

PHOTOGRAPHIC HOT SPOTS

GAME FARMS

As with most predators, game farms provide the only true "hot spots" for photographing bobcats. (See Appendix I.) If your heart is set on photographing wild bobcats, it would be worthwhile to check out the following locations.

BOSQUE DEL APACHE NATIONAL WILDLIFE REFUGE, NEW MEXICO

Embracing more than 57,000 acres of marsh, grasslands, and desert uplands, this refuge straddles the Rio Grande in the shadow of the Magdalena Mountains.

Bobcats are common throughout the refuge, though seldom observed. Refuge personnel can describe locations that have recently produced sightings.

CAUTION: This refuge is home to the western diamondback rattlesnake. Watch where you place your feet.

For complete directions and additional information, see Chapter 3.

HEYBURN STATE PARK, IDAHO

Heyburn State Park, along the shore of Lake Chatcolet, is comprised of shallow lakes, extensive marshes, and verdant forests. Six trails meander among 400-year-old ponderosas.

Close to 8,000 acres of forest, along with considerable amounts of dense under-growth near marshes and shallow lakes, provide large areas of habitat suitable for bobcats. Work the areas of dense cover near the lakes and marshes.

From Coeur d'Alene, drive south 35 miles along U.S. 95 to Plummer. Go east 5 miles on State Highway 5 to the park entrance. For additional information contact Heyburn State Park (208-686-1308). During winter, the park headquarters is closed on weekends.

KOOTENAI NATIONAL WILDLIFE REFUGE, IDAHO

Situated in the Idaho panhandle only 20 miles from Canada, this refuge is bounded by the Kootenai River on the east and the Selkirk Mountains on the west. Bobcats prefer dense cover near water, and they find this type of habitat along the park's western boundary.

For complete directions and additional information, see Chapter 3.

RED ROCK LAKES NATIONAL WILDLIFE REFUGE, MONTANA

Red Rock Lakes National Wildlife Refuge, embracing over 44,000 acres, is located in a remote section of Beaverhead County in southwestern Montana. Your best bet for finding bobcats is to work the higher elevations south of Red Rock Pass Road.

CAUTION: Hazardous bogs and sinkholes are found throughout the refuge. Be careful when traveling through wet areas.

For complete directions and additional information, see Chapter 3.

Wapiti (American Elk)

DESCRIPTION — Grayish brown sides; blackish brown neck and head; yellowish tan rump patch and tail; summer coat more reddish

    Bulls: 750 pounds

    Cows: 500 pounds

SCIENTIFIC NAME — *Cervus elaphus nelsoni*

FAMILY — Deer (Cervidae)

BREEDING SEASON — Mid- to late September

GESTATION PERIOD — 250 days

NUMBER OF YOUNG — 1 calf (twins rare)

The early morning air is crisp. The mountains are bathed in the golds and yellows of autumn. From the distance comes the unmistakable "bugle" of a bull wapiti in rut.

The rut, or annual breeding season, begins in September, as bulls defend their harems of up to 50 or 60 cows. By early November, the rut is over.

Bulls are in their prime in the fall. Winter coats, which started growing in August, are now complete, and antler development has ceased. Larger bulls shed their antlers in March; yearlings keep theirs until April or early May. A bull with antlers that have six points on each side is called a "royal." An "imperial" has seven points to a side, and a "monarch" has eight points to a side.

Bull wapiti in the Madison River, Yellowstone National Park

Calves, born in late May or early June, remain hidden for about a week after birth before joining the herd.

Wapiti are primarily nocturnal. They feed in open areas, then seek sanctuary in the forest during the day, remaining inactive from midmorning until midafternoon.

Better able to tolerate winter's harshness than summer's sweltering heat, wapiti typically seek cooler elevations during the summer. Winter finds them in lower montane, pinon-juniper, and sagebrush habitats.

Females, calves, and yearlings assemble in small herds during the summer, while mature bulls stay in small bachelor groups of up to three or four animals. Winter herds may include as many as 400 or 500 individuals.

As wapiti populations increase, herd dynamics and migration patterns often change. For example, some animals may stay in lower elevations year-round.

Wapiti, meaning "white deer," comes from the Shawnee and is the most appropriate name for American elk. In Europe, the term elk is applied to the animal we know as a moose. If we insist on calling a wapiti by the name elk, we should refer to it as the American elk.

PHOTOGRAPHIC TECHNIQUES

You will need at least a 300 mm lens for most of your shooting. 500 mm would be better.

Techniques vary with location. In general, wapiti habituated to people are more easily approached than those found in remote locations. I have been able to get surprisingly close to wapiti in Estes Park, Colorado, and Mammoth, Wyoming. Yet, I find it almost impossible to get within photographic range of these same animals once they move back into remote locations.

Use the "grazing approach," described in Chapter 2, when approaching wapiti in remote locations. If there is any secret to getting within range, it is GO SLOW. And, as with all ungulates (hoofed mammals), approach them from the downhill side to avoid cutting off their potential uphill escape route.

CAUTION: Bull wapiti can be very dangerous during the rut. They have been known to charge humans.

TIME OF YEAR

Bulls enter the rut, usually around Labor Day, in prime condition. Photograph them between early September and late October. During this time, you should have numerous opportunities to photograph bugling bulls. By the time the rut ends in early November, wapiti coats are roughed-up and patchy, and the animals are not very photogenic.

Calves are best photographed in June, soon after birth.

Trail Ridge Road in Rocky Mountain National Park offers photographic opportunities from June through August. During summer, bands of wapiti often congregate on the tundra and in the krummholz near the Alpine Visitor Center. Krummholz is a German word meaning "crooked wood."

Winter photography near Mammoth Hot Springs and Old Faithful, in Yellowstone National Park, should produce elk images you'll be proud to show others.

PHOTOGRAPHIC HOT SPOTS

ROCKY MOUNTAIN NATIONAL PARK, COLORADO

The open meadows left behind as melting glaciers receded in the Rockies are known as "parks." Beginning in early September, bulls bring their newly formed harems into these parks every evening, arriving a little before sunset. Bugling echoes throughout the valleys. The following morning, they return to the protection of the forests. As the rut continues, some harems will remain in these open areas throughout the day.

The only drawback to photographing wapiti in Rocky Mountain National Park is the large crowds of people that assemble to observe this spectacle. As a result, all foot travel in Moraine Park, Horseshoe Park, and Beaver Meadows is restricted to trails between the hours of 5 p.m. and 7 a.m. during the rut. In spite of these restrictions, I still believe the park is one of the top wapiti photography locations in the Rockies. Great photographs can be obtained from the trails and roads.

My favorite location is Moraine Park. Wapiti can be photographed from the access road into Moraine Park, the trail paralleling the south lateral moraine, and the Cub Lake Trail. I prefer the Cub Lake Trail. Harems often enter and exit Moraine Park where this trail intersects the trail along the south lateral moraine.

Parking spaces in Moraine Park are limited, so arrive early. I recommend arriving an hour before sunrise for morning shooting sessions, or in early afternoon if you plan to photograph wapiti entering the area late in the day.

To reach the Cub Lake Trail, go south along the Bear Lake Road, from its junction with U.S. 36, just inside the Beaver Meadows entrance. Turn right (west) opposite the Moraine Park Museum onto the Moraine Park Road, then continue approximately 2 miles to the Cub Lake Trailhead.

Beaver Meadows, Horseshoe Park, and the area along the road between park headquarters and the Beaver Meadows entrance station often provide photo opportunities. Also, wapiti are occasionally present at Sprague Lake.

On the west side of the park, scout the area along U.S. 34 between the entrance kiosk and the Never Summer Ranch. Check the forest clearings early in the morning and just before sunset. Once wapiti are located, they can be photographed from the road.

Don't overlook the town of Estes Park while you're in the area. Wapiti begin gathering right in town during November and stay well into the month of April. In fact, many wapiti remain in or near town all year. Three areas you will want to explore: Fall River Road, Fish Creek Road, and State Highway 7 along the south side of town.

For additional directions and information, see Chapter 3.

NATIONAL ELK REFUGE, WYOMING

For sheer numbers of wapiti, the National Elk Refuge in Jackson, Wyoming, is without equal. Up to 10,000 wapiti gather here each winter, beginning in mid-November.

Horse-drawn sleigh rides into the refuge are available from December through March. A sleigh will get you closer to wapiti than you would ever dream of getting on foot. Your 80-200 mm, f2.8 lens is ideal. It's almost always cold here in winter, and you will be sitting still for at least 30 minutes. Dress warmly!

You can also access the refuge in your private vehicle via nine miles of county roads. Unfortunately, some of these roads are closed during the winter. Wapiti also can be photographed in the refuge from a number of pull-offs along U.S. 26 north of Jackson during November and December.

The refuge is open during daylight hours all year; however, the huge wapiti concentrations occur only during the winter.

Refuge headquarters and the visitors' center are located near the east end of Broadway in Jackson. The refuge entrance is a quarter-mile east of refuge headquarters.

For additional information, see Chapter 3.

YELLOWSTONE NATIONAL PARK, WYOMING

Yellowstone National Park is home to more than 30,000 wapiti. Pack your bags, load your cameras, and let's go.

During September and October, a number of bulls assemble their harems in the Mammoth Hot Springs area. They can be found near the hot springs, in the campground, and even wandering the streets among the administration buildings.

Don't overlook open areas near the Norris campground. Wapiti herds frequently congregate here.

I have photographed wapiti along the Madison River west of Madison Junction. Check the open meadows between Madison and West Yellowstone.

Yellowstone becomes a magical winter wonderland during January and February. Photograph snow-encrusted wapiti wandering among steaming geysers and hot springs near Old Faithful and Mammoth Hot Springs. Mammoth has the only winter accommodations accessible by automobile. The Old Faithful area is accessible only by snowmobile, or by snow coach from Flagg Ranch (near the South Entrance) or West Yellowstone. Regardless of where you decide to stay, rent a snowmobile. For lodging and snow-coach reservations, call TW Recreational Services, Inc., (307-344-7311).

For additional information, see Chapter 3.

NATIONAL BISON RANGE, MONTANA

Wapiti can be photographed along the short scenic loop located just past the visitor center, and along the Red Sleep Mountain Scenic Drive. Bugling takes place during September.

All visitors, including photographers, must remain at their car and on the road at all times. The exceptions to this rule are along the Nature Trail and in the picnic area.

For directions and additional information, see Chapter 3.

BANFF NATIONAL PARK, ALBERTA

Believe it or not, the best location to photograph wapiti in the park during the rut is the ballpark in Banff Townsite. To reach the ballpark, follow Banff Avenue past the bridge to Cave Avenue. Turn right on Cave Avenue. After a little over a mile, you will come to Birch. Turn right on Birch to find the ballpark.

Two other locations worth checking out are the golf course and the east end of Vermilion Lakes. To reach the golf course, go south on Banff Avenue. Make the first left immediately after crossing the Bow River onto Cave Avenue. Take the first left onto Spray Avenue, followed by another first left onto Rundle. Rundle ends at Glen Avenue. Turn right onto Glen, which ends at the golf course.

The Vermilion Lakes area is accessed from the Mount Norquay Road. The first access is immediately north of the railroad tracks. You will find the Fenland Trail on the west side of the road. Near the trail, a waterway connects Echo Lake with the first Vermilion Lake. Wapiti gather near this location. Your other alternative is to turn west, just before reaching the Trans Canada Highway, onto Vermilion Lakes Drive. Wapiti gather in the meadow along the north and east sides of the first lake.

For additional directions and information, see Chapter 3.

JASPER NATIONAL PARK, ALBERTA

The Whistler Campground and surrounding area is the place to photograph wapiti during the rut. This campground is located just a little over 2 kilometers (1.2 miles) south of Jasper Townsite, along the west side of the Icefields Parkway.

For additional information, see Chapter 3.

Mule Deer

DESCRIPTION — Reddish brown in summer, gray in winter; white rump patch; black-tipped tail; large ears; antlers fork and fork again.

SCIENTIFIC NAME — *Odocoileus hemionus*

FAMILY — Deer (Cervidae)

BREEDING SEASON — November and December

GESTATION PERIOD — 200 days

NUMBER OF YOUNG — 1 in first year, twins thereafter (occasionally triplets)

The life of the mule deer is governed by the seasons of the year. The deer's antler growth and sexual behavior correspond directly to the day's light, or "photoperiod," as the days shorten and the winter solstice approaches.

Spring and summer are easy times for mule deer, but by October things change. The deer's antlers, which grew all summer, stop growing. The velvet covering that once carried nutrients to the antlers is shed. Soon the rut, or breeding season, will begin.

By mid-November, the bucks are in prime condition. Necks begin to swell in size. The males thrash bushes and small trees with their antlers, marking their territory with scent from glands located near their eyes. When a rival approaches, ears are laid back. Tails flair. Glands on the legs emit a scent. Snorts and bluff charges may follow. If this show of force fails to intimidate the intruder, a brutal battle for male dominance — although rare — may ensue. By mid-December, the rut ends.

Antlers are shed beginning in February. Older, mature males are the first to shed their antlers, followed by the younger bucks. By March, all antlers have dropped, and new antler growth begins almost immediately.

Following a gestation of 200 days, does give birth in June or early July. A doe's first offspring is a single fawn. However, in succeeding years, she will give birth to twins. Triplets, while not common, are seen occasionally.

Within a few hours of birth, the young fawns are able to get around on their own. They will remain motionless for two or three days, camouflaged by their spotted coat. The newborn fawns are said to be odorless, thus given an added measure of protection from predators. (However, there seems to be some disagreement over this.) During these first few days, the mother approaches the fawns several times each day to nurse them.

At three to four weeks of age, the young fawns will begin following their mother wherever she goes. At this time, does and fawns form small herds with yearlings from the previous year. These small bands remain together throughout the winter.

Feeding usually takes place early in the morning and late in the day. Deer browse on chokecherry, bitterbrush, serviceberry, mountain mahogany, and even sagebrush. They also graze on a variety of grasses and succulent forbs.

Mule deer scat, or fecal pellets, is dropped in small clusters. The pellets are approximately 0.5 inch in diameter and concave on one end, with a small nipplelike protrusion on the other. Deer and wapiti ranges often overlap, and the scat from both species is often observed in the same area. However, deer scat is much smaller than that of the wapiti.

Spooked mule deer often flee with a unique gait — a bouncing, springlike motion called "stotting." The stott allows the deer to change directions almost instantaneously.

Seasonal migration of mule deer allows them to avoid snow deeper than about 18 inches. Mule deer, a western species, can be found in suitable habitat from the plains to alpine tundra.

PHOTOGRAPHIC TECHNIQUES

First, locate your subject. Search for fresh scat. Take your time, stop often, and scout the area with binoculars. When feeding, the deer are much easier to spot. After feeding, they will lie down and chew their cud, often selecting a willow stand along a creek, or the shade of a large tree. A deer lying down is difficult to see. Look for two big ears sticking up.

Do not attempt a sneak approach. Stay in the open and near the edges of clearings. The deer will be aware of your presence long before you are aware of its. If you try sneaking up, it will think you are a predator and will be in the next county before you can spell M-U-L-E D-E-E-R. If the deer can anticipate your actions and determine that you present no threat, it usually will accept your presence.

Once you have located your subject, wait before continuing. Use the "grazing approach" (see Chapter 2). It is important for the deer to be able to see you at all times. Avoid loud noises and sudden movements. If your subject runs off, stay still for a few minutes before continuing. In all likelihood, the deer will not go very far.

Do not approach mule deer from their uphill side. This blocks their preferred escape route and tends to makes them extremely nervous — reason enough for your subject to flee.

A lens in the 400 mm to 500 mm range is ideal for this type of shooting, as it will provide frame-filling images from a comfortable working distance. I like using my 200-400 mm, f4 zoom lens when photographing mule deer. If I want a habitat shot, all I have to do is zoom to 200 mm. Or, I can put on a 1.4X teleconverter, which will give me 560 mm and an eyeball-to-eyeball look at my subject.

TIME OF YEAR

November and December are my favorite times to photograph bucks, because they are in prime condition at that time. July through August is best for photographing bucks in "velvet." Also, July is the best month for photographing newborn fawns.

PHOTOGRAPHIC HOT SPOTS

GREAT SAND DUNES NATIONAL MONUMENT, COLORADO

Sand dunes 700 feet high. No vegetation. These are sights one would expect to see in the Gobi or Sahara deserts, not in the mountains of Colorado. However, the park is not all sand. This area is surrounded by excellent deer habitat, and mule deer are everywhere. Does and their fawns are seen along the roads in late spring. Mature bucks make their presence known in the fall. It would be easier to tell you where not to look for deer; however, I prefer the areas along Medano and Mosca Creeks. The campground is another location you might want to investigate.

The national monument can be reached from U.S. 160, east of Alamosa, or from State Highway 17, north of Alamosa. Along U.S. 160, go east from town 14 miles. Turn left onto State Highway 150. Go 19 miles to the monument. Along State Highway 17, go north from Alamosa. Turn east 1 mile past Mosca onto Six Mile Lane. Go 16 miles, turn left, and follow State Highway 150 for 6 miles to the monument.

For additional information, contact Great Sand Dunes National Monument (719-378-2312).

ROCKY MOUNTAIN NATIONAL PARK, COLORADO

My favorite locations for photographing mule deer are along Beaver Creek and the south side of Deer Mountain. To locate deer along Beaver Creek, enter the park at the Beaver Meadows Entrance Station. After going 0.25 mile, turn left onto Bear Lake Road. Park at the first pull-off. The creek runs from west to east. Hike east, parallel to the creek. Don't walk along the creek bed; remain higher in order to scout more terrain. After hiking for about a mile, you will see several National Park Service houses. Carefully search this area, because deer are often observed among the houses.

Also search the hillsides along the road between park headquarters and Deer Ridge Junction. Another location is along Bear Lake Road, between U.S. 36 and the Moraine Park Museum.

For complete directions and additional information, see Chapter 3.

BIG FLAT, FISHLAKE NATIONAL FOREST, UTAH

Big Flat, a large mountain meadow encircled by fir, aspen, and Englemann spruce, is located east of Beaver, Utah, in the Tushar Mountains. It is the best summer location in Utah for photographing mule deer.

Mule deer are typically observed in the meadows along the main road early in the morning. A side road to the east makes a short loop and often produces results.

Most photography can be conducted from the roads. However, walking some of the wildlife trails can often be productive.

Stop at the U.S. Forest Service Station, located near the split-rail-fenced meadow. The staff there can advise you of significant sightings, such as newborn fawns.

For complete directions and additional information, see Chapter 3.

JASPER NATIONAL PARK, ALBERTA

Mule deer are frequently observed in this park in a number of locations. The following areas should be enough to keep you busy: Maligne Lake Road, Pyramid Lake, Highway 93A, and Highway 16 East and West.

To access the Maligne Lake Road, go north on Highway 16 approximately 2 kilometers (1.2 miles) from the intersection of Connaught Drive and Highway 16, on the north side of Jasper Townsite. Turn right as if you were going to the Jasper Park Lodge. However, after crossing the Athabasca River turn left on Lodge Road (instead of going right to the lodge). After going 2 kilometers (1.2 miles), Lodge Road turns to the right and becomes Maligne Lake Road. Follow it to the lake, searching for deer along the way.

Pyramid Lake can be reached from Jasper Townsite, by going northwest on Pine Avenue. Pine eventually turns into Pyramid Lake Road. Follow it until you arrive at the lake.

Highway 93A, beginning 7 kilometers (4.2 miles) south of town, follows the old highway for 23 miles, ending near Athabasca Falls. Several side roads leave the main highway. Take them all as you scout the area for mule deer.

Begin your search along Highway 16 East at the turnoff to the Snaring River Campground, 16 kilometers (10 miles) north of Jasper Townsite. Follow Highway 16 East, looking for deer along the way, to the Miette Hotsprings turnoff, a distance of 28 kilometers (17 miles).

Highway 16 West, crossing the Icefields Parkway south of Jasper Townsite, provides access to British Columbia to the west, a distance of only 25 kilometers (15 miles). Mule deer are often observed along this stretch of highway.

Mule deer are also frequently sighted in Jasper Townsite.

For complete directions and additional information, see Chapter 3.

WATERTON LAKES NATIONAL PARK, ALBERTA

Mule deer are often present along Red Rock Parkway. Go northeast from Waterton Townsite for 3 kilometers (1.8 miles), and turn left onto the parkway. Drive 15 kilometers (9 miles) to the road's end, searching for mule deer along the way.

Waterton Townsite holds a "tame" population of mule deer, providing willing and easy subjects. Unfortunately, the backgrounds are not always desirable.

For complete directions and additional information, see Chapter 3.

BOSQUE DEL APACHE NATIONAL WILDLIFE REFUGE, NEW MEXICO

Mule deer are often observed along the 15-mile auto tour through the refuge. Work them early in the morning when the lighting is good. CAUTION: The refuge is home to the western diamondback rattlesnake. Watch where you place your feet.

For complete directions and additional information, see Chapter 3.

NATIONAL CENTER FOR ATMOSPHERIC RESEARCH, BOULDER, COLORADO

Resting majestically on the hills west of Boulder is the National Center for Atmospheric Research (NCAR). Mule deer are plentiful here. As you enter the complex, you may see them grazing in the meadows along the road. They often bed down in the tall grasses near the hillside to your left. Do not stop along this road; park in the lot atop the hill. From there, you can hike wherever you like. You may want to follow the hiking trails west, past the NCAR buildings. Deer are often observed among the nearby foothills.

NCAR can be reached by going west along Table Mesa Drive, from its intersection with South Broadway (State Highway 93). Follow Table Mesa west to the NCAR area.

SEEDSKADEE NATIONAL WILDLIFE REFUGE, WYOMING

A herd of approximately 300 mule deer hangs out near the bottoms along the Green River. Three refuge roads provide access to the river — two on the river's west side and one on the east.

For complete directions and additional information, see Chapter 3.

CAMAS NATIONAL WILDLIFE REFUGE, IDAHO

Come to Camas in mid-October when the rut occurs. That's the time to photograph mule deer. They often congregate in the fields near headquarters.

For complete directions and additional information, see Chapter 3.

White-tailed Deer

DESCRIPTION — Winter coat: grayish brown
Summer coat: reddish brown Tail: white below, brown above

SCIENTIFIC NAME — *Odocoileus virginianus*

FAMILY — Deer (Cervidae)

BREEDING SEASON — Late October to mid-December

GESTATION PERIOD — 200 days

NUMBER OF YOUNG — 1 to 3

The whitetail's raised "white flag," flicking from side to side high above its rump, warns of nearby danger as the deer bounds away into a brushy thicket. Jan Wassink, in his book *Mammals of the Central Rockies*, writes of this shy and elusive deer: "Where it is hunted, it is as formless and shifty as a wisp of wood smoke. But where it is protected, as in national parks and hunting preserves, the whitetail is bold and obvious."

White-tailed deer seem to prefer the dense woodlands along river corridors. However, it is not uncommon for them to take up residence in treeless grasslands.

The home range of a whitetail covers 2 to 3 square miles. Movement patterns become established and are followed religiously. Does tend to stay within their home range. However, bucks roam about during fall and early winter as they play the mating game.

Feeding takes place at dawn and dusk. Large quantities of vegetation are rapidly consumed. After feeding, the deer retreat to protected bedding areas. The food is then regurgitated, a little at a time, and rechewed. The process of rechewing food reduces the deer's grazing time in open meadows, thus reducing their exposure to predators.

In winter, several small groups often congregate in an area of dense cover. Here they feed, protected from the harshness of winter winds. These areas become laced with a network of packed trails, providing easier walking. This trail network is called a "deer yard."

Bucks withdraw into bachelor groups for most of the year. A bachelor group may contain as few as two bucks and as many as six. Does form their own group, comprised of at least one doe, her yearlings, and her fawns. Other doe families may join in. Only in the fall, when a doe is in estrus, will a buck abandon his bachelor group.

The rut, or mating season, takes place from late October through mid-December. Does begin coming into estrus by the end of October. They are receptive for about 24 hours. If the females do not mate, they will come into estrus again in 28 days.

In May or June, after a gestation period of 200 days, the new arrivals enter the world. The first birth is usually a single fawn. However, in years following, does usually give birth to twins, and triplets are occasionally born.

Newborn fawns remain hidden and rarely move more than a few feet from their birthplace during their first month. This provides their greatest protection from predators. After the first month, they join their mother, following her everywhere.

All members of the deer family — deer, wapiti, moose, and caribou — grow antlers. Antlers are shed and regrown every year. Whitetails shed their antlers during January and February. New growth begins almost immediately. By September, growth is complete and the velvet covering is shed. The antler tines of the whitetail branch from one main beam.

PHOTOGRAPHIC TECHNIQUES

In general, white-tailed deer are very shy and elusive. Some have allowed me to walk within 50 feet and continued feeding. Others have vanished into the next county before I was able to get my car stopped.

For shy subjects, your automobile can serve as a fantastic blind. Set up your camera before stopping. Often, I've spotted deer while driving along backcountry roads; I just drive past until I'm out of sight before stopping. After positioning my camera and window mount (see Chapter 2), I return and begin photographing from my car window.

In Glacier National Park, I've been able to follow whitetails on foot without startling them, as they browsed on vegetation.

In either case, a 400 mm telephoto usually will be all you need for lens power. Whitetails are usually active when light levels are low. A fast lens (large aperture) is often needed to stop the action and still provide enough light to properly expose your film. My 200-400 mm, f4 is ideal for this type of photography.

TIME OF YEAR

All members of the deer family molt twice a year. Whitetails molt in May or June, and again during September. They are not very photogenic during these times.

Bucks are in their prime between September and December. Antler development is complete, and they are in top condition for the coming winter. However, bucks in "velvet" are best photographed in July and August.

Fawns can be photographed shortly after birth in May and June. CAUTION: Do not touch a fawn. Your scent, imparted to the newborn fawns, will make it easier for predators to locate them.

PHOTOGRAPHIC HOT SPOTS

CEDAR FLATS, NEZPERCE NATIONAL FOREST, IDAHO

Cedar Flats wetland is a well-known whitetail fawning area. Photographic opportunities are exceptional. If photographing fawns is your priority, I recommend planning your trip between late June and mid-August. Early morning and late afternoon hours are best.

From Kooskia, drive east 23 miles along U.S. 12 to the town of Lowell. At Lowell, turn right and follow the Selway River Road to the Cedar Flats wetland, a distance of 5.5 miles. I recommend stopping at the Fenn Ranger Station and informing U.S. Forest Service personnel of your intentions. They can supply you with a wealth of information.

For additional information, contact the U.S. Forest Service (208-926-4258).

GLACIER NATIONAL PARK, MONTANA

Glacier is host to both species of deer found in North America: the white-tailed deer and mule deer. Mule deer will be found in open woodlands, while whitetails prefer the protection of dense forests.

One area particularly worth checking out is McGee Meadow. It can be reached from Apgar by following the road around the south end of McDonald Lake to Fish Creek Campground. From the campground, go north 4 miles along the Inside North Fork Road. McGee Meadow will be on your left. Whitetails are frequently observed at this location early in the morning.

I would also keep a close watch on both Fish Creek and Sprague Creek Campgrounds.

For complete directions and additional information, see Chapter 3.

KELLY ISLAND, MONTANA

Whitetails are often observed early in the morning, peacefully grazing in the meadows, and, occasionally, resting in someone's yard in the nearby subdivision. As you hike the numerous wildlife trails, you are sure to come in contact with one of the island's many deer.

For complete directions and additional information, see Chapter 3.

NATIONAL BISON RANGE, MONTANA

Many species of wildlife can be photographed along the National Bison Range's 19-mile loop road, including the white-tailed deer. Look for them along Mission Creek, near the range's northern boundary.

For complete directions and additional information, see Chapter 3.

Moose

DESCRIPTION — Dark brown; dewlap (or bell) under throat; palmate antlers; males average 1,100 pounds; females average 700 pounds.

SCIENTIFIC NAME — *Alces alces*

FAMILY — Deer (Cervidae)

BREEDING SEASON — Mid-September to November

GESTATION PERIOD — 8 months

NUMBER OF YOUNG — 1 or 2 (usually 1)

Moose are the largest members of the deer family. Seven subspecies are recognized worldwide, and four of these are native to North America, with the largest occurring in western Canada and Alaska.

Moose inhabit the northern regions of North America, southward into the central Rockies. A plentiful water supply is the single most important requirement of moose. They especially like willow bottoms.

The average bull moose will weigh in at 1,100 pounds. In Alaska, mature bulls can stand over 7 feet at the shoulder, reach an antler spread of close to 80 inches, and weigh as much as 1,800 pounds.

Like other members of the deer family, moose grow a new set of antlers every year. Older bulls are the first to shed their antlers, usually in December. Those with smaller "racks" may not drop theirs until March. Growth of the new antlers is usually complete by late August or September. At that time, bulls begin losing the velvet in preparation for the rut. During the rut, bulls are extremely aggressive toward anything that moves, including people. By mid-October, the mating season comes to an end.

Usually, a single calf is born in May or June. Twins are not uncommon, but triplets are extremely rare. As with many species of wildlife, food supply affects fertility. A higher percentage of twins is born when food is abundant.

Unlike young deer and wapiti, newborn moose calves do not have spots. The young calf follows its mother two to three days after birth, making spots unnecessary for camouflage. A cow with a calf is dangerous and unpredictable.

Cathy and Gordon Illg, in their book *Rocky Mountain Safari*, relate the comment of a wildlife researcher concerning the moose's ungainly appearance: "Anyone who is mistaken for a moose and shot is better off dead anyway."

PHOTOGRAPHIC TECHNIQUES

In certain locations moose are quite approachable. However, because of their unpredictability, always maintain a safe working distance. This isn't always easy. Once, in Yellowstone, I literally stumbled upon a cow lying among the willows. Fortunately for me, she jumped to her feet and ran away; she was almost as rattled as I was.

A safe distance will vary depending on the individual animal and the habitat. Greater distances should be observed in open areas. When possible, stand next to a sizable tree. If the moose decides to charge, it's a simple matter to put the tree between you and the moose.

In areas near the highway where moose are unapproachable on foot, use your car as a blind. Use a bean bag or window mount for steadying a long lens.

Early morning hours are best. During the heat of the day, moose seek cover in heavy timber. The exception is cold winter days, when moose are often observed in the open, soaking up sunshine.

I recommend using at least a 400 mm telephoto lens for moose photography. Anything with less power will not allow a safe working distance.

Moose have very dark coats and reflect little light. If you meter on the moose and do not correct the meter reading, your slides will be overexposed when you get them back from the lab (see Exposure, Chapter 2).

TIME OF YEAR

Bull moose are most photogenic from mid-September through November. Newborn calves can be photographed beginning in early June. Images showing a cow with her newborn calf are welcome additions to anyone's file.

PHOTOGRAPHIC HOT SPOTS

GRAND TETON NATIONAL PARK, WYOMING

The Grand Teton skyline, one of the most impressive mountain vistas in North America, towers more than a mile above Jackson Hole.

The Snake River and its tributaries immediately east of Jackson Lake provide the most consistent photo opportunities for large bull moose south of the Canadian border. Oxbow Bend and Willow Flats — these names should bring joy into the heart of every wildlife photographer in their quest for the ultimate moose image. Moose browse among the willows lining Pilgrim Creek, Christian Creek, and the slow-moving waters of Oxbow Bend. This prime moose habitat lies only a few miles west of the Moran entrance station.

For complete directions and additional information, see Chapter 3.

YELLOWSTONE NATIONAL PARK, WYOMING

How do you spell moose? W-I-L-L-O-W P-A-R-K! In fact, the National Park Service has installed an interpretive display about moose at Willow Park. Willow Park is near Indian Creek Campground, between Mammoth and Norris.

Be sure to check out the area between Fishing Bridge and Pelican Creek. It, too, is noted for moose activity, as is the area along the Lewis River, near the south entrance to the park.

For complete directions and additional information, see Chapter 3.

CAMAS NATIONAL WILDLIFE REFUGE, IDAHO

There are so many species of waterfowl in Camas that being able to photograph moose is like having icing on your cake. The moose are difficult to locate when they're bedded down. By driving the refuge roads you may compel some moose to stand, allowing you to observe and photograph them. Be sure to check out the willows along Camas Creek.

For complete directions and additional information, see Chapter 3.

ELK VALLEY MARSH, CARIBOU NATIONAL FOREST, IDAHO

If it's moose you're after, go to Elk Valley Marsh. Beaver dams have created a 200-acre marsh, which attracts many species of wildlife, including the state's largest moose population.

From the town of Soda Springs, go north 11 miles along State Highway 34. Turn right onto the Blackfoot River Road, which becomes Forest Road 102. After following Diamond Creek approximately 12 miles, Forest Road 102 intersects Forest Road 146. Follow 146, the Wells Canyon Route, 4 miles to its junction with Forest Road 111. Go south on 111, the Crow Creek Road, for 5 miles to the junction with Road 147. Follow this road for 6 miles to the Elk Valley Marsh.

The marsh is on the east side of the road. Search carefully, taking your time. Even standing, a moose can be completely obscured by the profusion of willows.

When you've taken all the images your shutter finger can endure, return to Forest Road 111. By continuing south 10 miles, you connect with Highway 89, 6 miles east of Montpelier.

For additional information, contact the U.S. Forest Service (208-547-4356).

LOCHSA RIVER CANYON, CLEARWATER NATIONAL FOREST, IDAHO

The Lochsa River Canyon, designated part of the National Wild and Scenic River System, features abrupt canyon walls covered with deciduous shrubs and conifers. The place to go for moose: Elk Summit Cabin. During late summer and fall, moose descend upon the natural mineral licks at this location.

To reach the cabin from Kooskia, take the scenic Lewis and Clark Highway (U.S. 12) northeast to the Powell Ranger Station, near Milepost 162. Turn right and go 2 miles. Upon crossing the Lochsa River, turn left onto Forest Road 111. After traveling 4 miles, you will come to a fork in the road. Take the right fork, Forest Road 360, and continue 12 miles to Elk Summit and the cabin.

For additional information contact the U.S. Forest Service (208-926-4275).

MUSSELLSHELL MEADOWS, CLEARWATER NATIONAL FOREST, IDAHO

Every spring, cow moose and their calves are attracted to this 100-acre boggy meadow, situated in the midst of a lush evergreen forest. Moose can be photographed as you wade among the bogs, leisurely stroll the nature trail, or drive along the roads encircling the meadow.

From Kamiah, go east along Forest Road 100 from its junction with U.S. 12, south of the Clearwater River bridge. Stay on Forest Road 100 for 25 miles until you reach the Mussellshell Meadows parking area.

For additional information, contact the U.S. Forest Service (208-476-4541).

JASPER NATIONAL PARK, ALBERTA

Several locations are worth investigation: Highway 93A, Maligne Lake Road, Highway 16 West, Snaring River Road, and Sunwapta Falls.

Highway 93A, beginning 7 kilometers (4.2 miles) south of Jasper Townsite, follows the old highway for 23 miles, ending near Athabasca Falls. Two tarns on the west side of the road, 3 to 5 kilometers (1.8 to 3 miles) north of Athabasca Falls, attract moose.

To access the Maligne Lake Road, go north on Highway 16 approximately 2 kilometers (1.2 miles) from the intersection of Connaught Drive and Highway 16, on the north side of Jasper Townsite. Turn right as if you were going to the Jasper Park Lodge. However, after crossing the Athabasca River turn left on

Lodge Road instead of going right to the lodge. After 2 kilometers (1.2 miles), Lodge Road turns to the right and becomes Maligne Lake Road. Follow it to Maligne Lake, searching for moose along the way.

Highway 16 West, crossing the Icefields Parkway south of Jasper Townsite, provides access to British Columbia to the west, a distance of only 25 kilometers (15 miles). The highway parallels the Miette River along the way, with abundant moose habitat.

Begin your search along the Snaring River Road where it intersects Highway 16 East, approximately 10 kilometers (6 miles) north of Jasper Townsite. From this intersection north to Jasper Lake there is abundant moose habitat.

The area along the Icefields Parkway near Sunwapta Falls, 55 kilometers (33 miles) south of Jasper Townsite, often is good for moose photography in the evenings.

For complete directions and additional information, see Chapter 3.

The following locations are not "hot spots," but they are places where moose are frequently seen.

NORTH PARK

North Park is located in an intermountain glacial basin in north-central Colorado, with pristine mountain lakes, crystal-clear streams, verdant forests, and sagebrush country. North Park is generally productive for moose photography from June through October.

In 1978, the Colorado Division of Wildlife began moose reintroduction in Colorado with the release of 12 animals near the town of Rand, 8 miles west of Rocky Mountain National Park. The release group consisted of three bulls, seven cows, one yearling male, and a female calf. In 1979, an additional 12 moose from the Jackson Hole area were released in Colorado. Today, the Colorado moose population numbers around 600 animals. They continue to be observed in North Park, in the area surrounding the initial release site.

In your search for moose, begin at the town of Walden. Investigate the willows along the Illinois River, southwest of the Arapaho National Wildlife Refuge headquarters.

Continue your search along Highway 125. South of Rand, turn left at the Old Homestead Lodge. After about 5 miles, the road forks, with one road going to Old Teller City and the other to Bowen Pass. Explore both, searching for moose in the tall timber where they often rest during the heat of the day.

Continuing your quest for moose, go back to Highway 125 and turn south. Approximately 3 miles after re-entering the highway, turn right and follow Road 106 to Troublesome Pass, searching for moose along the way.

Before you leave the area, stop at the Rand Store, a great place for coffee and information. The store is generally open from Memorial Day through the end of big-game hunting season in late fall

Another location where moose are often observed is between Cameron Pass and Gould. From Rand, go northwest along Road 27, which connects with Highway 14 west of Gould. Turn right, following Highway 14 to Gould. Take time out at the restaurant (the only one in town) in Gould. They serve a mean Texas-style burrito. After you finish your burrito, explore the willows along the highway between Gould and Cameron Pass to the east, investigating all side roads and campgrounds.

ROCKY MOUNTAIN NATIONAL PARK, COLORADO

Moose seem to prefer the Kawuneeche Valley, on the park's west side. During spring and summer, I recommend searching the willows along U.S. 34, between the Onahu Creek Trailhead and the Timber Creek Campground. Winter finds moose in the area bordered on the north by Onahu Creek and on the south by the town of Grand Lake.

For complete directions and additional information, see Chapter 3.

KOOTENAI NATIONAL WILDLIFE REFUGE, IDAHO

Spring and fall is the time to gear up for moose in Kootenai. In the early morning hours, and again in late afternoon, moose are frequently observed grazing the refuge marshes. One area you may want to investigate is Cascade Pond, near the refuge's northwest corner. A permanent blind — the Moose Overlook Blind — is provided by the refuge. During the heat of day, moose seek refuge in the conifer forests bordering the refuge's western boundary.

For complete directions and additional information, see Chapter 3.

BANFF NATIONAL PARK, ALBERTA

Several locations in Banff often provide opportunities for moose photography: Vermilion Lakes, Fenland Trail, and the area between Bow Lake and Waterfowl Lakes.

Vermilion Lakes is immediately west of Banff Townsite. Turn west onto Vermilion Lakes Drive from Mount Norquay Road, just south of the Trans Canada Highway. Follow this to the lakes.

The Fenland Trail is on the west side of Mount Norquay Road, just north of the railroad tracks.

Bow Lake is about 90 kilometers (54 miles) northwest of Lake Louise along the Icefields Parkway. Moose are frequently observed between Bow Lake and Waterfowl Lakes, 20 kilometers (12 miles) to the north.

For complete directions and additional information, see Chapter 3.

YOHO NATIONAL PARK, BRITISH COLUMBIA

Moose are frequently observed among the sloughs and fens in the park. Of particular note is the area near the lake along the Ice River Road as you approach the park's western boundary. Beaverfoot River and its shrub margins are also worth checking out.

During winter, you may want to scout the shrub margins along the Otterhead or Porcupine Valley fire roads. In the Porcupine Valley, I would suggest examining the lower areas of the burn approximately 2 kilometers (1.2 miles) past the end of the fire road.

For the more adventuresome, I recommend the west side of the Ottertail valley, near the Hurd burn, and the areas along both Float and McArthur Creeks. Or, you might want to investigate the avalanche chutes along the west slopes of Mount Clawson, near the Beaverfoot River. Moose can be found in these areas all year. However, hiking between 5 and 10 kilometers (3 and 6 miles) is required.

A couple of natural mineral licks in the park also provide plenty of photo opportunities. The Wapta Falls lick is located at the intersection of the Trans Canada Highway and the Wapta Falls Road, 4.5 kilometers (2.7 miles) east of the park's western boundary. The Ottertail lick requires a little more effort. It is located 3.2 kilometers (2 miles) up the Ottertail Trail.

For the moose's protection, I have chosen not to include several other locations where they may be photographed. If, in your wanderings, you should happen across any of these locations, share them only with the moose.

For complete directions and additional information, see Chapter 3.

Bull moose grazing in meadow

Pronghorn

DESCRIPTION — Russet-tan upper body; white lower body and sides; males have black cheek patch; black horns with forward-pointing prong; female horns short; 75 to 140 pounds.

SCIENTIFIC NAME — *Antilocapra americana*

FAMILY — Goat-Antelope (Antilocapridae)

BREEDING SEASON — Mid-September

GESTATION PERIOD — 230 to 250 days

NUMBER OF YOUNG — 2 (occasionally 3)

In the early days of this country, it is estimated that some 75 million pronghorn roamed the western plains. By the early 1900s, market hunters and habitat destruction had reduced this number to less than 25,000 animals. Today, thanks to state and federal wildlife agencies, some 750,000 pronghorn populate the continent.

North America's fastest mammal, the pronghorn is capable of attaining speeds up to 84 miles per hour.

Home for the pronghorn is the prairie and sagebrush country of the West. Well-suited for wide-open spaces, the pronghorn's exceptionally large eyes can detect the slightest movement of a predator miles away. Their eyes are shaped somewhat like a fisheye lens, allowing them to see both front and rear without moving their head.

Because both males and females grow horns, the black chin-strap found only on males is the best way to differentiate between the sexes. Unlike other animals that grow horns, pronghorns shed the outer horn sheath annually, usually in late November, leaving only a bony protuberance.

Territories, established by dominant bucks in March, are maintained through the breeding season in mid-September. During this time, non-territorial bucks form bachelor groups elsewhere, while does remain with their fawns. As the breeding season begins, bucks attempt to keep does and their fawns within these territories. Once breeding season has ended, both sexes of all ages assemble on their winter range.

Fawning begins in late May. Over half of first-year does give birth to twins, and triplets are occasionally born. Fawns spend most of their first few days sleeping alone.

Pronghorn are often incorrectly called antelope. They evolved solely in North America and are not even closely related to the true antelope found in Africa.

PHOTOGRAPHIC TECHNIQUES

In general, pronghorn are extremely nervous, high-strung animals. It doesn't take much for them to become anxious. In many areas, simply stopping your car is enough to send them scurrying away.

However, in Yellowstone National Park pronghorn have become so habituated to people that I've been able to approach them on foot. In fact, I even had one walk up to me. In situations like these, I find my 200-400 mm, f4 zoom lens to be ideal.

In other areas, pronghorn behavior may require photographing them from your automobile. At times like these, you might wish you had something in the 600 mm range or larger.

When approaching pronghorn on foot, watch for changes in their behavior. For example, if your subject stops grazing and looks up, or begins stomping the ground with one of its front hooves, freeze in your tracks. Wait until the pronghorn resumes grazing before continuing. Also, never walk directly toward your subject. Use the "grazing" approach (see Grazing Approach, Chapter 2).

TIME OF YEAR

Bucks are best photographed between June and November. In late November, the outer horn sheath is dropped. Several months will pass before the new covering is complete. Pronghorn are not very photogenic in spring while their winter coat is being shed.

Fawns can be photographed beginning in early June. Since they grow rather rapidly, it's usually best to photograph them within the first two months following birth.

PHOTOGRAPHIC HOT SPOTS

YELLOWSTONE NATIONAL PARK, WYOMING

What does the area surrounding the Gardiner entrance into Yellowstone have in common with the Denver Zoo? The world's most approachable pronghorn. These pronghorn actually come into the edge of town and graze on the manicured lawns.

You will find pronghorn along the North Entrance Road, within two miles of the large Rock Arch Entrance. At the entrance kiosk, a one-way gravel road intersects the entrance road. From this road, pronghorn are often observed among the rolling hills to the west. Access to the gravel road is in Mammoth, behind the Mammoth Hot Springs Hotel. Inside the park, approximately 0.75 mile past the entrance kiosk, a trail leads to the east. Pronghorn often graze in the fields along this trail.

For complete directions and additional information, see Chapter 3.

WIND CAVE NATIONAL PARK, SOUTH DAKOTA

Wind Cave National Park is more than an underground network of geological wonders. Its most significant features are the stunning ponderosa forests and vast prairie grasslands.

Pronghorn can be photographed in the grassy valley along Beaver Creek Canyon. NPS Roads 5 and 6 also provide marvelous photo opportunities.

Beaver Creek Canyon, located north of the Visitor Center, can be reached from State Highway 87. Hike along Fire Road 8 into the valley shaded by high cliffs.

NPS Road 5 can be accessed from State Highway 87, near the park's northern boundary. Drive east, following NPS 5 into the park's eastern section, where it joins NPS 6.

For additional information, contact Wind Cave National Park (605-745-4600).

NATIONAL BISON RANGE, MONTANA

Many species of wildlife can be photographed along the bison range's 19-mile loop road, including pronghorn, which are frequently observed in the grassy hillsides along the last 5 miles of the tour route.

The 19-mile Red Sleep Mountain Scenic Drive, traversing grassy prairies and montane forests, is open from mid-May until late October. During the remainder of the year, only a 5-mile section of Red Sleep Mountain loop is open. However, a smaller loop, taking a half-hour to drive, is open all year. Refuge personnel suggest taking two hours to drive the 19-mile loop.

All visitors, including photographers, must remain at their car and on the road at all times. The exceptions to this are along the Nature Trail and in the picnic area.

For complete directions and additional information, see Chapter 3.

Bigborn Sheep

DESCRIPTION – Brown with white muzzle and underparts; cream-colored rump patch; rams weigh 127 to 316 pounds, ewes 74 to 200 pounds.

SCIENTIFIC NAME – *Ovis canadensis*

FAMILY – Sheep (Bovidae)

BREEDING SEASON – Mid-November to early December

GESTATION PERIOD – 180 days

NUMBER OF YOUNG – 1 (twins extremely rare)

Bighorn sheep, at home in high, rugged landscapes, are the "monarchs of the mountains." Ewes, lambs, and immature males live together, while rams separate into small "bachelor" groups, except during the "rut," or breeding season. Each fall the sheep migrate to lower elevations as deepening snow covers their food supply. At this time, ewes and rams come together and the rut begins.

During the rut, beginning in November, rams challenge one another for dominance, first by flank bumping and kicking, followed by violent head butting. Starting 30 or 40 feet from each other, on some imperceptible signal the rams rush head-on. The resultant rifle-sounding clash, as horns and skulls meet, can be heard half a mile or more away.

Breeding is complete by January. Ewes usually give birth to a single lamb during the months of May and June. They remain with their newborn lambs in remote, inaccessible places for about two weeks before reassembling into small bands.

PHOTOGRAPHIC TECHNIQUES

Bighorn sheep escape their predators by fleeing uphill. Make your approach from the downhill side. By avoiding the sheep's potential escape route, you won't stress them. Always use the "grazing" approach, described in Chapter 2, when attempting to move close to your subject.

For bighorn photography, I find the 80-200 mm, f2.8, autofocus to be a good all-around lens. The autofocus mode allows me to capture sudden action. For those tight head shots, I prefer something in the 500 mm range.

TIME OF YEAR

Fall is the best time to photograph adult sheep. They are in prime physical condition then, and there is the chance of catching rams during their spectacular head-butting displays. Young lambs are best photographed during June, shortly after birth.

PHOTOGRAPHIC HOT SPOTS

ROCKY MOUNTAIN NATIONAL PARK, COLORADO

One of my favorite locations for photographing bighorn sheep is along the Fall River Road, between the town of Estes Park and the park entrance. Bighorn rams begin arriving in this area around the first of November and stay until the following February, before going back into the high country. The sheep actually congregate outside the park on private property. Most of the time, they can be photographed from the road. Go from November through the first half of December, while they look their finest.

To reach this area, go northwest along Fall River Road from Estes Park. The sheep can be anywhere along this or the side roads, between Castle Mountain and McGregor Mountain.

For complete directions and additional information, see Chapter 3.

WHISKEY RIVER BASIN, SHOSHONE NATIONAL FOREST, WYOMING

Each winter, more than 1,000 bighorn sheep gather in the Whiskey River Basin, south of Dubois, providing endless photo opportunities.

Stay alert upon arrival in this valley; the sheep can be anywhere. Scout the hillsides, using your binoculars. Frequently they descend into the valley, at times congregating in the middle of the road.

Bighorns begin gathering in the area during mid-November, and they stay through the following March. Photography is best during November and December. Afterward, the sheep are not as photogenic.

To reach the Whiskey River Basin from Dubois, drive southeast along U.S. 287 for 4 miles. Turn right onto Forest Road 111, and go 7 miles to the Whiskey River Basin.

During your visit to the area, I recommend visiting the National Bighorn Sheep Interpretive Center in Dubois. The center is a non-profit organization, formed "to promote education, research, and conservation of wildlife and its habitat." (See Appendix I.)

YELLOWSTONE NATIONAL PARK, WYOMING

One of the best bighorn locations in Yellowstone is Mount Everts, immediately east of Mammoth. In the summer, look for sheep high on the mountain. However, beginning in the fall and continuing through the winter, they drink from the Gardner River along U.S. 89, between Gardiner and Mammoth, near the town of Mammoth. If you do not see them along the river, look among the cliffs above the river.

Sheep can be photographed on Mount Washburn in the summer. Two different trails will take you to the summit. To reach the area, take the road from Canyon Village and head toward Tower Junction. After approximately 5 miles, you will see the Dunraven Pass parking area on the right. This parking lot is also the trailhead for a 3.6-mile hike to the summit of Mount Washburn. It is a moderately easy hike to the summit, with a 1,400 feet elevation gain.

Another approach is to continue past Dunraven Pass another four miles. You will see a road on the right and a sign proclaiming "Mt. Washburn." Don't get too excited. The road leads to the Chittenden parking area, and it is still a 3-mile hike to the summit. Use binoculars and take your time as you search for sheep. They often appear to blend into the rocks and can be difficult to locate.

Specimen Ridge is another location where bighorn can be photographed in spring and summer. The ridge lies 3 miles southeast of Tower Junction. To reach the Specimen Ridge Trailhead, travel east approximately 2.5 miles from Tower Junction, along the Northeast Entrance Road. The trailhead will be on your right.

For complete directions and additional information, see Chapter 3.

GLACIER NATIONAL PARK, MONTANA

Logan Pass is a name well-known to wildlife photographers. It's a great location for photographing bighorns and mountain goats. To reach Logan Pass, take the Going-To-The-Sun Road from either the east or the west entrance, and drive until you reach the pass. This road is closed during the winter.

To locate the sheep, scout the mountainside across the road from the visitor center with your binoculars. If no bighorns are in this area, hike the Highline Trail, also located across the road. Near the 3-mile point, you will come to Haystack Butte on the left. Sheep are often observed in this area. After passing Haystack Butte, the trail climbs rather steeply into an open area, where bighorns often congregate.

For complete directions and additional information, see Chapter 3.

NATIONAL BISON RANGE, MONTANA

Bighorn sheep can be photographed in the refuge along the Red Sleep

Mountain Scenic Drive in spring and summer. Refuge rules dictate that photography must be performed from the road. This usually presents no problem if you have a lens in the 500 mm to 600 mm range. If the sheep are not close to the road, simply wait until they move within range.

The sheep usually congregate between the Bitterroot Trail trailhead and the High Point turnoff. However, they may sometimes be found along the switchback northeast of the trailhead. Look carefully among the rocks, using your binoculars. They can be difficult to spot when they are bedded down.

For complete directions and additional information, see Chapter 3.

WATERTON LAKES NATIONAL PARK, ALBERTA

Red Rock Canyon usually has a number of semi-tame bighorns present. To reach the canyon, located at the end of Red Rock Parkway, go 3 kilometers (1.8 miles) northeast of Waterton Townsite, and turn left onto the parkway.

During much of the fall and winter, bighorns also hang out in downtown Waterton.

For complete directions and additional information, see Chapter 3.

The following locations are not "hot spots" but are worth investigating:

BABCOCK MOUNTAIN BIGHORN SHEEP VIEWING AREA, LOLO NATIONAL FOREST, MONTANA

Babcock Mountain features hillsides dressed in green, merging into steep, rocky cliffs fringed with stands of evergreens. The herd of bighorn sheep here can be photographed from your car or while hiking. Photography is best during spring and winter.

Hikers can choose between the Babcock Creek and the Spring Creek trails. The Babcock Creek Trail goes about a mile along the front of the sheep range, while the Spring Creek Trail proceeds into the heart of their range. During lambing — April through mid-May — both trails are closed to hiking. However, the ewes often bring their week-old youngsters onto the cliffs, introducing them to their human brothers and sisters below.

To reach the sheep viewing area from Missoula, go east along Interstate 90 a distance of 20 miles. Take the Rock Creek exit. Go south 4.5 miles, along Rock Creek Road. An interpretative sign provides information on the bighorns. For additional information, contact the U.S. Forest Service (406- 329-3814).

KOOKOOSINT SHEEP VIEWING AREA, LOLO NATIONAL FOREST, MONTANA

The KooKooSint Sheep Viewing Area, a quarter-acre meadow bordered by rock outcroppings, is not large. However, the photo opportunities are worth the drive. One of the benefits of the small viewing area is up-close photography, and bighorns are often spotted along the highway for several miles on either side of the viewing area.

Herds of 75 to 100 animals are occasionally observed. Interpretive signs share information concerning the bighorns. The best viewing months are from early March to late May, and from mid-November until the end of December.

From the town of Thompson Falls in northwestern Montana, go east along State Highway 200 for 8 miles to the viewing area. For additional information, contact the U.S. Forest Service (406-826-3821).

JASPER NATIONAL PARK, ALBERTA

The area around Tangle Hill along the Icefields Parkway, six kilometers (3.6 miles) north of the Columbia Icefields, is worth checking into, as is the area along the parkway near Mount Wilcox.

North of Jasper Townsite, investigate a couple of areas along Highway 16 East. The first is Cinquefoile Ridge, approximately 15 kilometers (9 miles) north of town. The other location is Syncline Ridge, just north of Rocky River, located 30 kilometers (18 miles) north of town.

For complete directions and additional information, see Chapter 3.

YOHO NATIONAL PARK, BRITISH COLUMBIA

Glacier-carved rock cliffs and the blue-green waters of Emerald Lake provide one of the most breathtaking backdrops for photographing bighorns in the Canadian Rockies.

To reach Emerald Lake, go west on the Trans Canada Highway from Lake Louise through the town of Field. One mile southwest of Field, a road leads off to the right. Take this side road for 5 miles to Emerald Lake. To locate the sheep — and the deer and moose that also live here — hike along the lake shore in the early morning or late in the day. The animals will allow you to approach, as long as you stay on the trail.

Another location where bighorns often congregate is near the intersection of Highway 1A and the Trans Canada Highway, near the park's east entrance.

For complete directions and additional information, see Chapter 3.

Mountain Goat

DESCRIPTION – White coat; beard; shoulder hump; short tail; 7- to 12-inch, black horns; 200 to 325 pounds.

SCIENTIFIC NAME – *Oreamnos americanus*

FAMILY – Sheep (Bovidae)

BREEDING SEASON – November and December

GESTATION PERIOD – 150 days

NUMBER OF YOUNG – 1 (occasionally 2)

Short summers, winter winds exceeding 100 miles per hour, blizzards lasting weeks, 50-foot snowdrifts, and temperatures dropping to 50, 60, and 70 degrees below zero — this is the world of the mountain goat.

Mountain goats inhabit some of the most inhospitable regions in North America. They are at home among precipitous mountain terrain and alpine meadows. Feeding on a variety of forage, including grasses, sedges, forbs, shrubs, and lichens, they have little competition from other species.

Breeding takes place between November and mid-December. Nannies usually breed during their second year, giving birth to a single kid; they give birth every other year thereafter. The young are born in late May or early June. Twins, though not common, occasionally come into the world.

Mature billies are loners, except during the rut, while immature males typically form small groups. During the summer, large nursery groups comprised of nannies, their kids, and immature billies, often form. These nursery groups number upwards of 15 or 20 goats.

Mountain goats, like sheep and bison, grow true horns. Both billies and nannies produce horns. In fact, both sexes are so similar that it is often difficult to distinguish a male from a female. One difference is the horns of the billy are wider at the base and more sharply curved backward than the gently curving horns of the nannie.

The mountain goat is not a true goat, but is more closely related to the antelope of Asia and eastern Europe.

PHOTOGRAPHIC TECHNIQUES

Mountain goats, unlike deer and sheep, are not intimidated when approached from above. In fact, many appear more comfortable when approached in this manner. By moving slowly and avoiding sudden movements, you will be accepted within a relatively short time. While conducting a workshop on Mount Evans, I had a nannie lie down beside me as I sat watching others take photos.

A telephoto lens in the 300 mm to 400 mm range usually will provide all the magnification you need.

TIME OF YEAR

It is usually best to avoid photographing adult goats from mid-June through July. During this time they are shedding their winter coats, and they do look shaggy! However, June and July are the best months for photographing young kids.

PHOTOGRAPHIC HOT SPOTS

MOUNT EVANS, ARAPAHO NATIONAL FOREST, COLORADO

Mount Evans, only a few hours from Denver, has a paved road to its 14,264-foot summit, providing some of the most spectacular vistas in Colorado, plus opportunities for photographing several wildlife species. It is my opinion that Mount Evans is the best location in North America for photographing mountain goats.

Begin looking for goats 2 miles after passing the Mount Goliath area. Search the mountain directly in front of you. From this distance, goats will appear as white specks. Occasionally, they'll be along the roadside.

Another location worthy of investigation is the area surrounding Summit Lake. While facing Summit Lake from the parking area, use your binoculars to examine the mountain directly across the lake and the hills on your right. If you do not see any goats, follow the trail along the right side of the lake. Once you get to the overlook, search the boulderfield to your right. Sit down on a rock and take your time. Even with binoculars, goats are often difficult to spot.

You are likely to see goats anywhere between Summit Lake and the summit of

Mount Evans. Goats frequently hang out at the summit. Another location worth investigating is the first switchback past Summit Lake, on your way to the top. Park at the switchback and hike the old roadway.

For complete directions and additional information, see Chapter 3.

GLACIER NATIONAL PARK, MONTANA

Three locations in Glacier are a definite must for photographers seeking goats: Hidden Lake Trail, Highline Trail, and the Walton Goat Lick.

Hidden Lake Trail, a 1.5-mile boardwalk, begins at the Logan Pass Visitor Center and ends at Hidden Lake Overlook. Goats often congregate near the overlook.

Highline Trail also begins at the Logan Pass Visitor Center. After hiking approximately 3 miles, you will come to Haystack Butte on your left. This is another location often frequented by goats.

The Walton Goat Lick is heavily used by goats between April and mid-July. Goats are typically at the lick early in the morning, and again in late afternoon. The mineral lick is located along U.S. 2, near the park's southern boundary. From the Walton entrance station, go south for 2 miles to the lick.

For complete directions and additional information, see Chapter 3.

JASPER NATIONAL PARK, ALBERTA

A "Goat Lookout" is located along the Icefields Parkway, approximately 40 kilometers (24 miles) south of Jasper Townsite, and 3 kilometers (1.8 miles) north of the Mount Christie picnic area. Look for the stylized goat sign on the east side of the highway. Park in the designated site at the top of the hill, go to the viewpoint, and scan the area.

Two "animal lick" overlooks should be scouted from time to time. One is along the west side of the Icefields Parkway, just north of Athabasca Falls, and the other is along Highway 16 East, approximately 35 kilometers (21 miles) north of Jasper Townsite. These mineral licks are popular with the goats during late spring and early summer.

For complete directions and additional information, see Chapter 3.

KOOTENAY NATIONAL PARK, BRITISH COLUMBIA

Mountain goats frequently congregate along the highway near Mount Wardle. The main attraction is a roadside mineral lick. The lick, located midway into the park on the east side of the highway, is about halfway between Vermilion Crossing and the Hector Gorge View Point.

For complete directions and additional information, see Chapter 3.

YOHO NATIONAL PARK, BRITISH COLUMBIA

Mountain goats are often observed along the Yoho Valley Road to Takakkaw Falls. However, due to snow conditions, this road is only open from mid-June to mid-October. The road is located off the Trans Canada Highway, 3 kilometers (1.8 miles) north of Field.

Goats also congregate near the intersection of Highway 1A and the Trans Canada Highway, near the park's east entrance.

For complete directions and additional information, see Chapter 3.

The following locations also offer excellent opportunities for mountain goat photography. However, hiking is required.

MALLARD-LARKINS PIONEER AREA, IDAHO PANHANDLE NATIONAL FOREST, IDAHO

The Mallard-Larkins Pioneer Area includes high mountain lakes, lush evergreen trees, and 30,000 acres of breathtaking scenery. Every July, a large herd of mountain goats congregates around the Black Mountain Lookout. The goats are extremely tame and provide wonderful photography subjects in a scenic setting.

The round-trip hike is approximately 16 miles. Start early, take your time, and enjoy a memorable day with our woolly brothers and sisters of the mountains.

From Pierce, located in north-central Idaho, go north 13 miles along State Highway 11 to the town of Headquarters. Bear left and follow Forest Road 247 to the North Fork Clearwater River bridge, a distance of approximately 21 miles. Turn left, and go 2 miles along Forest Road 700, then bear right and follow Forest Road 705 for 1.5 miles to the Isabella Creek Trail. The remainder is on foot. Hike along Trail 95 to its intersection with Trail 97, a distance of approximately 5 miles. Go south on Trail 97 about 3 miles to Black Mountain.

For additional information, contact the U.S. Forest Service (208-476-3775).

OUR LAKE, FLATHEAD NATIONAL FOREST, MONTANA

Our Lake, a scenic alpine lake with commanding views of the Bob Marshall Wilderness, provides breathtaking backdrops for your mountain goat images.

The goats are typically by the lake or hanging out on the nearby rocky cliffs. As sure as you can count on taxes, you can count on the goats awaiting your arrival at Our Lake.

July and August are the months to plan your trip. Any earlier or later, and you quite possibly may have to deal with harsh, winterlike weather conditions, including heavy snows.

From Choteau, 52 miles northwest of Great Falls, drive northwest 5 miles along U.S. 89. Turn left onto Road 144. Go 15 miles to the Ear Mountain Ranger Station sign. Turn left onto Road 109, the South Fork Teton Road, and continue 9 miles to its end. From the trailhead to Our Lake along Forest Service trail is a distance of 3.5 miles.

For additional information, contact the U.S. Forest Service (406-466-5341).

Bison

DESCRIPTION – Dark brown; calves reddish brown; dark, woolly hair on head, shoulders, and front legs; beard; shoulder hump; black horns; weight up to 2,200 pounds.

SCIENTIFIC NAME – *Bison bison*

FAMILY – Sheep (Bovidae)

BREEDING SEASON – Mid-July to September

GESTATION PERIOD – 9 1/2 months

NUMBER OF YOUNG – 1 (occasionally twins)

American Indians, cowboys, Buffalo Bill Cody, gun fight at the OK Corral — these are some of the images conjured up when one reminisces about the bison. Sometimes called buffalo, bison are normally considered part of the American West.

Bison once inhabited much of this continent, from New York to Georgia, westward to the Rocky Mountains and eastern Oregon and Washington, and northward from northern Mexico all the way to the Yukon. Today, they can be found in only a few isolated locations in a handful of western states, including the Canadian province of Alberta.

The bison is at home on the prairies, both short-grass and long-grass, as well as in open forests, where they appear to enjoy escaping severe weather, hot sun, and insects.

Two subspecies are recognized: the plains bison (Bison bison), and the wood bison (B. bison athabascae). The plains bison roamed the open plains, while the wood bison was more at home on montane meadows.

Breeding takes place between mid-July and September, peaking during the month of August. During May the following year, a single reddish brown calf usually is born. Before calving, the pregnant cow wanders off in search of a secluded location where she can give birth to her calf in private.

When it comes to eating, bison are not particular. They'll eat just about any vegetation, as long as there's plenty of it.

Bison normally assemble into groups of eight to twelve animals. These groups are made up of cows and their calves, along with several immature bulls. Often, several groups will come together to form a large herd. A good indication that the rut is in progress is the presence of mature bulls within the group.

PHOTOGRAPHIC TECHNIQUES

Safety is one of the main considerations when photographing bison. Most of the time they will ignore you. Just when you think there is no problem, WATCH OUT!

Use a lens in the 500 mm to 600 mm range. However, even this will not always give you a safe working distance. Stay close to your automobile, or stand next to a large tree. If your subject charges, you can duck behind the tree or jump into your vehicle. Just remember, bison may wheel about and charge very quickly.

The best way to meter for bison, assuming your subject is filling a major portion of your view finder, is to meter off a neutral object (18 percent gray card, grass, tree trunk, etc.) and open up one-half stop to compensate for their dark coloring. In fact, if you're shooting a tight head-shot, I would open up one full stop.

TIME OF YEAR

Late May and June are the best months to photograph young calves.

Adult animals shed their winter coat in the spring. Therefore, it is best to avoid photographing them at this time. I prefer fall and winter. A bison standing in deep snow, with its head and back covered with powder, is an awesome sight.

PHOTOGRAPHIC HOT SPOTS

YELLOWSTONE NATIONAL PARK, WYOMING

If you're looking for a choice location to photograph bison, Hayden Valley is Numero Uno. It provides the most opportunities to shoot bison with a great variety of backdrops.

For complete directions and additional information, see Chapter 3.

WIND CAVE NATIONAL PARK, SOUTH DAKOTA

Wind Cave National Park is more than an underground network of geological wonders. Its most significant features are the stunning ponderosa forests and vast prairie grasslands.

Bison can be photographed in the grassy valley along Beaver Creek Canyon. NPS Roads 5 and 6 through the park's grasslands also provide marvelous photo opportunities.

Beaver Creek Canyon, located north of the Visitor Center, can be reached from State Highway 87. Hike along Fire Road 8 into the valley shaded by high cliffs.

NPS Road 5 can be accessed from State Highway 87, near the park's northern boundary. Drive east, following NPS 5 into the park's eastern section, where it joins NPS Road 6.

While you're in the area, don't overlook Custer State Park, adjoining Wind Cave along its northern boundary. Custer's bison herd numbers more than 1,000 animals.

For additional information, contact Wind Cave National Park (605-745-4600).

NATIONAL BISON RANGE, MONTANA

The National Bison Range was established in 1908 to maintain a representative bison herd, thus preserving the species from extinction. This herd fluctuates between 300 and 500 animals. They are most numerous in the Alexander Basin, the rolling, grassy hills in the northeast section of the range. Newborn calves can be photographed from mid-April through May.

For complete directions and additional information, see Chapter 3.

BANFF NATIONAL PARK, ALBERTA

A fenced buffalo paddock north of the Banff Townsite, is home to several wood bison, a subspecies larger than the plains bison. To reach the area, go northeast along Banff Avenue. At the end of town, a sign instructs you to turn left. Cross the Trans Canada Highway, and follow the signs to the paddock.

For complete directions and additional information, see Chapter 3.

WATERTON LAKES NATIONAL PARK, ALBERTA

Waterton Lakes' "bison paddock" offers the opportunity to photograph bison against breathtaking backgrounds. The entrance to the drive-through paddock is located along Highway 6, 2 kilometers (1.2 miles) northwest of the park entrance station.

For complete directions and additional information, see Chapter 3.

Great Blue Heron

DESCRIPTION — 46 inches from head to tail; 72-inch wingspan; gray-blue; black stripe extending above eye; long yellowish bill.

SCIENTIFIC NAME — *Ardea herodias*

FAMILY — Herons (Ardeidae)

NESTING BEGINS — Mid-February through late April

INCUBATION — 28 days; 1 to 7 eggs (usually 3 to 5)

TIME TO FLEDGE — 56 to 60 days

The Great Blue Heron, with wings arching gracefully downward and feet trailing behind, flies like a modern-day pterodactyl. Many visitors to the Rocky Mountains, who identify these magnificent creatures with coastal marshes and swamps, are surprised when they first witness a heron flying overhead near the mountains.

Herons often are observed standing motionless along streams and in ponds, staring intently into the water as they scrutinize everything that moves for their next meal.

Great Blues traveling from their wintering grounds in the southern United States and Mexico begin arriving along the southern Rockies in February. Those nesting farther north may not reach their rookeries until sometime in April.

Herons return to the same nesting area year after year. Their conspicuous nests are located in the tops of tall cottonwood trees along lakes, reservoirs, and rivers. These nesting colonies are called heronries or, more commonly, rookeries. Many have been in use for decades and contain large numbers of nests.

Courtship begins on the selected nest within a few weeks of the birds' arrival at the rookery. Old nests are repaired and expanded, and new nests are occasionally built. Sticks several feet long and up to a half-inch in diameter are used in the nests.

Young herons often regurgitate food onto an unsuspecting trespasser below the nest. This is a defensive reaction to an uninvited intruder.

In fall, Great Blues depart for warmer climates, beginning in mid-September and continuing through October. A few birds remain all winter, especially in the southern regions covered by this book.

PHOTOGRAPHIC TECHNIQUES

Great Blue Herons have walked within 15 feet of me as I stood in the open, photographing them in saltwater marshes in their winter range. Yet, many of these same birds will flush when you come within a quarter-mile as they hunt for prey in their summer breeding range. In general, these are very wary birds. It is difficult to get close without a blind of some type.

Great Blues can be photographed along waterways as they hunt for food, or in the tops of tall trees in the rookery.

When hunting for prey, they will often return to the same location several days in a row. To find them, drive back roads along canals, streams, and ponds. Quite often you will locate your subject on private land. It is important to locate the owner and obtain his or her permission before entering the property.

Once you have obtained permission, set up your blind where you observed the heron feeding — taking lighting and background into consideration. Return to your blind before sunrise the next morning and wait. Herons leave the rookery early, just as daylight begins.

In the rookery, you can photograph nesting herons by standing in the open or while concealed in a blind on a high scaffold or in a nearby tree.

CAUTION: Extreme caution should be exercised while photographing Great Blue Herons in a rookery. Heron rookeries are very sensitive to human disturbance. Ravens and other predators frequently take advantage of these disturbances to prey upon unprotected eggs and nestlings.

If you will be photographing when eggs or young are in the nest, do so only from a blind, and plan to spend the day there, arriving before daylight and remaining until after dark.

If you intend to photograph the birds high in the treetops while you remain on the ground, you will need at least a 500 mm lens. I have obtained nice images using this technique.

If you intend to photograph Great Blue Herons on the nest, your work will begin during the winter before they arrive. It is likely that not all nests will be used, and some nesting pairs may not successfully raise their young to fledgling stage. Therefore, it is important to place your blind in a position from which you can photograph several nests. The blind can be placed atop well-secured scaffolding or in a nearby tree about the same height, or better yet, slightly above the height of the nests. Great Blue Herons build their nests 50 to 80 feet above the ground, so be extremely careful.

Remember, when you go into a rookery, you are a guest of the herons. Respect their rights.

TIME OF YEAR

Great Blue Herons can be photographed as they stalk prey along waterways, beginning in mid-February and continuing until fall migration. I find it somewhat easier after the young have fledged, simply because there are more birds at that time.

To photograph in the rookery without a blind, go in February before any eggs have been laid, or in June after the young have fledged. February is usually best. The trees are without leaves at this time of year, giving you an unobstructed view.

If you intend to photograph from an aerial blind, have it in position and ready for use by mid-February.

These suggested times could be pushed as much as two months later in the northern regions covered by this book.

PHOTOGRAPHIC HOT SPOTS

The following locations are certainly not the only places where Great Blue Herons may be photographed. There are heron rookeries throughout the Rockies. Grand Teton, Yellowstone, and Glacier National Parks all have nesting colonies. However, it is much easier to obtain a permit to set up a portable blind within a national wildlife refuge. Because of the sensitive nature of heron rookeries, I have not given specific directions. Inquire with refuge personnel for permission to photograph and for directions to the rookeries.

BOSQUE DEL APACHE NATIONAL WILDLIFE REFUGE, NEW MEXICO

Bosque hosts a non-breeding population of Great Blue Herons. They are commonly seen in the refuge during the spring, as they search for food along the water's edge. Photography can be accomplished from your vehicle as you drive along the auto-tour route, or from a portable blind.

CAUTION: The refuge is home to the western diamondback rattlesnake. Watch where you place your feet.

For complete directions and additional information, see Chapter 3.

ARAPAHO NATIONAL WILDLIFE REFUGE, COLORADO

A small colony of Great Blue Herons nests in cottonwood trees along the Illinois River. Contact the refuge headquarters, and inform the staff of your intentions. They can direct you to the rookery. Headquarters is located along State Highway 125, 7 miles south of Walden. Turn east at the refuge entrance onto a gravel road, and follow the signs.

For complete directions and additional information, see Chapter 3.

OURAY NATIONAL WILDLIFE REFUGE, UTAH

Ouray National Wildlife Refuge, encompassing almost 12,000 acres along the banks of the Green River, features miles of hiking trails and a 10-mile auto tour. The refuge's habitat diversity — desert shrub to cattail marshes, grasslands to cottonwood bottoms — contributes to a wide assortment of wild-life species.

Some 200 Great Blue Herons nest high in the tops of cottonwood trees along the Green River. Refuge personnel can give you information and directions to the rookery. The headquarters is in Vernal (see Appendix I for the address).

To reach the refuge from Vernal, drive southwest along U.S. 40 for 14 miles. Turn left onto State Highway 88, and follow this 15 miles to the refuge. For additional information, contact the U.S. Fish and Wildlife Service (801-789-0351).

SEEDSKADEE NATIONAL WILDLIFE REFUGE, WYOMING

Five Great Blue Heron colonies are located on private land near the refuge in the tops of tall cottonwoods along the Green River. Stop at refuge headquarters, introduce yourself, and inform the personnel of your intentions. They will tell you how to contact the landowners and give you directions to the rookeries. You will need a canoe or boat.

For complete directions and additional information, see Chapter 3.

CAMAS NATIONAL WILDLIFE REFUGE, IDAHO

Great Blue Herons are particularly abundant during summer. Look for nests in the tops of tall cottonwood trees. Off-road travel is prohibited between February 1 and July 15. Permission to erect a blind is granted on a case-by-case basis.

For complete directions and additional information, see Chapter 3.

Kelly Island, Missoula, Montana

Like the swallows returning to San Juan Capistrano every March, Great Blue Herons return to the rookery on Kelly Island. In addition to the photographic opportunities at the rookery, you can set up a blind along one of the many backwater sloughs and photograph herons as they stand motionless, waiting for their next meal to swim by.

In all likelihood, you will flush one of the herons upon your arrival at a slough. However, once a heron has picked its hunting ground, it will return to the same location time and again, so have patience.

For complete directions and additional information, see Chapter 3.

Sandhill Crane

DESCRIPTION – Gray with red crown; immature birds lack red patch

SCIENTIFIC NAME – *Grus canadensis*

FAMILY – Crane (Gruidae)

NESTING BEGINS – May

INCUBATION – 28 to 32 days; 1 to 3 eggs (usually 2)

TIME TO FLEDGE – 65 days

Nature's last great spectacle — the migration of the Sandhill Crane. Gone forever are the flocks of passenger pigeons darkening skies with their numbers as they flew overhead. The great herds of bison that once roamed the plains of the American west have disappeared. Only the crane migration remains among the truly gigantic movements of animals.

Sandhill Cranes are separated into six subspecies: lesser, greater, Canadian (intermediate), Mississippi, Florida, and Cuban. Only minor differences divide the six. And, since several subspecies share the same habitat, field identification is next to impossible.

Each spring, 80 percent of the world's population of Sandhill Cranes —500,000 birds — migrate through the Platte River Valley in western Nebraska. The "lesser" subspecies makes up about 80 percent of this flock, "greaters" five percent, and Canadians the remainder.

Approximately 20,000 sandhill cranes — all greaters — migrate through the Monte Vista National Wildlife Refuge in Colorado, en route to their nesting grounds at Grays Lake National Wildlife Refuge in southern Idaho. While I recommend putting Monte Vista on your agenda, the big show takes place in Nebraska.

The largest concentration occurs along the Platte River between Kearney and Grand Island. Cranes begin arriving around St. Valentine's Day. Peak migration occurs between mid-March and early April. During the second week in April, a mass exodus takes place.

As sunset approaches, cranes begin returning to their roosts on sandbars in the river's shallow waters. Fifteen-thousand cranes have been counted in a half-mile stretch of river. At dawn, the birds leave the river for nearby corn and alfalfa fields, where they spend the day feeding and dancing.

Nesting takes place in marshes, grasslands, and on the tundra. In the Rockies, nesting is closely associated with beaver ponds, where the birds nest along the water's edge, or even directly on top of a beaver or muskrat lodge.

Nesting occurs between mid-May and late June. The nest consists of sticks, reeds, and grasses, and is usually located on the ground. Between one and three (usually two) colts, or chicks, hatch between mid-June and late July. The young birds remain with their parents for 10 months.

Birds remain on their breeding grounds until mid-October, when, once again, they will begin their southward migration.

PHOTOGRAPHIC TECHNIQUES

After attempting to get within photographic range of Sandhill Cranes you'll understand how they have been around 10 million years — they're very wary!

To photograph cranes you'll need the biggest lens your pocketbook can afford. For portraits, a 600 mm or 800 mm lens is ideal. By working from a blind I have had success using my 200-400 mm f4, with a 1.4X converter.

In Nebraska, you have three choices: photograph from a blind, from your vehicle, or along the river at sunset. I recommend taking advantage of all three.

A blind is the only way you'll get close-up portraits. Photographers can reserve a blind through the Fort Kearney State Historical Park. (See Appendix I.) You must remain in the blind as long as cranes are nearby. This may be until 10 a.m., or, as once happened to me, until sunset.

Using your vehicle as a blind, cranes can be photographed in the fields where they feed or from the county roads paralleling the river. A sturdy window mount or bean bag is helpful for supporting those long lenses.

At sunset, set up your tripod on a bridge and photograph the birds returning to their roosts. Images showing cranes silhouetted against a colorful sunset are often taken in this manner.

Use your vehicle as a blind in Bosque del Apache and Monte Vista National Wildlife Refuges. This is a great way to photograph cranes from the refuge roads.

In Idaho or Montana, you might find the opportunity to photograph nesting sandhill cranes. PLEASE DON'T! Incubating cranes should never be disturbed. Wait until the colts are several days old before attempting any photography.

TIME OF YEAR

The time to be in Nebraska or Monte Vista is the last two weeks of March. People flock to these locations, so make your reservations several months in advance. Crane activity at Bosque del Apache is best from Thanksgiving through January. Time your visits to Grays Lake and Red Rock Lakes National Wildlife Refuges sometime between early May and late September.

PHOTOGRAPHIC HOT SPOTS

BOSQUE DEL APACHE NATIONAL WILDLIFE REFUGE, NEW MEXICO

In 1941, only 17 Sandhill Cranes wintered at the refuge. Today those numbers reach as high as 17,000. Cranes, being extremely wary birds, are best photographed from the confines of your car along the 15-mile auto-tour.

For complete directions and additional information, see Chapter 3.

MONTE VISTA NATIONAL WILDLIFE REFUGE, COLORADO

The Monte Vista National Wildlife Refuge, in Colorado's San Luis Valley, is made up of ponds and cattail marshes surrounded by fields of grain and alfalfa.

Large concentrations of Sandhill Cranes stop at Monte Vista during March and April on their way to Grays Lake National Wildlife Refuge in eastern Idaho. Each year, during the third weekend of March, the town of Monte Vista hosts its annual Crane Festival. The cranes can be photographed at the refuge and along county roads in the area.

Administration of the Monte Vista refuge is handled from the Alamosa National Wildlife Refuge, located 4 miles east of Alamosa on Highway 160. Turn right on El Rancho Lane, and go 2.5 miles south to headquarters.

From the town of Monte Vista, go south along State Highway 15 for six miles to the refuge. During March and April, the office there maintains a regular schedule. The rest of the year, the hours are irregular.

For additional information, contact the Alamosa National Wildlife Refuge (719-589-4021).

PLATTE RIVER VALLEY, NEBRASKA

The Platte River Valley is the hot spot for photographing Sandhill Cranes. Each spring 80 percent of the world's Sandhill Crane population —approximately 500,000 birds — congregates along the Platte River Valley before continuing its northward migration.

A few "early birds" (pun intended) begin arriving in February. However, the main migration does not begin until early March. Numbers peak by the second and third week in March. By mid-April, all is quiet again along the Platte.

The largest concentrations of cranes occurs between Lexington and Grand Island. Roosting along the river sandbars at night, the birds spend the day feeding, resting, preening, and dancing in the meadows and corn fields, typically within five miles of the river.

In your quest for crane images, the time of day dictates where you should be. The birds leave the protection of the river at sunrise, or a little before. Therefore, you should be in your blind in one of the grain fields or meadows by 5:30 a.m. Your other option is to drive the back roads and photograph from your car.

The cranes return to the river each evening, beginning a little before sunset, and continuing until after dark. If you have a river blind, you should be in it and ready for action by 5 p.m., and you should be prepared to spend the night. Your alternative, if you don't have a blind, is to station yourself at one of the overlooks along the river. Near Kearney, there are three such overlooks: the Gibbon Bridge, the bridge along State Highway 10, or the old railroad bridge along the Hike & Bike Trail at Fort Kearney State Park.

Remember, most land in this area is privately owned. Obtain permission from the landowner before erecting any photo blind. One source of semi-public blinds is through Gene Hunt, the superintendent of Fort Kearney State Park.

For complete directions and additional information, see Chapter 3.

Grays Lake National Wildlife Refuge, Idaho

Grays Lake, home to the world's largest breeding population of Greater Sandhill Cranes, has also been a reintroduction site for endangered Whooping Cranes. "Whooper" eggs were placed with surrogate sandhill parents for incubation.

Cranes begin arriving in April. "Dancing," along with other forms of courtship display, begin as soon as the birds arrive. By early October, as many as 3,000 cranes will gather before beginning their exodus to warmer climates in New Mexico, Arizona, and Mexico.

From the town of Soda Springs, follow State Highway 34 north and east for 33 miles to the refuge sign. Turn left at a sign for the refuge, and go 3 miles to refuge headquarters. For additional information, contact the U.S. Fish and Wildlife Service (208-574-2755).

Red Rock Lakes National Wildlife Refuge, Montana

Approximately 400 Sandhill Cranes summer in the Centennial Valley each year. Photo opportunities are best between mid-April and late August. Search the open fields, along creeks, and near wetlands. The area south of Upper Red Rock Lake is often productive, as are the fields west of Lower Red Rock Lake. Odell Flats, which can be viewed from an overlook along the road one mile west of Shambo Pond, almost always has cranes.

CAUTION: Hazardous bogs and sinkholes are found throughout the refuge. Caution is advised when traveling through wet areas.

For complete directions and additional information, see Chapter 3.

Hooded Merganser

DESCRIPTION – Male: black and white; rounded head crest
   Female: brownish

SCIENTIFIC NAME – *Lophodytes cucullatus*

FAMILY – Swans, Geese, Ducks (Anatidae)

NESTING BEGINS – Late June to late July

INCUBATION – 32 or 33 days; 7 to 13 eggs (usually 10 to 12)

TIME TO FLEDGE – 71 days

The cocky, little Hooded Merganser is found only in North America. Migrating northward from their wintering grounds, a few Hooded Mergansers choose western Montana as their destination, becoming summer breeding residents, while others continue into Canada before stopping. Canada-bound birds usually reach Alberta and British Columbia by early May.

By mid-July, the merganser hen will have selected her nest site, an abandoned tree cavity or nest box, where she will lay 10 to 12 white eggs. Nest preparations, incubation, and rearing the young are her chores. The male takes no part.

In about a month, several tiny, brownish fuzz balls will start dropping, one by one onto the ground, or, if they're lucky, into the water. In either case, the fall causes no harm. After a month and a half, the young ducklings will make their first flight.

Hooded Mergansers seem to prefer quiet, sheltered backwaters, streams, and woodland ponds. If the water is clear and the fish are plentiful, the "hoodie" more often than not will be there.

PHOTOGRAPHIC TECHNIQUES

The best way to obtain close-up images of Hooded Mergansers is to work from a blind, either at a nest location or by a small body of water. A small pond will allow you to be within photographic range most of the time.

If you want to photograph birds at a nest cavity, first select an area that has a resident "hoodie" population, such as a nature center, state park, or waterfowl management area. Talk with personnel at the facility. Inquire about the location of nest boxes or nest cavities. Chances are good that the same nest location will be used year after year.

Prepare your blind prior to the bird's arrival. Use natural materials collected locally for its construction. Make sure it will command a good view of the female entering and leaving the nest. You might want to set up two blinds, each at a different nest site, in case one of the sites is not used. Make certain you enter and exit the blind while the female is away from her nest.

If nest photography does not interest you, simply locate a small pond or marsh frequented by "hoodies." Network with personnel as described above, asking for their assistance in locating such a pond. Set up your blind, taking lighting and background into consideration. In this case, it is not necessary to erect the blind days in advance. Simply set it up the night before you plan to shoot. A good portable blind can be handy for this type of situation.

To photograph Hooded Mergansers, you'll want a lens in the 500 mm to 600 mm range.

TIME OF YEAR

In western Montana, nesting begins in late June and continues for about a month. These birds spend their winter farther south, arriving in Montana near the end of February. If you want to photograph them at a nest cavity, you will probably need to set up your blind in early February, so it will be ready when they arrive.

If you're not interested in nest-cavity photography, but simply want to photograph the birds in their habitat, this can be accomplished between late February and October. However, you'll see more birds if you plan your photography during spring (late February to early April) or fall migration (September to October).

July is the best month to photograph baby "hoodies" following their mother around.

PHOTOGRAPHIC HOT SPOTS

DENVER ZOO, DENVER, COLORADO

The Denver Zoo, home to more than 1,300 exotic animals, provides many photographic opportunities. In addition to these species, the zoo is also home to several "wild" mergansers. You can photograph them displaying, swimming, preening, and taking a "quick five" at the waterfowl pond, near the west end of the zoo.

The main zoo entrance and parking area are on 23rd Avenue, between York Street and Colorado Boulevard, east of downtown Denver. For more information, contact the Denver Zoo (303-331-4100).

MACLAY FLAT RECREATION AREA AND NATURE TRAIL, MONTANA

Maclay Flat, situated along the Bitterroot River, embraces a mixture of aspen, cottonwood, and ponderosa woodlands. The lushness of the area provides cover and protection to a numbers of bird species, including the Hooded Merganser. The "hoodies" are often cautious, but with a little effort you should be able to go away with some really nice images.

In Missoula, exit Interstate 90 at Orange Street. Drive south on Orange to Stephens, then continue south on Stephens to Brooks. At Brooks, turn right. After crossing the Bitterroot River, turn right and follow Blue Mountain Road to Maclay Flat.

OWEN SOWERWINE NATURAL AREA, KALISPELL, MONTANA

Owen Sowerwine Natural Area, an urban-wildlife setting at the confluence of the Stillwater and Flathead Rivers, is home to a breeding Hooded Merganser population.

From U.S. 93 (Main Street) in Kalispell, go east along 2nd Street East, turning south onto Woodland Avenue. Go to Leisure Lane (sign on your right) and turn left. Follow Leisure Lane across the narrow, wooden bridge. Turn left into the natural area. Park at the posted signs, and hike to the river on your left.

BANFF NATIONAL PARK, ALBERTA

Two Locations in the park are worth your attention: Vermilion Lakes and Waterfowl Lakes.

Vermilion Lakes is located just west of Banff Townsite. One of the better photo locations is along the Marsh Trail. A photo blind is available for photographers and birders on a first-come, first-serve basis. Go south on Banff Avenue, cross the bridge over the Bow River, and turn right onto Cave Avenue. Go to the end of the avenue and park in the lot. You can access the Marsh Trail from here.

Waterfowl Lakes is approximately 120 kilometers (72 miles)) northwest of Lake Louise along the Icefields Parkway. Late summer and fall are very good in this area.

For complete directions and additional information, see Chapter 3.

Northern Pintail

DESCRIPTION — Male: brown head; white underparts; thin white line extending onto head; long, slender tail.

Female: mottled brown.

SCIENTIFIC NAME — *Anas acuta*

FAMILY — Swans, Geese, Ducks (Anatidae)

NESTING BEGINS — Late April to mid-July

INCUBATION — 22 to 25 days; 6 to 12 eggs (usually 6 to 9)

TIME TO FLEDGE — 36 to 57 days

The Northern Pintail is fittingly described as sleek, elegant, graceful, and poised. Although the pintail is distributed throughout most of North America, higher population densities exist in the West.

Pintails have adapted to life on open prairies, where they are associated with lakes, ponds, and marshes. They are seldom found in densely wooded wetlands.

The Northern Pintail is a summer or year-round resident throughout most of the region. In Montana, for example, pintails are quite common between March and October. From November through February, despite decreasing population numbers, sightings are still not unusual.

Pintails are fast flyers, and with narrow, pointed wings they are extremely agile, as they gracefully dart from one prairie pothole to the next. With a distinctive, short whistle they call out to other members of their clan for a point of reference. In winter, they often feed in grain fields.

Breeding begins in late April and often continues into July. Peak breeding activity occurs during May. Early nesting and re-nesting following initial nest failure account for the extended breeding season.

The hen builds the nest by scraping a shallow depression in the earth and lining it with down. Six to nine cream-colored eggs are laid. Often, the nest is placed in an exposed location away from water. Although nest-building and incubation duties belong to the female, the male is often nearby. Within 23 days the newly hatched ducklings enter the world.

PHOTOGRAPHIC TECHNIQUES

Networking with park rangers, biologists, and birders is always important. Knowledgeable people can advise you on the whereabouts of pintails, as well as their nest locations.

You will need a blind. A good 500 mm or 600 mm telephoto lens goes without saying, as does a good sturdy tripod. Once you've decided on a location, arrive early enough to set up your blind and be situated inside before daylight. Or, you can set it up the night before and arrive the next morning while it is still dark.

If you're interested in photographing nesting waterfowl, it's best to erect your blind while the female is away from her nest. Position yourself several hundred feet from the nest, so you can see when she leaves. After she is gone, quickly erect your blind. This is when a good portable blind comes in handy. Enter and leave the blind while she is away.

TIME OF YEAR

Large numbers of pintails are encountered during the spring and fall migrations. However, since the fall migration is spread out over several months, higher concentrations are experienced during spring.

In spring, numbers peak between late March and early April. By early May, it is all over. The fall migration begins in September and continues into December.

A substantial population of summer residents can be photographed between March and October. Ducklings can be photographed between mid-May and mid-June.

PHOTOGRAPHIC HOT SPOTS

BOSQUE DEL APACHE NATIONAL WILDLIFE REFUGE, NEW MEXICO

During migration, up to 25,000 ducks pass through the refuge, including Northern Pintails. In fact, not all pintails depart; many spend the summer here, nesting and raising their young.

To photograph Northern Pintails, you can erect a temporary blind or shoot from your "four-wheel, motorized blind" along the 15-mile auto tour.

For complete directions and additional information, see Chapter 3.

MAXWELL NATIONAL WILDLIFE REFUGE, NEW MEXICO

Northern Pintails can be photographed during spring and fall migrations on any of the refuge lakes. Stop at refuge headquarters to get acquainted, and inform the staff of your intentions. If your plans include erecting a portable blind, permission is granted on a case-by-case basis.

For complete directions and additional information, see Chapter 3.

ARAPAHO NATIONAL WILDLIFE REFUGE, COLORADO

Beginning in early spring, Northern Pintails are a common sight in the refuge. Nesting takes place near most of the reservoirs.

Several reservoirs are located along the refuge's 6-mile auto tour. On occasion, I've photographed waterfowl from the window of my vehicle. However, a portable blind usually provides more opportunities.

The Self-Guided Auto Tour loop is located along State Highway 125, 3 miles south of Walden, on the west side of the highway.

For complete directions and additional information, see Chapter 3.

SEEDSKADEE NATIONAL WILDLIFE REFUGE, WYOMING

A variety of ducks, including the Northern Pintail, nest on the refuge each year. Although not abundant, pintails can be photographed in the lakes and ponds along the refuge's auto-tour route.

For complete directions and additional information, see Chapter 3.

CAMAS NATIONAL WILDLIFE REFUGE, IDAHO

Large numbers of pintails nest in the refuge. Beginning in spring and continuing into fall, you should have plenty of photo opportunities. In a couple of areas, refuge roads parallel canals.

For complete directions and additional information, see Chapter 3.

BENTON LAKE NATIONAL WILDLIFE REFUGE, MONTANA

Northern Pintails are present on the refuge in large numbers. They can be photographed occasionally while driving the 9-mile Prairie Marsh Wildlife Drive, or while walking along the Prairie Marsh Trail Boardwalk.

For complete directions and additional information, see Chapter 3.

RED ROCK LAKES NATIONAL WILDLIFE REFUGE, MONTANA

Upwards of 50,000 ducks and geese pass through the refuge during spring and fall migrations, including the Northern Pintail. Many remain throughout the summer.

Pintails are common throughout the refuge. Culver and Wigeon Ponds can be good when pintails are on the water. Upper Red Rock Lake always has large pintail concentrations. However, the smaller ponds and marshes are better suited to photography.

For complete directions and additional information, see Chapter 3.

Wood Duck

DESCRIPTION — Male: colorful, iridescent plumage; full crest.
Female: dark upper parts; teardrop-shaped eye patch; short crest.

SCIENTIFIC NAME — *Aix sponsa*

FAMILY — Swans, Geese, Ducks (Anatidae)

NESTING BEGINS — May to early July

INCUBATION — 28 to 37 days; 6 to 15 eggs (usually 10 to 15)

TIME TO FLEDGE — 56 to 70 days

If coloration and markings have anything to do with it, the male Wood Duck should have the largest ego in the duck family. The Wood Duck is a summer resident in many of the northern areas covered by this book.

The Wood Duck's scientific name — Aix sponsa — is revealing. Aristotle used the word Aix to describe a waterfowl, and sponsa is Latin for the word "bride." Ornithologist E. Coues, in 1882, wrote that this name is "prettily applied to this lovely duck, as if the bird were arranged for a bridal." With bold markings and iridescent colors, the little "woodie" is the most beautiful and highly colored duck in North America.

In flight, female Wood Ducks vocalize with a squealing whistle, a loud, ascending o-eek. Male woodies produce a similar whistling call.

Wood Ducks prefer woodlands supporting fairly large trees with suitable nest cavities, near lakes, marshes, or streams. Trees producing nuts, such as acorns, are like icing on the woodies' cake. Wood ducks consume vegetation, such as berries, seeds, acorns, and grains, as well as aquatic invertebrates, including crayfish, shrimp, and snails.

Courtship begins in September, although mating does not actually take place until the following spring, usually during June. Like most species of ducks and geese, woodie pairs form tight bonds. Each year, during a series of prolonged and elaborate courtship displays, including the bill-jerk and wing-and-tail-flash, these bonds are renewed.

Just as her offspring return to the area where they were raised, the female typically returns to the same breeding area each year in search of nesting sites. She selects a suitable location, usually a natural cavity of a hollow tree or an abandoned woodpecker nest, where she will lay her eggs. Although some nest entrances may be 60 feet or higher, most are less than 30 feet above the ground. The tree may be a mile away from the nearest water.

Once egg-laying day arrives, both male and female arrive at the nest site early in the morning. The female enters the nest cavity alone and lays her first egg, while the male woodie waits nearby. Returning each day thereafter to lay an egg, she continues until a dozen or so creamy white, glossy eggs have been laid.

After about a month, the eggs hatch. The female does not feed the newly hatched ducklings. The day following hatching, they leave the nest on their own. The mother gives her kuk kuk kuk call, and almost at once the ducklings begin climbing up the side of the nest cavity, which may be several feet deep. Since their feet are equipped with claws, this presents no problem. As soon as they reach the nest opening, one by one, they jump. With their wings outstretched, they hit the ground, bounce a few times, and head for their mother, who leads them to the nearest water, where they feed for the first time.

PHOTOGRAPHIC TECHNIQUES

Both the Wood Duck and the Hooded Merganser share similar nest sites and habitat, so the techniques used for obtaining images of the "hoodie" also apply to the "woodie." Photograph them from a blind.

To get images of birds coming and going from a nest cavity, select an area with a known Wood Duck population. The easy way to locate a nest site is by talking with people who frequent the area where you plan to shoot.

Set up your blind ahead of the birds' spring arrival. Use natural material collected in the area to construct your blind. As with setting up a "hoodie" blind, you might want to erect a blind at two different nest locations, in case one of them is not used. By setting up the blind in advance, you will avoid disturbing the birds once nesting has begun. Make sure you enter and exit the blind while the female is away from the nest.

If photographing "woodies" at the nest cavity is not your thing, locate a small pond or marsh frequented by Wood Ducks. Set up your blind, taking into consideration suitable background and lighting. Set it up either the night before or the morning you plan on using it. In either case, make sure you're in it before daylight.

For this type of photography, you'll need a lens in the 500 mm to 600 mm range.

TIME OF YEAR

Male Wood Ducks are best photographed between late September and May. During the summer, they wear "eclipse plumage," which is not as colorful as their highly iridescent breeding plumage.

Plan to photograph nest activity between May and early July. Young ducklings can be photographed during June and July.

Spring migration usually occurs during the month of April, while fall migration typically begins during mid-September and continues into mid-November.

PHOTOGRAPHIC HOT SPOTS

CHAIN OF LAKES, COEUR D'ALENE RIVER, IDAHO

This beautiful stretch of country along the Coeur d'Alene River, dotted with numerous shallow lakes and marshes, is home to many species of waterfowl, and it's a major Wood Duck breeding area. Verdant evergreen forests, coupled with dense undergrowth, enshroud the adjacent mountain slopes.

In your quest for Wood Ducks, investigate the many side roads. In addition, I would consider using either a shallow-draft boat or canoe as you search for nest cavities among the numerous lakes.

Talk with personnel at the Idaho Department of Fish and Game headquarters, at Thompson Lake. They can supply you with a map of the area and may provide information that will shorten your search.

From the town of Coeur d'Alene, go east 12 miles, following Interstate 90. Turn south along State Highway 3, and go to Rose Lake. State Highway 3 bisects the Chain of Lakes district, which ends at Thompson Lake. For additional information, contact the Idaho Department of Fish and Game (208-765-3111).

HEYBURN STATE PARK, IDAHO

Heyburn State Park, along the shore of Lake Chatcolet, is comprised of shallow lakes, extensive marshes, and verdant forests. Six trails meander among 400-year-old ponderosas.

Extensive marshes and shallow lakes provide suitable habitat for a variety of waterfowl species, including Wood Ducks. The park has placed a number of nest boxes at these locations. The increased Wood Duck population resulting from the nest boxes should provide you with many photo opportunities.

Close to 8,000 acres of forest, along with considerable amounts of dense undergrowth near marshes and shallow lakes, provide large areas of habitat suitable for wood ducks. Work the areas of dense cover near the lakes and marshes.

From Coeur d'Alene, drive south 35 miles along U.S. 95 to Plummer. Go east 5 miles on State Highway 5 to the park entrance. For additional information contact Heyburn State Park (208-686-1308). During winter, the park headquarters is closed on weekends.

KOOTENAI NATIONAL WILDLIFE REFUGE, IDAHO

Wood Duck nesting in the refuge has been facilitated by the addition of a number of nest boxes, supplementing the natural cavities used by the "woodies." One such nest box is located along the Island Pond Wildlife Trail. Other nest boxes and natural cavities can be found at tree-lined ponds around the refuge.

For complete directions and additional information, see Chapter 3.

KELLY ISLAND, MISSOULA, MONTANA

A number of nest boxes have been placed on trees along the backwater sloughs. These locations will provide many wonderful photo opportunities. A number of well-worn wildlife trails crisscrossing the island will assist you in your search for these nest sites.

For complete directions and additional information, see Chapter 3.

TWO MOON COUNTY PARK, MONTANA

Two Moon County Park, an urban park in the northeast section of Billings, consists of cottonwood river bottoms, dense underbrush, and cattail-lined sloughs along the Yellowstone River.

Wood Ducks can be photographed in their nesting areas among the cottonwoods situated along the backwater sloughs. Stop by the caretaker's house, and inform them of your intentions.

In Billings, go north on Main Street and east onto Bench Boulevard. Follow Bench approximately 5 miles, turning right onto a gravel road. Go to the parking area at the bottom of the hill.

For additional information, contact Yellowstone County (406-256-2703).

INGLEWOOD BIRD SANCTUARY, ALBERTA

This is an urban wildlife sanctuary only a few kilometers from the heart of downtown Calgary. A number of ponds and backwaters provide secluded nesting sites for many species of waterfowl. Without question, this is the best location in Alberta for observing and photographing Wood Ducks.

From Blackfoot Trail, go southeast on 9th Avenue SE to Sanctuary Road. Turn right, and go to the parking area. For additional information, contact Calgary Parks and Recreation (403-269-6688) or the Alberta Fish and Wildlife Division in Calgary (403-297-6423).

Trumpeter Swan

DESCRIPTION – White; black bill

SCIENTIFIC NAME – *Cygnus buccinator*

FAMILY – Swans, Geese, Ducks (Anatidae)

NESTING BEGINS – Late May

INCUBATION – 33 to 37 days; 2 to 9 eggs (usually 4 to 6)

TIME TO FLEDGE – 1 to 119 days

The stately Trumpeter Swan, dressed in snowy white feathers and a coal-black bill, was once common in much of the West. The breeding range covered an area from the Bering Sea eastward through most of Canada and south into Illinois, Indiana, and Missouri.

By the early 1900s, however, the trumpeter had been hunted nearly to extinction. Research in 1932 revealed that the Centennial Valley in southwestern Montana hosted the only population of trumpeters known in the world — 68 swans remained. Immediate steps were taken to preserve this location, and in 1935 Red Rock Lakes National Wildlife Refuge was established. Today, through much hard work, the Trumpeter Swan's numbers in this area have stabilized to somewhere between 250 and 300 birds.

Some 20 years later, a large, previously unknown population of trumpeters was discovered in Alaska and western Canada. Today, estimates place their numbers close to 15,000, of which approximately 14,500 reside in Alaska and Canada.

The Trumpeter Swan, with its 8-foot wingspan and weight of close to 30 pounds, is the largest swan in the world and the largest waterfowl in North America.

Trumpeters are at home in marshes, ponds, and lakes in prairies and open wooded areas. In the Arctic, nesting takes place among the many marshes on the tundra. While in the Rockies, trumpeters most often construct their nest near a moderately sized, secluded lake, often over 30 acres in size. Open water is required by these heavy birds for takeoffs and landings.

Trumpeter Swans require at least a 15-acre breeding territory, which they defend religiously against all large birds. It is not uncommon for a pair to demand ownership of several hundred acres.

Nests are built during the month of May, usually close to shore or on a small island. In the Rockies, a muskrat or beaver lodge is often selected as the choice location.

Both the "cob" (male) and the "pen" (female) are actively involved in nest building. The cob gathers the nest materials, including bulrushes, horsetail, cat-tails, and sedges, and brings them to the pen for proper positioning. Nest building continues through the incubation period. The final nest may be anywhere from 6 to 12 feet in diameter, and a foot and a half in height. The same nest is often used for many breeding seasons.

After completion of the nest, the pen lays anywhere from two to nine eggs; a single egg is laid every other day until the clutch is complete. During incubation, the cob stands guard nearby, ready to defend against all intruders; he may occasionally sit on the eggs while the pen is away feeding.

After an incubation period of approximately 100 days, the young cygnets hatch. This usually occurs by early July. Family bonds are tight. Not only are the adult pairs usually bonded for life, they band together to protect their newly hatched, downy cygnets.

In the Rockies, family groups usually remain near their breeding areas until freezing occurs, at which time they seek ice-free lakes and rivers.

Sago pondweed and duck potato tubers are significant foods for the Trumpeter Swan. However, the leaves, roots, and seeds of other aquatic vegetation, along with insects and crustaceans, also find their way into trumpeter diets.

The call of the Trumpeter Swan is sonorous and vibrant, employing a series of loud, low-pitched trumpeting honks. Witnessing a flock of trumpeters flying overhead, calling to one another, is an experience long remembered.

PHOTOGRAPHIC TECHNIQUES

Trumpeter Swans in Yellowstone, acclimated to the presence of people, can be photographed easily with a 400 mm or 500 mm telephoto lens. On occasion, they've come close enough for me to use my 80-200 mm, f2.8, autofocus lens.

TIME OF YEAR

I prefer July to early August. During these months the cygnets are still small. By September, the young swans are no longer little, although they still make good photo subjects.

PHOTOGRAPHIC HOT SPOTS

YELLOWSTONE NATIONAL PARK, WYOMING

As far as I'm concerned, Yellowstone is the only location that can really be described as a "hot spot" for photographing Trumpeter Swans. And in Yellowstone I only consider one area: Seven Mile Bridge, located on the Madison River, 7 miles east of the town of West Yellowstone, Montana.

For complete directions and additional information, see Chapter 3.

RED ROCK LAKES NATIONAL WILDLIFE REFUGE, MONTANA

This refuge has the largest breeding population of Trumpeter Swans south of the Canadian border, with close to 500 swans. Shambo Pond, situated along Red Rock Pass Road, typically has a pair of nesting trumpeters. Although the area surrounding the pond is closed, nice images can often be produced from the road.

Another location often providing photo opportunities is the western end of Lower Red Rock Lake, along the northern shore, a half-mile east of the dam. Culver Pond is also occasionally productive.

For complete directions and additional information, see Chapter 3.

Canada Goose

DESCRIPTION — Black neck and head; white chin strap; gray body.

SCIENTIFIC NAME — *Branta canadensis*

FAMILY — Swans, Geese, Ducks (Anatidae)

NESTING BEGINS — Mid-March to mid-July

INCUBATION — 25 to 30 days; 4 to 10 eggs (usually 4 to 7)

TIME TO FLEDGE — 40 to 73 days

High-flying, V-shaped flocks of Canada Geese mark the seasons as they fly south in autumn and north in winter. Canada Geese are permanent, year-round residents of many parts of the Rockies, moving to open stretches of lakes and rivers once their breeding areas freeze over. As soon as the spring sun melts the ice from these locations, they return.

Naturalist Aldo Leopold, in his book *A Sand County Almanac*, writes, "In thus watching the daily routine of a spring goose convention, one notices the prevalence of singles — lone geese that do much flying about and much talking. One is apt to impute a disconsolate tone to their honkings, and to jump to the conclusion that they are broken-hearted widowers, or mothers hunting lost children.... After my students and I had counted for half a dozen years the number of geese comprising a flock, some unexpected light was cast on the meaning of lone geese. It was found by mathematical analysis that flocks of six or multiples of six were far more frequent than chance alone would dictate. In other words, goose flocks are families, and lone geese in spring are probably just what our fond imaginings had first suggested. They are bereaved survivors of the winter's shooting, searching in vain for their kin. Now I am free to grieve with and for the lone honkers."

Many geese, however, migrate with the changing seasons, renewing each spring and fall that inner urge imprinted millenniums ago. In Montana and Wyoming, for example, spring migration for non-resident birds peaks near the end of March, while the fall migration peaks during November.

Nesting times vary with location. In Colorado, nesting often begins during the month of March, while birds in Jasper National Park usually wait until the first week of May, and some even wait until mid-July.

"Honkers" build their nests in a variety of habitats, from forests to prairies, and even within major cities. They are always near water. Favored sites include hummocks surrounded by water, as well as atop beaver or muskrat lodges. Often nests are placed among grasses alongside small ponds or lakes.

Strong family ties unite the male and female for life. Both sexes are involved in selecting their nest site and rearing their offspring. Once a nest site has been selected, the female hollows out a shallow depression. While standing in the middle of this depression, she collects everything in her reach — dry grasses, twigs, mosses, aquatic plants, even evergreen needles and bark chips in some areas. She literally fabricates the nest around herself.

The female lays her first egg soon after the nest is finished, usually within an hour. She then lays one egg every day until she has completed her clutch of four to seven eggs. The male stands guard for the next 28 days, while the female handles the chore of incubation.

One interesting note: the male is normally responsible for leading the young goslings on their swimming forays. At the first sign of danger, he executes a diversion as the young dive. The young remain with their parents through the winter and into the following spring.

"Honkers" seek the security of lakes during the night, while feeding in fields and pastures during the day. Sentinels stand guard while the flock feeds. Sometime during mid-morning, most will return to the lake to take their midday nap, often in the shade of a tree. In the afternoon, when the hunger urge strikes again, the morning routine is repeated. As darkness begins settling, the geese return to the lake, where they spend the night on the security of its waters.

Canada Geese molt during mid-summer. Having lost their flight feathers, they are unable to fly until new feathers grow out, usually by mid-August.

As a young boy, I remember one cold, dreary winter morning along the Texas Gulf Coast. Wading in thigh-deep muck and ooze, wearing an old pair of hip boots, I looked up into gray, overcast skies and watched with awe as flight after flight after flight...of "honkers" passed by. The air was filled with their musical calls. In every direction, V-shaped flights of Canada Geese filled the skies. Never before, nor since, have I witnessed so many honkers at any one time. And ever since I've had a reverence for the Canada Goose.

PHOTOGRAPHIC TECHNIQUES

Techniques vary, depending on when and where you intend to photograph geese.

Most birds around city parks and lakes are semi-tame. Many are accustomed to receiving handouts from people. To get their attention, all you have to do is start rattling a snack-food bag. However, for their own well-being, do not feed them.

An 80-200 mm zoom lens usually will provide all the magnification you need for city geese. Then again, there may be times when you want something in the 400 mm range. Go prepared.

Many of our national wildlife refuges have roads adjacent to canals, ponds, and lakes. Your car makes a fantastic blind. I've photographed many species from the window of my vehicle, using a window mount for my telephoto lens. I set up everything in advance, ready for action as I drive the refuge roads. Although you can get by with less, a lens in the 600 mm range is best suited for shooting geese from your car window.

A blind becomes necessary for photographing truly wild Canada Geese. As mentioned before, your car can be used as a blind under some circumstances, but not all. A blind made from local grasses and reeds is usually best if you plan to leave it up for any length of time, such as when photographing nesting geese. Otherwise, a portable blind is easier to erect and take down.

Canada Geese often use the same nest for years. This makes it easy to plan for photography once you've located a suitable nest site. Erect your blind prior to any breeding activity. Once nesting begins, you'll be ready to occupy the blind. If you plan to enter and leave the blind during daylight, do so when both birds are away from the nest.

Canada Geese will inform you of their nest location if you understand their language. Listen for loud honking. This could be the male and female greeting each other, or it could be a territorial dispute between the male and an intruder. A lone, aggressive male should also alert you. The nest will not be far away. In the southern regions covered by this book, mid-March is the time to begin looking for these telltale signs, while June is best throughout the more northern regions.

The best times of day to photograph geese in flight are sunrise and sunset. Find a lake where they "roost." Geese remain on the water at night, rather than roost in trees. When taking off, waterfowl head into the wind. Likewise, they land into the wind. Knowing this, place yourself along the anticipated flight path. By panning — following the birds with your camera aimed at them — you should be able to use a shutter speed of 1/250 second.

If you're shooting on a morning with an exceptionally colorful sky, you might want to consider shooting silhouettes of the geese. Anticipate the position of the birds at the moment of shutter release and take a meter reading from the sky in that area. This will give you a silhouette of geese in flight, with a colorful background. The larger the birds appear in your viewfinder, the more difficult it will be to follow them in flight. Start with something in the 200 mm range, and work up as you gain more experience.

TIME OF YEAR

Molting birds are unable to fly and often avoid people, making photography more difficult. The molt is typically completed by mid-August. In certain areas — Rocky Mountain Arsenal in Denver, for example — I've found semi-tame geese acting no different during this time of the year.

Nesting geese can be photographed beginning in mid-March in the Southern Rockies, and through mid-July in Jasper National Park.

Goslings can be photographed between mid-April and August, depending upon their location in the Rockies.

PHOTOGRAPHIC HOT SPOTS

DENVER ZOO, DENVER, COLORADO

The Denver Zoo, home to over 1,300 exotic animals, provides many photographic opportunities. In addition to these species, the zoo is home to many free-roaming "wild" Canada Geese. You can photograph them being chased by young children, and you can photograph them as they chase young children. Or, you can photograph them incubating their eggs among colorful red and yellow tulips. In mid-spring, adult geese can be photographed leading their young goslings among zoo visitors and across ponds.

The main zoo entrance and parking area are located on 23rd Avenue, between York Street and Colorado Boulevard, east of downtown Denver.

For more information, call the Denver Zoo (303-331-4100).

ROCKY MOUNTAIN ARSENAL, DENVER, COLORADO

The Rocky Mountain Arsenal once was prairie grasslands, home to Native Americans and wildlife. In 1942, the U.S. Army acquired the land and began producing chemical and incendiary weapons. After weapons production ceased, the facility was leased to private corporations for the production of agricultural pesticides. This continued until 1982. Chemical wastes produced during these years resulted in high contamination levels. Cleanup is in progress.

In October 1992, the U.S. Congress set aside the area as a national wildlife refuge, with official designation pending cleanup. Until then, it is called the Rocky Mountain Arsenal National Wildlife Area.

The Canada Goose is a common sight around Lake Mary, next to the visitor center. The geese, having adapted to the presence of people, are quite approachable and make easy photographic subjects.

Until the cleanup is complete, permission to enter the arsenal must be procured in advance by phone (303-289-0232). Due to cutbacks in government funding, permission is granted on a case-by-case basis, as personnel are available.

From Interstate 70, go north on Havana Street to the South Entrance of the arsenal.

CHAMBER OF COMMERCE INFORMATION CENTER, JACKSON, WYOMING

Jackson, Wyoming, gateway to the Tetons, is immediately south of Grand Teton National Park. Canada Geese can be photographed in the marshy pond behind the Chamber of Commerce Information Center. The pond is actually part of the marshlands of the National Elk Refuge. Being used to people, the geese are relatively tame and easy to photograph. Late afternoon provides the most favorable lighting conditions.

The Information Center is north of town at 532 North Cache. (307-733-3316).

BENTON LAKE NATIONAL WILDLIFE REFUGE, MONTANA

Canada Geese can be photographed from the Prairie Marsh Trail Boardwalk, or from your car while driving the 9-mile Prairie Marsh Wildlife Drive.

For directions and additional information, see Chapter 3.

JASPER NATIONAL PARK, ALBERTA

Canada Geese inhabit several locations within the park. The following sites should provide plenty of action.

The Miette River and its sloughs make up the first noteworthy location. Immediately south of town, Highway 16 crosses the Icefields Parkway. Take Highway 16 West along the river. I suggest scouting the river and its sloughs along the valley all the way to the park boundary.

Talbot Lake is also worthy of your consideration. Located 26 kilometers (16 miles) north of town, the lake is along the east side of Highway 16 East.

For directions and additional information, see Chapter 3.

The following locations are not "hot spots" but are worth investigating:

BOSQUE DEL APACHE NATIONAL WILDLIFE REFUGE, NEW MEXICO

Canada Geese are a common year-round sight in the refuge. They can be photographed from a portable photo blind or from your car along the 15-mile auto tour.

For directions and additional information, see Chapter 3.

MAXWELL NATIONAL WILDLIFE REFUGE, NEW MEXICO

Maxwell National Wildlife Refuge, established in 1966 among the open prairies and farmland of northeastern New Mexico, attracts more than 20,000 migrating ducks and geese each year. Upwards of 10,000 Canada Geese come through the refuge during spring and fall migrations. Many geese also winter on the refuge, making this the best time of year to plan your photo safari.

For directions and additional information, see Chapter 3.

CAMAS NATIONAL WILDLIFE REFUGE, IDAHO

Large numbers of Canada Geese nest in the refuge, providing wonderful opportunities for photographing adults and their goslings. Check out the lakes and ponds. In a couple of areas, refuge roads parallel canals, allowing you to photograph waterfowl from your car window. Off-road travel is prohibited between February 1 and July 15.

For directions and additional information, see Chapter 3.

KOOTENAI NATIONAL WILDLIFE REFUGE, IDAHO

With over 800 acres of wetlands and nearby stands of tall, dense grass providing suitable nesting cover, many families of Canada Geese consider the refuge their home. From Bonners Ferry, a sign along U.S. 95 directs visitors to turn west and follow Riverside Road for 5 miles to the refuge.

For complete directions and additional information, see Chapter 3.

KELLY ISLAND, MISSOULA, MONTANA

Over 600 acres of tranquil meadows bordered by stands of cottonwoods, backwater sloughs, and ponderosa woodlands provide ideal habitat for a variety of birds and mammals, including the Canada Goose.

Canada Geese will be found nesting among the tall grasses near some of the backwater sloughs, or atop one of the several nesting platforms erected on the island. However, a pair may occasionally commandeer a heron nest high in the top of a cottonwood.

For directions and additional information, see Chapter 3.

American Avocet

DESCRIPTION – Black and white above; white below; long, slender, upturned bill.

Breeding Plumage: head and neck rusty.

Winter Plumage: head and neck gray

SCIENTIFIC NAME – *Recurvirostra americana*

FAMILY – Stilts, Avocets (Recurvirostridae)

NESTING BEGINS – Mid-April to July

INCUBATION – 22 to 29 days; 3 to 5 eggs (usually 4)

TIME TO FLEDGE – 28-35 days

Adorned in spring breeding plumage, American Avocets are among the most strikingly beautiful of all shore birds. The American Avocet ranges from alkaline marshes in the dry, parched plains of the United States northward into Alberta's park lands. They are common along stretches of exposed shoreline containing meager amounts of vegetation. Mud flats, lake shores, and shallow, alkaline bodies of water often provide suitable habitat.

Nesting can begin as early as mid-April in New Mexico. From Colorado northward to Montana, most nesting activity occurs during May and June. In Canada, nesting takes place between mid-June and July. Avocets are rarely seen after the end of August.

Both male and female prepare the nest and tend the young after they have hatched. Nests are often placed on bare ground, near the water's edge. However, they also may be placed among stubby, sparse vegetation. The nest consists of nothing more than a shallow depression, sparsely lined — if at all — with small amounts of vegetation. Nesting in ill-defined colonies, several breeding pairs will be in the general area.

The clutch usually consists of four olive-buff eggs, marked with brownish-black splotches that are often impossible to see. Incubation is shared by the female and the male. The male takes on the majority of incubation duties during the first week, while the female is the primary incubator during the following weeks.

American Avocets vigorously defend their nesting territories from all intruders. Usually the first indication of their presence is a repeated series of sharp, raspy calls — kleek ... kleek ... kleek — as they "mob" the unwelcome intruder.

Avocets have a unique way of locating submerged food. By sweeping their bill back and forth under water, they locate their food by feel. Their primary diet of crustaceans and insects is often supplemented with seeds and aquatic vegetation.

PHOTOGRAPHIC TECHNIQUES

Individual members of any wildlife species have personalities as varied as the personalities of humans. American Avocets are no exception. I often use a blind when photographing avocets, and even then some are very "spooky." In contrast, on some occasions when I have not used a blind, some individuals have continued feeding, undaunted by my presence. With one particular bird, I had to stop shooting until he moved farther away. He was too close for my 600 mm lens. When a blind is needed, a good portable blind is best.

TIME OF YEAR

Wintering in the southern United States and Mexico, American Avocets do not arrive in the Rocky Mountains until spring. By then, they are usually adorned in their handsome breeding plumage.

Avocets begin arriving in Colorado in mid-March and stay until the end of November. In Wyoming and Montana, they show up anytime from mid- to late April. It is typically the end of September before they leave. Birds show up in Alberta in early May. In Canada, it is rare to see a single bird after the end of August.

Nesting usually begins in mid-April in New Mexico. From Colorado northward into Montana, nesting does not begin until May. In Canada, nesting starts in late May and continues through July.

PHOTOGRAPHIC HOT SPOTS

MAXWELL NATIONAL WILDLIFE REFUGE, NEW MEXICO

This is a great location for photographing American Avocets. Look for them wading shallow waters in search of tasty morsels. Stop at refuge headquarters to get acquainted and to inform the staff of your intentions. If your plans include erecting a portable blind, permission to do so is granted on a case-by-case basis.

For directions and additional information, see Chapter 3.

ARAPAHO NATIONAL WILDLIFE REFUGE, COLORADO

Several reservoirs are located along the 6-mile Self-Guided Auto Tour. Wherever you find water, you will generally find avocets. If you intend to use a blind, you will need to obtain permission from refuge headquarters.

The Self-Guided Auto Tour is located 3 miles south of Walden along State Highway 125, on the west side of the highway. Headquarters is another 4 miles south. Turn east at the refuge entrance sign onto a gravel road, and follow the signs to headquarters.

For complete directions and additional information, see Chapter 3.

CAMAS NATIONAL WILDLIFE REFUGE, IDAHO

Avocets are common here all year, except during winter. They can be photographed along the mud flats and wading the shallow areas of lakes and ponds. Off-road travel is prohibited between February 1 and July 15. For directions and additional information, see Chapter 3.

BENTON LAKE NATIONAL WILDLIFE REFUGE, MONTANA

Almost 200 bird species find their way into the refuge, including the American Avocet. They are often observed incubating their eggs along the water's edge as you drive the 9-mile Prairie Marsh Wildlife Drive.

For directions and additional information, see Chapter 3.

RED ROCK LAKES NATIONAL WILDLIFE REFUGE, MONTANA

Avocets are frequent sights along mud flats. The shallow ponds near the dam at the western end of Lower Red Rock Lake should provide plenty of photo opportunities.

For directions and additional information, see Chapter 3.

Red-tailed Hawk

DESCRIPTION – Plumage variable, from brown to nearly all white to black; reddish brown tail.

SCIENTIFIC NAME – *Buteo jamaicensis*

FAMILY – Kites, Hawks, Eagles (Accipitridae)

NESTING BEGINS – Mid-February to early April

INCUBATION – 30 to 35 days; 1 to 5 eggs (usually 2 or 3)

TIME TO FLEDGE – 45 or 46 days

The call of the Red-tailed Hawk is an eerie, harsh, descending kee-e-e-er, which can be heard for some distance. These hawks are often seen perched on telephone poles or a lone cottonwood next to the highway, scrutinizing the ground for rodents. It is said that a redtail can spot a mouse up to half a mile away. Rodents make up 85 percent of the redtail diet. Next in importance are rabbits, followed by a variety of other vertebrates.

Two notable subspecies exist: the nearly all-white Krider's of the Great Plains, and the dark Harlan's, found in Alaska and Canada.

From Alaska across central Canada, southward into Mexico and Central America, the Red-tailed Hawk holds the unchallenged title as the most common and widely distributed buteo in North America. Buteos, the broad-winged, soaring hawks, occupy a variety of ecosystems, from plains to open woodlands. Regardless where they live, they always choose a nest site with a commanding panorama: a tall cottonwood, a rock ledge along a cliff face, or even a large saguaro cactus in the desert.

Redtails are early nesters, beginning in mid-February in the southern regions. In the northern regions, they are often required to deal with a spring snowfall, as nesting activities begin in early April. Both male and female share in refurbishing an old nest or building a new one.

Redtails return year after year to their nesting territory, and old nests are reused many times. In fact, if one mate dies, another hawk will acquire the surviving mate and the territory. Only death will separate a pair. Actual size of the territory can range from half a square mile up to several square miles. The size is determined by prey density and number of suitable observation perches.

Redtails are easily stressed during nest-building and incubation. If pressed too closely by humans, they will desert their nest and eggs.

Redtail nests are bulky structures of twigs, lined with bark and smaller stems. Greenery is added throughout the nesting period.

The bluish white eggs, marked with brown spots, are incubated by both the male and the female. However, most of these duties fall on the shoulders of the female. The male regularly brings her food. In about a month, two or three white, downy fluff-balls appear, and the real work for both parents begins.

PHOTOGRAPHIC TECHNIQUES

You have two primary choices for producing images of the redtail: photographing captive birds or working from a blind. Occasionally, you may be able to photograph a redtail sitting in a tree or on a fence post from your car, using a window mount. Most of the time, however, as soon as you stop your car the bird will fly away, leaving you with nothing but an empty viewfinder.

CAPTIVE REDTAILS

Captive birds are often found at bird rehabilitation facilities. Also, many falconers fly Red-tailed Hawks. Rehabilitation facilities and falconers are required to have a federal permit issued by the U.S. Fish & Wildlife Service, and most states require a permit too. Contact your state for a listing of falconers and rehabilitation facilities. (See Appendix I.)

To photograph captive redtails, you can use anything from a 20 mm wide-angle to a 500 mm or 600 mm telephoto.

WILD REDTAILS

Wild redtails, either individuals or nesting birds, are best photographed from a blind. You'll need a lens in the 600 mm range. Remember, redtails have phenomenal vision. They can spot reflections in your lens from quite a distance. Sometimes a long lens hood will help, as will having the sun at your back. You might try keeping the lens pointed toward the ground or covering it until you're ready to take pictures.

When working with individual birds, you can either call them to you or photograph them on their favorite perch. Redtails will respond to a variety of calls, including injured rabbit, owl, or even another redtail. An electronic caller is easier to use. Simply slip in the desired tape and begin calling. The mistake most people make when calling wildlife is using too much volume. Most birds and mammals can hear at least five times better than humans.

To call a Red-tailed Hawk, locate your blind near a suitable tree. If none is available, locate a fallen dead tree (one that you can carry), with a suitable limb for a perch. Dig a hole and place the tree upright in the hole. If you have a remote speaker for your caller, place the speaker in a concealed position directly under the limb. Play the call for one to three minutes. Wait five minutes, then repeat. Continue until a redtail responds.

CAUTION: Do not call birds during nesting season. This forces the birds to spend unnecessary time away from their nest, placing their eggs or young chicks at risk.

Your other option for photographing an individual bird is locating a favorite perch. Since each pair of redtails has its own, somewhat limited territory, this makes it easier to locate one of these perches. Observe a redtail for a few days, noting where it flies and where it perches. After a week or so, you'll have a good idea where its favorite perches are located and when they are used. The next step is to erect a blind near one of these perches. Make the blind as unobtrusive as possible, locating it among shrubs or against a tree.

One other idea. When photographing individual birds, you might try baiting them with a road-killed bird or rabbit.

NESTING REDTAILS

Photographing nesting Red-tailed Hawks is a major undertaking. In most instances their nest will be located high in tree, with few trees nearby. You'll need to locate your blind slightly higher than their nest. If a suitable tree in which you can erect a blind is nearby, you're in luck. Otherwise, you'll need to erect tower scaffolding to the right height, and locate your blind at the top.

Locating a redtail nest is a fairly easy matter. It will always be in a prominent location, with a commanding view. Locate the nest during the breeding season, a year in advance. This will assure you have selected an active nest; with luck, they'll use the same nest the following year.

During late winter, before the breeding season begins, erect your blind. When it's time to begin photographing activities on the nest, you'll be ready.

CAUTION: Stay away from the area during nest construction and incubation. Do not attempt any photography until the eggs have hatched. Even the slightest interruption prior to this time may cause the pair to abandon their nest and eggs.

Changes in behavior will tell you when the eggs have hatched. For information on redtail behavior, I strongly recommend the Stokes Nature Guide book *A Guide To Bird Behavior, Volume 3*, by Donald and Lillian Stokes.

Arrive and depart from the blind in darkness. Avoid all unnecessary movement, and remain quiet. Like I said, photographing redtails on the nest is a major undertaking. However, by carefully following these directions, you'll come away with wonderful images and memorable experiences, and, more importantly, you will not have disturbed a redtail family.

TIME OF YEAR

Redtails are year-round residents in many areas, and can be photographed throughout the year.

Migrant birds begin entering an area during February, and usually stay until sometime in September or October.

Nesting begins in mid-February in the south and continues until early April in the north. Adjust your photography schedule accordingly.

PHOTOGRAPHIC HOT SPOTS

Unfortunately, there is no such thing as a "hot spot" for photographing Red-tailed Hawks. In fact, nest photography is usually best on private land. Most landowners will give permission. Simply inform them of what you want to do. Usually, all they will want in return are some photographs.

The following public lands have redtail populations and are worth looking into.

SEEDSKADEE NATIONAL WILDLIFE REFUGE, WYOMING

Red-tailed Hawks are common sights along the 20-mile stretch of Green River flowing through the refuge. Using binoculars, carefully scrutinize the cottonwood trees lining the river for their presence.

Stop at refuge headquarters, introduce yourself, and inform the personnel of your intentions. If you want to erect a temporary blind, you will first need to obtain a permit.

For directions and additional information, see Chapter 3.

KOOTENAI NATIONAL WILDLIFE REFUGE, IDAHO

Redtails are a common sight during spring and summer. They are often observed in the trees along the Kootenai River. From Bonners Ferry, a sign along U.S. 95

directs visitors to turn west and follow Riverside Road for 5 miles to the refuge.

For directions and additional information, see Chapter 3.

SNAKE RIVER BIRDS OF PREY AREA, IDAHO

Embracing almost 500,000 acres with a dense ground-squirrel population, it is not surprising this area supports a high population of nesting Red-tailed Hawks.

For directions and additional information, see Chapter 3.

KELLY ISLAND, MISSOULA, MONTANA

Over 600 acres of tranquil meadows bordered by stands of cottonwoods, backwater sloughs, and ponderosa woodlands provide ideal habitat for a variety of birds and mammals, including the Red-tailed Hawk.

Redtails will typically select a nest site in a conspicuous cottonwood, with a commanding view of one of the grassy meadows. As you hike the trails on the island, keep your eyes trained skyward. A soaring redtail, in search of its next meal, will help you pin-point its territory.

For directions and additional information, see Chapter 3.

RED ROCK LAKES NATIONAL WILDLIFE REFUGE, MONTANA

Large numbers of Red-tailed Hawks are attracted to the Centennial Valley, drawn by the population of prey produced by the diverse habitat. The area surrounding Elk Lake, just outside the refuge's eastern boundary, can be productive. Go north along Elk Lake Road from its junction with Red Rock Pass Road. The lake is reached in 4 miles.

For directions and additional information, see Chapter 3.

EAST PORCUPINE HILLS, ALBERTA

The fir and limber pine dotting the hillsides of the area remind one of a porcupine's quills — thus the name. This Natural Area is located in southwestern Alberta, 124 kilometers (75 miles) west of Lethbridge.

To reach the area, go west from Claresholm on Road 520, a well-maintained gravel road. After 25 kilometers (15 miles), you will come to a road to the south. Take it. After 7 kilometers (4 miles), you will arrive at East Porcupine Hills. Red-tailed Hawks are found on the prairie.

For information, contact the Alberta Forest Service in Blairmore (403-381-5473), or the Alberta Fish and Wildlife Division in Claresholm (403-625-3301).

Golden Eagle

DESCRIPTION — Brown; golden wash over head and nape

SCIENTIFIC NAME — *Aquila chrysaetos*

FAMILY — Kites, Hawks, Eagles (Accipitridae)

NESTING BEGINS — Mid-February to June

INCUBATION — 43 to 45 days; 1 to 4 eggs (usually 2)

TIME TO FLEDGE — 66 to 75 days

Golden Eagles are considered by many to be the noblest representative of North American birds. Unfortunately, this has not always been the case. More than 20,000 Golden Eagles were destroyed during one 10-year period, chiefly by sheep ranchers, despite little evidence of sheep depredation. In fact, one individual prided himself on killing 12,000 eagles — bald and golden — over a period of 20 years. After receiving federal protection in 1962, Golden Eagle populations are finally recovering.

Inhabitants of the western United States, Golden Eagles can be found in a variety of habitats: semidesert, plains, pinon-juniper, ponderosa woodlands, and even alpine tundra. They establish territories in mountainous or rim-rock country adjacent to meadows and prairies. These open hunting grounds supply the eagles with their primary diet of small mammals.

Jackrabbits, cottontails, and rodents comprise nearly 90 percent of the diet of the Golden Eagle. During winter, when live prey is often scarce, carrion becomes an important food source.

Golden Eagles are huge birds with impressive 6- to 7-foot wingspans. The golden wash over the head and nape feathers, noticeable at close range, furnishes the bird with its name.

In the southern Rocky Mountains, goldens tend to be permanent residents, while in the northern areas they are somewhat migratory, especially the immature eagles.

Nesting may begin as early as February in New Mexico. In northern regions, it is often delayed until June. In Montana, for example, nesting extends from mid-April into June.

Rock ledges or cliffs are usually chosen as a nest site. However, in some areas, trees are sometimes selected. Both male and female labor together to build their nest, using thick branches interwoven with smaller twigs and leaves. Aromatic leaves, which tend to discourage insect pests, are often used. It is not uncommon for the pair to alternate between two or even three nest sites within their territory. In fact, construction has been observed on two different sites during the same season.

The creamy white eggs (usually two) are laid during a three- or four-day interval. While most eggs have a reddish brown, blotched pattern, one egg often remains unmarked. The task of incubation falls mainly on the female, although she may receive occasional help from the male. The male is the major "bread winner," hunting the majority of food and even feeding the female on the nest. Long-term pair bonds develop between male and female Golden Eagles.

As with many raptors, the smaller sibling is often killed by the larger.

PHOTOGRAPHIC TECHNIQUES

Locating a Golden Eagle nest is not as difficult as it may seem. Prime territory is rock ledges and cliffs, with nearby open meadows or fields. Look for eagles soaring high above these open areas in the early mornings in search of food. Once eagles have been located, their nest site will not be far away. Search nearby rock ledges for "whitewash" deposited by successive generations of young.

More often than not, eagle nests are located in inaccessible places. You have two choices: conduct photography from a blind suspended on rope, or locate a more accessible nest.

I know of one individual who, upon locating the territory of a pair of goldens, placed branches and shredded bark on a ledge adjacent to a good spot for a blind. It worked. The eagles built their nest on the ledge, and he was able to obtain some wonderful images.

CAUTION: Nesting Golden Eagles may abandon their nest site as a result of human disturbance. The chances of this happening can be greatly reduced if photography is delayed until their eggs have hatched.

Wait until the young eagles are about a week old before attempting any photography. Even then, it is important to be cautious. Enter and leave the blind during hours of darkness, or when the adults are away from the nest. Learn all you can about eagle behavior, and how you can minimize your impact on the birds before attempting any nest photography.

Networking is important. State or federal wildlife agencies can often direct you to a good location, as can local birders. Nesting areas are often closed to human activity, in which case it will be necessary to obtain permission from those in charge.

Goldens can sometimes be lured into photographic range using a road kill. Take a dead deer or pronghorn to a suitable location, erect a blind nearby, and wait. Golden Eagles are smart and extremely cautious. It is important for the blind to be as inconspicuous and as natural looking as possible.

The alternative to photographing wild Golden Eagles is to locate a captive bird and make arrangements for photography. A few falconers work with the magnificent birds. Your other choice is to contact a rehabilitation facility. (See Appendix I.) A cash donation will be appreciated, and is often required.

Photographing wild Golden Eagles will require all the lens power you can afford — preferably something in the 600 mm range. I have successfully used my 80-200 mm, f2.8, autofocus lens to photograph captive birds.

TIME OF YEAR

In New Mexico, Utah, and southern Colorado, nesting Golden Eagles can be photographed between mid-April and late June. In the northern regions covered by this book, this period may be delayed for one or two months.

Goldens are more easily lured to road kills during winter, when small mammals often become scarce prey. Northern populations tend to be somewhat migratory. Therefore, winter photography is best accomplished in New Mexico, Utah, Colorado, and southern Wyoming.

Captive goldens may be photographed throughout the year. However, fall colors added to your eagle images are worth considering. Fall colors peak during early September in Alberta and British Columbia, and early October in southern Utah and New Mexico.

PHOTOGRAPHIC HOT SPOTS

PAWNEE NATIONAL GRASSLANDS, COLORADO

The Pawnee National Grasslands were formed from land bought by the federal government from bankrupt farmers during the dust-bowl days of the 1930s. It is administered by the U.S. Forest Service today, and close to 30 percent of the land is owned by the federal government.

Golden Eagles nest along the rocky ledges of the buttes and in isolated trees in the area. Due to the sensitivity of the buttes during nesting season, I recommend contacting Forest Service or Colorado Division of Wildlife personnel before attempting any nest photography.

To reach Pawnee Buttes from Fort Collins, go east 53 miles along State Highway 14 from its intersection with Interstate 25. Fourteen miles past the town of Briggsdale, turn left onto Road 105. Follow this road as it makes a half-mile jog to the left and then back to the right through the community of Keota, a total distance of 7 miles. Turn right on Road 104. Go 3 miles, then turn left on Road 111. Go 4 miles to the end, turn left onto Road 112, then immediately back to the right. Follow the small dirt road, bearing right at the fork. Continue to the trailhead. Follow the foot trail to the edge of the escarpment, where you have a good view of the buttes.

For additional information, contact the U.S. Forest Service (303-353-5004) or the Division of Wildlife (970-484-2836).

OURAY NATIONAL WILDLIFE REFUGE, UTAH

Ouray National Wildlife Refuge, encompassing almost 12,000 acres along the banks of the Green River, features miles of hiking trails and a 10-mile auto tour. The refuge's habitat diversity — desert shrub to cattail marshes, grasslands to cottonwood bottoms — contributes to a wide assortment of wildlife species.

The refuge supports a breeding population of Golden Eagles. Search the cliffs along the north end of the refuge for their nests.

Include refuge personnel in your plans to photograph nesting Golden Eagles. Their office is located in Vernal. (See Appendix I.) To reach the refuge from Vernal, drive southwest along U.S. 40 for 14 miles. Turn left onto State Highway 88, and go 15 miles to the refuge.

For additional information, contact the U.S. Fish and Wildlife Service (801-789-0351).

SNAKE RIVER BIRDS OF PREY AREA, IDAHO

The Snake River Birds of Prey Area, consisting of desert-like habitat bordering vertical cliffs that tower 700 feet above the Snake River, supports North America's densest concentration of nesting raptors. With 81 miles of basalt cliffs, containing innumerable crevices for potential nest sites, plus a high population density of ground squirrels, it is no wonder that nesting Golden Eagles are common here.

For directions and additional information, see Chapter 3.

WRITING-ON-STONE PROVINCIAL PARK, ALBERTA

Sandstone, cottonwoods, and the picturesque Milk River mark one of Alberta's most fertile wildlife locations. Writing-On-Stone Provincial Park, located 178 kilometers (107 miles) southeast of Lethbridge, has up to 60 species of nesting birds, including the Golden Eagle.

From Lethbridge, go southeast on Highway 4 to the town of Milk River. Turn left (east) onto Highway 501 and travel 42 kilometers (25 miles). At this point the roadway becomes gravel. Turn south, and go 8 kilometers (4.8 miles), then east for 2 kilometers (1.2 miles) to the park entrance.

For additional information, contact the Provincial Park Service (403-647-2364), or the Alberta Fish and Wildlife Division in Foremost (403-867-3826).

Bald Eagle

DESCRIPTION—White head and tail; blackish brown body; large yellow bill.

SCIENTIFIC NAME—*Haliaeetus leucocephalus*

FAMILY—Kites, Hawks, Eagles (Accipitridae)

NESTING BEGINS—Mid-February to April (in the Rockies)

INCUBATION—34 to 36 days; 1 to 3 eggs (usually 2)

TIME TO FLEDGE—70 to 98 days

The Bald Eagle, symbol of freedom, strength, and power, was adopted as the United States national emblem in 1782. Bald Eagles reach full adult plumage — white head and tail feathers — by age four or five. Breeding begins at this time and continues until death, usually at age nine or ten. Captive birds have been known to live to the ripe old age of forty.

Nesting trees are usually located near a lake, large river, or sea coast. The nest is typically placed in the fork of a prominent, tall tree adjacent to an open area. It is a conspicuous, massive structure of sticks and branches. Both male and female are involved with the construction. Used annually, and added to each season, the nest may attain a height of 5 or 6 feet, be 9 or 10 feet in diameter, and weigh upwards of 2,000 pounds.

In the Rockies, two bluish white eggs are laid sometime between February and April. In other areas, Florida for example, nesting may occur as early as November. Both parents share in the incubation, and in rearing their offspring. Young Bald Eagles face many dangers, and mortality is high. The pair will be fortunate if two of their offspring reach maturity.

Bald Eagles are capable of capturing fish weighing up to 15 pounds. In addition, small mammals, waterfowl, seabirds, and carrion find their way into their diet.

In recent history, several factors contributed to plummeting bald eagle populations. The paying of bounties for dead eagles did not end until 1962. In Alaska, a pair of eagle feet brought two dollars. Eagle eggs were weakened by exposure to pesticides, drastically reducing the number of eagle chicks hatched. And, human development of critical breeding areas added to eagles' problems. Today, many of these problems are behind us, and Bald Eagles are making a comeback.

PHOTOGRAPHIC TECHNIQUES

Bald Eagles are endangered in many areas, and, like many raptors, they are extremely sensitive to human activity.

To photograph a nesting pair of birds, it will be necessary to work closely with the U.S. Fish & Wildlife Service, and, even then, you may not be able to obtain the necessary permits.

Never fear. There are a number of areas in the Rockies where you can photograph non-nesting, wild Bald Eagles. In most of these areas, you will have better success using your car as a blind. Set up your camera, lens, and window mount in advance. Once you locate a subject you want to photograph, stop your car and begin shooting. Some birds will fly the moment you stop your car; others will not. Keep trying until you find one that is cooperative. In any case, always exercise extreme caution when photographing these magnificent birds. They are easily disturbed. You'll find that a 600 mm or 800 mm lens will get you more "keepers."

Licensed falconers, rehabilitation facilities, and zoos provide an alternative method for obtaining Bald Eagle images (see Appendix I). When photographing captive birds, some situations will require the use of a 400 mm or 500 mm lens for tight head shots. On other occasions, you'll be able to get the images you want with a 200 mm lens. In fact, I once used a 28 mm wide-angle lens. It allowed me to get close to my subject and still provide the necessary depth of field for the scenic mountains in the background.

TIME OF YEAR

Captive Bald Eagles may be photographed throughout the year. Winter images with snow or an eagle surrounded by fall colors can be breathtaking. Fall colors occur between September and early October. In Colorado, for example, fall colors usually peak around September 22 or 23. However, rain or early snowfall will affect these dates.

Spring migration peaks during March. In the fall, migration is at its peak in

November. Wild eagles are best photographed during these times. Their numbers are higher, providing more opportunities for photography.

PHOTOGRAPHIC HOT SPOTS

CLARK FORK RIVER DELTA, LAKE PEND OREILLE, IDAHO

The Clark Fork delta is a blend of exposed mud flats, wetlands, grasslands, and cottonwoods. In addition to the thousands of shore birds and waterfowl present during spring and fall migrations, close to 400 Bald Eagles come to the delta each winter, making it northern Idaho's best location for Bald Eagle photography.

From Sandpoint, go north along U.S. 95 approximately 2 miles. Turn right, following State Highway 200 along the lake shore for 27 miles to the town of Clark Fork. To reach the delta, turn right and cross the river. Once across, turn right and continue 2 miles to the Johnson Creek Recreation Area. There are no trails on the delta. However, you can slip on a pair of waders and hike into the marsh. A portable blind erected close to the water is often productive for "flight shots." State Highway 200 provides several vantage points for making eagle images.

For additional information, contact the Idaho Department of Fish and Game (208-765-3111) or the U.S. Army Corps of Engineers (208-437-3133).

CANYON FERRY DAM, MONTANA

Each year, more than 200 Bald Eagles gather along the Missouri River, below the Canyon Ferry Dam, southeast of Helena. Stopping to feed on spawning kokanee salmon, they provide photographers with great photo opportunities before continuing their southward movement. This is Montana's top location for photographing Bald Eagles.

Certain parts of the river and surrounding land are closed to visitors from October 15 through December 31 to minimize disturbances to the eagles, although much of the area remains open.

Eagles begin arriving in late September. In 1995, 15 eagles were present by the end of the first week of October. By October 13, two days before the closure, 33 eagles were present. Highest densities occur between mid-November and the first week of December. On November 23, 242 eagles were counted.

Four viewing locations provide photo opportunities: Riverside, York Bridge, Hauser Dam/Black Sandy, and Beaver Creek.

Riverside Viewing Area is just below Canyon Ferry Dam. From Helena, drive 9 miles south along U.S. 287. Turn left onto State Highway 284, going 9 miles to the town of Canyon Ferry. At Canyon Ferry, turn left following the signs to Riverside Campground. You will be directed to the river overlook just before you get to the campground. This is one of the best locations along the river. Eagles are never very far away.

The York Bridge Viewing Area is northeast of Helena, along State Highway 280 where it crosses the Missouri River.

To reach the Hauser Dam/Black Sandy Viewing Areas, go north from Helena 8 miles along Interstate 15. Turn right onto State Highway 453. Bear left to find Hauser Dam. Black Sandy is on the right just before reaching the dam.

Beaver Creek Viewing Area is more remote. From Helena, go northeast along State Highway 280, as if you were going to the York Bridge area. However, continue to the town of York. At York, turn left onto a dirt road. Follow this until its junction with Beaver Creek Road, a distance of around 20 miles. Turn left, following the road to the river and the Beaver Creek Viewing Area.

For additional information, contact the U.S. Bureau of Reclamation (406-475-3310) or the Montana Department of Fish, Wildlife and Parks (406-444-1276).

KOOTENAI RIVER, MONTANA

Each fall, more than 100 Bald Eagles descend on the Kootenai River, concentrating their efforts below Libby Dam. They come to feed on the kokanee salmon.

Eagles begin arriving in early October. By mid-December, most of them are gone. The highest eagle count generally occurs during the first week of November. The largest concentrations of eagles occur just below the dam. One of the better viewing sites is the Alexander Creek Picnic Area.

From Libby, drive east along State Highway 37 for 13 miles. Just before Libby Dam, turn left onto Forest Road 228 and go to the Alexander Creek Picnic Area.

For additional information, contact the Army Corps of Engineers (406-293-5577).

White-tailed Ptarmigan

DESCRIPTION — Summer: mottled grays, blacks, and browns above; white wings, tail, and underside.
   Winter: all white, red eye-comb and black bill and eyes are visible

SCIENTIFIC NAME — *Lagopus leucurus*

FAMILY — Grouse, Ptarmigan (Phasianidae)

NESTING BEGINS — June to late July

INCUBATION — 22 to 24 days; 3 to 9 eggs (usually 4 to 7)

TIME TO FLEDGE — 7 to 10 days

The White-tailed Ptarmigan is a master of disguise. From its seasonal changes in coloration to its "snowshoe-fitted" feet, no other bird is so well adapted for life on the barren alpine tundra. In winter, these are the only birds to don a cloak of white.

The White-tailed Ptarmigan ranges throughout the mountainous areas of Alberta, British Columbia, and western Montana, and in scattered alpine habitats of Wyoming, Colorado, and northern New Mexico.

They are generally found in open forests near treeline or on tundra above 12,000 feet. During winter, ptarmigan customarily descend into mountain valleys, where willow tops remain exposed above the snow.

Climatic conditions control the beginning of the nesting season. The hen will not establish a nest until she is fully clothed in her summer plumage — a mixture of mottled grays, blacks, and browns. This usually occurs in June.

A nest site usually is selected next to a large, lichen-covered boulder. The female scoops out a shallow depression, lines it with grasses and lichens, and deposits four to seven eggs. She may also select a nesting place in the open or under a shrub.

The male remains nearby to warn the hen of any approaching danger. The female is so committed to incubating her eggs that she will often allow human intruders to pick her up and examine her eggs. However, don't try this!

After 22 days the eggs begin to hatch. Within 10 days the young ptarmigan are able to fly short distances. They will remain with the hen until the following spring.

As winter approaches, the White-tailed Ptarmigan is dressed in its showiest plumage, a rich mixture of the chocolate browns of summer and the whipped-cream whites of winter.

Winter diet in most areas consists of buds and woody twigs from the alpine willow. In summer, leaves, buds, and flowers are enjoyed, as are occasional insects.

When the snows return, the birds begin banding together in flocks of 20 or more. As the nights become colder and the snow gets deeper, they bury themselves beneath the snow and roost, allowing their body heat to warm their underground igloo.

With feathered toes that help them walk on soft snow, feathered eyelids and nostrils for added protection against extreme cold, and a camouflaged cloak to conceal them from enemies, the White-tailed Ptarmigan is masterfully adapted for its life on top of the world.

PHOTOGRAPHIC TECHNIQUES

Ptarmigan are easily photographed once they're located. The problem is locating them. Several clues will aid you, including tracks, scat, feathers, and their call. Tracks are easily spotted in the snow, as are excavated holes where ptarmigan roosted the night before, burrowed beneath the snow. Ptarmigan scat, reminding one of willow catkins, is easily recognized. Hen-like clucking also announces their presence in the vicinity.

In early spring before all the snows have melted, their spring molt is often incomplete. At this time, the birds often sport a combination of winter whites and summer browns, and the white stands out in sharp contrast to brush along the edges of the snowfields.

Take your time while searching. It's entirely possible for a bird to be no more than 10 feet away and remain unnoticed. Binoculars come in handy when searching for these masters of disguise.

Once you've located your subject, the rest is easy. Remember to correct your meter reading for a white subject or snow. (See Exposure, Chapter 2.) An 80-200 mm zoom lens is ideal. I once used a 28 mm wide-angle lens.

Lie on the ground while photographing these beautiful birds. This will place the camera at the same perspective as your subject.

TIME OF YEAR

The White-tailed Ptarmigan is a permanent resident wherever it is found, with limited altitude migration, usually occurring between summer and winter forage areas. The only thing limiting year-round photography is winter snow depths.

In Rocky Mountain National Park, ptarmigan can be photographed along Trail Ridge Road. However, the road traditionally stays closed until Memorial Day and is open only into October.

On Guanella Pass in Colorado, ptarmigan donned in their white attire are best photographed between late February and early March. On neighboring Mount Evans, July is the best month to photograph ptarmigan in their summer dress.

June is best to photograph nesting birds, while young chicks can be photographed between mid-July and mid-August.

PHOTOGRAPHIC HOT SPOTS

GUANELLA PASS, ARAPAHO NATIONAL FOREST, COLORADO

If you can only travel to one location to photograph White-tailed Ptarmigan, 11,669-foot Guanella Pass should be your priority. This is the best location in North America to photograph these birds in their all-white winter plumage.

To locate the birds, park at the pass above treeline. There is an interpretive sign here pertaining to ptarmigan. The birds will be found between one-quarter and one-half mile of the parking lot. As you stand at your car looking eastward, ptarmigan will be in one of two locations: the east side of the hill to your immediate right, usually near the trees, or down in the valley in front of you, seeking shelter among the willows.

The snow is deep here in winter. Snowshoes or cross-country skis are a must.

CAUTION: Blowing snow can produce severe "white out" conditions. Disorientation can occur. For your safety, do not go out on the tundra during these conditions.

To reach Guanella Pass, take the Georgetown exit from Interstate 70, 41 miles west of Denver. Turn south and go under the interstate. Continue one block to the first street and turn right. Go 0.3 mile to the next street, and turn left. Cross the stream. Turn right on Rose Street. At the west edge of town, Rose Street begins climbing a series of switchbacks on its way to Guanella Pass. Follow this road to the summit.

A trip to this area is never complete without a stop at Daylight Donuts in Idaho

Springs. It's amazing what a couple of donuts can do for one's outlook on life.

For additional information or a weather update, contact the U.S. Forest Service in Idaho Springs (303-567-2901).

MOUNT EVANS, ARAPAHO NATIONAL FOREST, COLORADO

The most consistent location for ptarmigan on Mount Evans is above Summit Lake. As you drive past Summit Lake, look for the barricade that blocks the road during bad weather. Go one-quarter mile past the barricade and climb the hill on your right, looking for ptarmigan as you go.

For complete directions and additional information, see Chapter 3.

ROCKY MOUNTAIN NATIONAL PARK, COLORADO

One of the better locations in the Rockies to photograph White-tailed Ptarmigan in the summer is along Trail Ridge Road, 2.25 miles west of Rainbow Curve. Limited parking is available on the left side of the road. Search the alpine tundra north of the road, being careful where you step. Due to the extremely short growing season, many alpine plants grow very slowly. One misplaced footstep could destroy a plant that took years to grow.

For complete directions and additional information, see Chapter 3.

WATERTON LAKES NATIONAL PARK, ALBERTA

White-tailed Ptarmigan can be photographed along a mountain trail paralleling the park's western boundary. The trail can be accessed at two different locations: Akamina Parkway or Red Rock Canyon.

From Akamina Parkway, go northwest from Waterton Townsite approximately 9 kilometers (5.4 miles) to a trailhead on your right. This trail will take you past Rowe Lake to South Kootenay Pass, 22 kilometers (13 miles) away. Fortunately, you will not have to hike that far. Unfortunately, you will have to hike 14 to 16 kilometers (8 to 10 miles). Oh well, who said life was going to be easy?

From Red Rock Canyon, hike 10.2 kilometers (6 miles) west to South Kootenay Pass, then southwest another 6 kilometers (3.6 miles) to a location about 2 kilometers (1.2 miles) past Lone Lake. Camouflaged ptarmigan are difficult to locate. Take your time, and search the area carefully. They're here!

For complete directions and additional information, see Chapter 3.

JASPER NATIONAL PARK, ALBERTA

Whistlers Mountain and Signal Mountain host White-tailed Ptarmigan populations.

Whistlers Mountain is reached by taking the Jasper Tramway to the top of the mountain. Go south from Jasper Townsite along the Icefields Parkway for 2.3 kilometers (1.4 miles) to Whistlers Road. Turn right and follow the signs to the tramway parking lot.

To reach Signal Mountain, go north on Highway 16 East approximately 2 kilometers (1.2 miles) from the intersection of Connaught Drive and Highway 16, on the north side of Jasper Townsite. Turn right as if you were going to the Jasper Park Lodge. However, after crossing the Athabasca River turn left on Lodge Road instead of going right to the lodge. After 2 kilometers (1.2 miles), Lodge Road turns to the right and becomes Maligne Lake Road. The Signal Mountain trailhead begins at a point along the Maligne Lake Road 5.5 kilometers (3.3 miles) after leaving Highway 16 East. From the trailhead to Signal Mountain is a 6-kilometer (3 mile) hike. If you fail to locate any White-tailed Ptarmigan, you may still find and photograph Willow Ptarmigan, which share the mountain with their white-tailed cousins.

For complete directions and additional information, see Chapter 3.

Sharp-tailed Grouse

DESCRIPTION — Mottled brown and black; narrow, pointed tail, edged in white.

SCIENTIFIC NAME — *Tympanuchus phasianellus*

FAMILY — Grouse, Ptarmigan (Phasianidae)

NESTING BEGINS — April and May

INCUBATION — 21 to 24 days; 5 to 17 eggs (usually 10 to 14)

TIME TO FLEDGE — 7 to 10 days

The morning sun was just beginning to make its presence known to the life forms on their ancient dancing grounds. From overhead came the winnowing sounds of snipe — their erratic, swooping flights would provide music for the ceremony about to unfurl. The dancers were ready to begin their ritualistic performance.

Sharp-tailed Grouse are the avian equivalent of Native American dancers. Watching Native American ceremonies and the courtship displays of these grouse, it's easy to see the similarity between the dances of the people and the birds.

Beginning in early April of each year and continuing through the first week or two of May, Sharp-tailed Grouse are drawn by some irresistible force to their courtship-display grounds, known as leks. The leks are found in grasslands, sagebrush country, and even some montane meadows. They are usually 50 to 100 feet across, bare of grass, and hard-packed and smoothed by generations of use. Just how many generations is not certain. One lek was known to have been in use for at least 50 years, while yet another was frequented by sharp-tails beyond the tribal memory of local Native Americans.

Just before daybreak, 15 to 30 birds assemble at the lek. Each male has his own territory within the lek and competes with other males for the females.

The dance is performed as the male drops his head and, with wings drooped, holds his pointed tail erect and vibrates it from side to side. He does all of this while rapidly stomping his feet and turning in a circle. The sound produced is similar to that of a muffled jack-hammer in operation. While dancing, he inflates purple air sacs on each side of his neck and extends bright yellow "eyebrow" patches over his eyes. Surely, this must be hard for a female sharp-tail to resist.

After the dance is complete, the female selects and mates with the male of her choice, then leaves to prepare her nest and lay her eggs.

The nest consists of a shallow depression in the earth, lined with grasses and leaves. Often it is located near the edge of an open area and concealed by some type of cover, such as sagebrush or a tree.

Between 10 and 14 light-brown eggs, sprinkled with fine, reddish brown specks, are laid. The eggs hatch in about 22 days. The young are tended by the female.

Food consists of leaves, buds, flowers, seeds, and fruit. Young sharp-tails also eat a large number of insects.

Many species of grouse have elaborate courtship displays, but none is quite as entertaining as that of the male Sharp-tailed Grouse, the bird world's Native American dancer.

PHOTOGRAPHIC TECHNIQUES

As far as I'm concerned, the only time to photograph the Sharp-tailed Grouse is when they're performing their courtship rituals. The best way to locate a lek is by networking. The personnel at state and federal wildlife areas are usually able to direct you to an active lek, as are local birders.

Arrive at the lek at least an hour before sunrise. Some people use their car as a blind. This works if you're close enough to the lek. I prefer using something that will allow me to photograph from ground level, so I often set up a portable blind. On a few occasions, I've cut sagebrush and placed just enough of it around my tripod to break up my outline. Other times, I've used camouflage netting around my tripod.

A 400 mm telephoto usually provides all the magnification you need. Activity usually begins when light levels are low. Pushing Fujichrome 100 four stops to ISO 400 will allow you to begin shooting when others are just thinking about it.

Sharp-tailed Grouse are not shy. In fact, I've had them come up and peck my camera.

TIME OF YEAR

Lek activity begins in early April and continues into early May. This is the time to photograph the sharp-tail.

PHOTOGRAPHIC HOT SPOTS

Due to the sensitive nature of breeding grounds, I have not given specific directions to lek locations. Instead, I have listed government agencies to contact. They are very helpful when working with knowledgeable and conscientious photographers.

ROUTT COUNTY, COLORADO

Cottonwoods in the river bottoms along the Yampa River, foothills blanketed in sagebrush, and the Elkhead Mountains to the north — this is Routt County, and the backdrop for the leks of the Sharp-tailed Grouse.

All of the sharp-tail leks of Routt County are on private land. You can make photo arrangements through the Division of Wildlife, District Wildlife Manager (970-276-3338).

One of my favorite leks is on the Lou Wyman Elk Ranch, south of Hayden. For additional information, contact Lou or one of his sons (970-824-6431).

BENTON LAKE NATIONAL WILDLIFE REFUGE, MONTANA

Almost 200 species of birds find their way into the refuge, including the Sharp-tailed Grouse. Each spring, approximately 50 sharp-tails perform the courtship dance near the refuge auto-tour loop. Reserve space in a refuge blind, or seek permission to erect your own portable blind.

For directions and additional information, see Chapter 3.

HAWKINS RESERVOIR, IDAHO

Hawkins Reservoir, a picturesque mountain reservoir, attracts many species of shore birds and waterfowl. Sharp-tailed Grouse have established their leks in the area among the stands of juniper and mountain shrub surrounding the reservoir. In searching for active leks, look for grouse scat as well as areas of hard-packed earth.

To reach Hawkins Reservoir, go south from Pocatello for 31 miles along Interstate 15 to the town of Virginia. Turn right onto Virginia Road, traveling west 8.5 miles to the reservoir.

For information, contact the Bureau of Land Management (208-766-4766).

SAND CREEK WILDLIFE MANAGEMENT AREA, IDAHO

Sand dunes, lava formations, sagebrush, and lodgepole pine forests, all situated among rolling hills — that's Sand Creek Wildlife Management Area. With such diverse habitat, you'd expect to find a diversity of wildlife, and this reasoning is not unfounded. At Sand Creek, you can see everything from

Trumpeter Swans to white-tailed deer. Sharp-tailed Grouse are found in and around the sand dunes.

From Idaho Falls, drive northeast for 35 miles along U.S. 20 to St. Anthony. Turn left, following Middle Street to the U.S. Forest Service Office. Turn right, and go 1.5 miles to Sand Creek Road. Turn left, following Sand Creek Road for 16.5 miles to Sand Creek Ponds, where you will find camping and rest rooms.

For additional information, contact the Idaho Department of Fish and Game (208-624-7065).

Ring-necked Pheasant

DESCRIPTION — Male: iridescent bronze; glossy green head; iridescent ear tufts, bare red eye patches, white neck ring, long, pointed tail.
   Female: mottled brown overall.

SCIENTIFIC NAME — *Phasianus colchicus*

FAMILY — Grouse, Ptarmigan (Phasianidae)

NESTING BEGINS — Mid-April to late July

INCUBATION — 23 to 25 days; 6 to 15 eggs (usually 10 to 12)

TIME TO FLEDGE — 12 days

The Ring-necked Pheasant was introduced into the United States from China in 1881. Today, ring-necks inhabit farmlands and prairie grasslands from southwestern Canada across the northern United States, and southward into northern Baja California, Arizona, and Texas.

In the Rockies, ring-necks are generally restricted to lower elevations. Corn fields are cherished, as are woodland edges and hedgerows.

Nesting begins in mid-April and continues until late July. Peak nesting activity occurs during early May. The hen selects and prepares the nest site, usually among tall plants or shrubs. The actual nest is nothing more than a shallow hollow on the ground, with little or no lining.

After an incubation of approximately 24 days, 10 to 12 olive-colored eggs hatch. The hen tends the young. In less than two weeks, the young chicks are able to fly short distances.

Ring-necks' primary food consists of berries and seeds, although insects, small vertebrates, and invertebrates find their way into the ring-neck diet.

Cocks commence "crowing" in late winter and early spring. The ring-neck's caaw-gock is a raspy, two-part call with an accent on the second part. This sound is preceded by several wing flaps and followed by a short burst of intense, rapid flapping. The crowing appears to serve two functions: attracting hens and claiming territory. Crowing usually begins just before sunrise and occurs again around sunset.

By April, the territory has been defined and established; crowing then increases in frequency and continues into May. Territories may range in size from 3 acres to as much as 10 acres. The cocks are polygamous. Once all the hens have departed to incubate their eggs, the crowing gradually comes to a halt.

PHOTOGRAPHIC TECHNIQUES

Ring-necked Pheasants are highly secretive. However, there are a couple of methods that will help you obtain photographs. One is to locate a "crowing" cock. The other involves baiting with corn.

A crowing cock is very noisy and easy to hear. The cock usually stands on a prominent stump, log, or rock, and he tends to use the same location several days in a row.

First locate a general area that pheasants are known to inhabit. (See Networking, Chapter 2.) Arrive at the selected location at least an hour before sunrise and listen. Once you've heard a cock crow, move to a new location and listen for the same bird. After hearing the cock again from your new position, you can use triangulation to help locate him. However, if you begin your search now, you may cause him to move to another crowing location. Wait until mid-day before investigating.

The presence of scat on or near a conspicuous perch will confirm that you have found the cock's crowing location. Set up your blind nearby. Photographs can often be obtained at dusk or dawn. In either case, enter the blind at lease two hours before sunrise or sunset. It is very important to remain quiet and still.

To bait with corn, first locate an area inhabited by pheasants. Build a permanent blind using local materials. Place cracked-kernel corn in a shallow depression where it will not show in your photographs. Broadcast additional corn over a 10- to 15-foot circle. It may take several days before the birds begin feeding. Replace the corn as needed. Once the feeding station has been established, enter your blind a couple of hours before sunrise. Be quiet. Be still. And keep your fingers crossed. You've done your part. The rest is up to the birds.

One other place where ring-necks can often be photographed is a privately owned game-bird farm. Not all such facilities have suitable backgrounds for photography, but some do. Contact the state wildlife agency in your area for a list of such farms. (See Appendix I.)

Photographing ring-necks requires a 500 mm to 600 mm telephoto lens.

TIME OF YEAR

Ring-necked Pheasants are permanent residents wherever they are found, and, as such, they may be photographed year-round.

April and May are the months for focusing on "crowing" cocks. Other things you might want to consider are fall colors or snow in your photographs. Even an October pumpkin can add considerable color to pheasant images. Fall colors usually peak during September. Fresh snowfalls can occur anytime between October and March.

PHOTOGRAPHIC HOT SPOTS

BOSQUE DEL APACHE NATIONAL WILDLIFE REFUGE, NEW MEXICO

Ring-necked Pheasants are commonly observed along the 15-mile auto-tour route. Your best chance of seeing one is early in the morning. After you've determined their general territory, it will be easier to locate individual birds and photograph them.

Upon arriving, stop by the refuge office, introduce yourself, and share your intentions. Refuge personnel will assist you in any way possible.

For directions and additional information, see Chapter 3.

MONTE VISTA NATIONAL WILDLIFE REFUGE, COLORADO

Monte Vista National Wildlife Refuge, located in Colorado's San Luis Valley, is made up of ponds and cattail marshes, surrounded by fields of grain and alfalfa.

Pheasants are typically observed early in the morning along the 12 miles of county roads crisscrossing the refuge. This is where you want to focus your attention.

Administration for the refuge is handled from the Alamosa National Wildlife Refuge, 4 miles east of Alamosa on U.S. 160. Turn right on El Rancho Lane and go 2.5 miles south to headquarters. Be sure to stop by and say hello.

From the town of Monte Vista, go south along State Highway 15 for 6 miles to the Monte Vista National Wildlife Refuge office. During March and April, this office maintains a regular schedule; hours are irregular the remainder of the year.

For additional information, contact the Alamosa National Wildlife Refuge (719-589-4021).

CAMAS NATIONAL WILDLIFE REFUGE, IDAHO

Pheasants are often seen in the meadows along the western edge of the refuge. Off-road travel is prohibited without special permission between February 1 and July 15. Permission is also required to erect a portable blind, and is granted on a case-by-case basis.

For directions and additional information, see Chapter 3.

BENTON LAKE NATIONAL WILDLIFE REFUGE, MONTANA

The refuge is home to almost 200 species of birds, including the Ring-necked Pheasant. Ring-necks typically can be observed at dawn from the 9-mile Prairie Marsh Wildlife Drive.

For directions and additional information, see Chapter 3.

TYRRELL AND RUSH LAKES AREA, ALBERTA

Tyrrell Lake, Rush Lake, and the adjacent marshes form a major staging area for shore birds and waterfowl. The area also provides copious amounts of cover for the local Ring-necked Pheasant population.

The area can be reached by going southeast from Lethbridge along Highway 4 for 38 kilometers (23 miles) to the town of New Dayton. Continue past New Dayton for 3 kilometers (1.8 miles) along Highway 4, and you will find access to Tyrrell Lake. Highway 36, to the west, provides additional access to the area.

For additional information, contact the Alberta Fish and Wildlife Division in Lethbridge (403-381-5281), or St. Mary's River Irrigation District in Lethbridge (403-328-4401).

Mourning Dove

DESCRIPTION — Grayish brown overall; underparts with pinkish wash; purple sheen on nape; long, pointed tail.

SCIENTIFIC NAME — *Zenaida macroura*

FAMILY — Pigeons, Doves (Columbidae)

NESTING BEGINS — May to September

INCUBATION — 13 or 14 days; 2 or 3 eggs (usually 2)

TIME TO FLEDGE — 12 to 14 days

The sad call of the Mourning Dove engendered its descriptive name. At home in fields with scattered trees, open woodlands, and urban areas, Mourning Doves are found in all vegetative habitats up to the lower coniferous life zone.

The dove's breeding season is extensive; it produces two, three, or more broods in a single year. In Colorado for example, breeding usually begins in early May and continues until mid-August.

Both the female and the male are involved in nest building. The male selects the twigs and brings them to the female, who constructs the nest. The nest, a simple platform of twigs, is 7 to 10 ten inches in diameter and is typically located in the fork of a horizontal tree branch.

The clutch is usually comprised of two white eggs. Male and female doves share incubation. The young are capable of flying within 10 days of hatching. However, they normally wait until 12 days unless disturbed.

Mourning Doves have two basic calls: the long who-oo, who-who-who-who and the short who-oo, who. With either call, the second note is higher pitched.

The longer call is used by the male to attract a mate. The short call is used by both male and female at the nest site. Upon selecting a nest site, the male invites the female to the chosen location using the short call. This is repeated for several days if necessary, until a female responds by flying to him at the proposed site. At that time, the call is usually repeated by both birds.

The male then begins bringing nest materials to the female, a twig at a time. This is repeated several hours each morning until the nest is completed. Complete construction may take several days.

PHOTOGRAPHIC TECHNIQUES

Look and listen among trees along the edge of open areas. The Mourning Dove's short call is the chief clue for locating a potential nest site. Also, look for the male walking around on the ground collecting nesting materials. He will lead you to the nest.

Nesting doves are easily photographed, and they usually accept the presence of a considerate photographer. A 500 mm lens will provide a comfortable working distance and eliminate the need for using a blind.

I often locate birds and photograph them from my car window. Set up your equipment in advance, and drive the back-country roads. Mourning Doves are often seen along these roadways, feeding on the ground and perching side by side on fences. When you find a subject, stop and begin shooting. Again, you will need a lens in the 500 mm range.

TIME OF YEAR

Colorado doves begin nesting in early May and continue until mid-August. In Montana, nesting activity takes place a month later, commencing in early June and lasting until mid-September.

Your best chances of photographing Mourning Doves from your car occur between the months of April and October.

PHOTOGRAPHIC HOT SPOTS

BOSQUE DEL APACHE NATIONAL WILDLIFE REFUGE, NEW MEXICO

Mourning Doves are common sights in many portions of the refuge. They can occasionally be photographed along the 15-mile auto-tour road, and you will often see them around refuge headquarters. Also, look for them along the fringe of wooded areas.

For directions and additional information, see Chapter 3.

ARAPAHO NATIONAL WILDLIFE REFUGE, COLORADO

Search for Mourning Doves in the willows and cottonwoods along the Illinois River. I recommend beginning among the trees approximately a quarter-mile southwest of refuge headquarters. First inform refuge personnel of your intentions. They can often be very helpful.

For directions and additional information, see Chapter 3.

SEEDSKADEE NATIONAL WILDLIFE REFUGE, WYOMING

Mourning Doves are abundant here all summer. They can often be photographed near refuge headquarters, or as they feed along the sides of the entrance road. Nesting typically occurs in the sagebrush uplands.

For directions and additional information, see Chapter 3.

CAMAS NATIONAL WILDLIFE REFUGE, IDAHO

Mourning Doves are often observed in the areas surrounding refuge headquarters. Carefully scrutinize the trees along the river for nesting doves.

For directions and additional information, see Chapter 3.

BENTON LAKE NATIONAL WILDLIFE REFUGE, MONTANA

Almost 200 species of birds are found on the refuge, including the Mourning Dove. Several pairs nest among the trees near refuge headquarters. Stop by and inform the refuge staff of your intentions. They may be able to assist you in your quest for doves.

For directions and additional information, see Chapter 3.

WYNDHAM-CARSELAND PROVINCIAL PARK, ALBERTA

Towering balsam poplars and cottonwoods line this section of the Bow Valley, providing nesting sites for many species of birds, including the Mourning Dove. Investigate the area around the park entrance. Open areas adjacent to cottonwood stands also should be carefully scrutinized.

The park is southeast of Calgary. Drive east 37 kilometers (22 miles) along the Trans Canada Highway. Turn south onto Highway 25, following it south and then east past Carseland, then south again across the Bow River. The park entrance is reached after a total distance of 35 kilometers (21 miles).

For information contact the Alberta Provincial Parks Service (403-934-3523), or the Fish and Wildlife Division in Strathmore (403-934-3422).

Great Horned Owl

DESCRIPTION — Grayish brown; white throat; horizontal barring on chest; long ear tufts; 19 to 25 inches from head to tail.

SCIENTIFIC NAME — *Bubo virginianus*

FAMILY — Typical Owls (Strigidae)

NESTING BEGINS — Mid-February to mid-March

INCUBATION — 26 to 35 days; 1 to 6 eggs (usually 2 or 3)

TIME TO FLEDGE — 35 days

Great Horned Owls occupy most of North America, from forests to cities to deserts. They are hunters of the night and the minutes after sunset, just before darkness arrives. In daylight, dense trees appear to swallow them as they roost, nearly invisible, near the trunk.

These owls have phenomenal hearing. Their ears are asymmetrically placed openings on each side of the head, one higher than the other. A ruff of highly specialized feathers encircling the face can be raised or lowered, much as a person cups a hand behind an ear, funneling sounds into the ear drum.

Owls also can discern objects at light levels 100 times lower than those required by humans. They are often observed moving their heads back and forth, up and down, and side to side — a technique used to pin-point sound sources.

Great Horned Owls are marvels of natural selection.

Courtship begins in November and continues until nesting, sometime between January and mid-March. A nest site may be selected on the plains or in the mountains. Females may lay eggs in an abandoned hawk or magpie nest, in a tree cavity, or in a crevice among the rocks. Left undisturbed, owls will use the same nest for several years.

One to five white eggs are laid, with three being the usual number. Young owlets begin hatching after 26 to 35 days. The young fledge between 63 and 70 days after hatching.

PHOTOGRAPHIC TECHNIQUES

First, locate your subject. One method involves searching leafless trees during the winter. Drive the back roads, looking for prominent trees in open meadows. Using binoculars, scrutinize each limb, especially where it joins the main trunk.

Another method is to call an owl with an electronic caller. This method works best at night. First, place your blind in an open area, near a tree containing a suitable perch for the bird. If no perch is available, get one. Use a fallen tree limb and place it where you want it. Locate the speaker directly below the perch.

Set up your flash, prefocus your camera, and wait until dark. When using a Great Horned Owl tape, the biggest problem is too much volume. Play the tape about the same volume as an owl would produce or lower. Play one or two calls and wait. Continue this for several hours, if necessary. Sooner or later, an owl will come to your perch.

CAUTION: Do not attempt to call nesting birds. This could cause them to stay away for extended periods, exposing the nest to predators.

The third method for locating owls is to find a potentially active nest. Carefully examine this with binoculars. The inhabitants will not always be visible at first. Don't overlook networking with the staffs of state and national parks and wildlife refuges, and with Audubon Society members, for possible nest sites.

CAUTION: Avoid disturbing incubating birds. Even minor disturbances can force some species to abandon their nest. Wait until you see nestlings before attempting any photography.

The last method for finding owls involves "whitewash." When a Great Horned Owl selects a prime roosting site, it will return to that location again and again. Under these roosts are large accumulations of white excrement, called whitewash. Locating whitewash can be easier than spotting an owl, especially after trees have leafed-out in the spring. Look beneath trees and thickets surrounded by open meadows.

Once you have located your subject, move cautiously. If the owl feels threatened, it may leave before you have a chance to set up your equipment. You'll need a 500 mm lens or larger.

Since owls roost in the densest cover they can find, more often than not you are forced to shoot at extremely low light levels. I recommend using fill-flash under these conditions.

TIME OF YEAR

Late fall through early spring is the best time to photograph Great Horned Owls. Increased activity and leafless trees during this time will make your job easier. Young "downy" owlets can be photographed during March and April.

PHOTOGRAPHIC HOT SPOTS

Unlike many mammals and bird species, Great Horned Owls are not concentrated in specific locations. They are found throughout the area covered by this book, national parks, wildlife refuges, and even city parks and backyards.

I have observed and photographed Great Horned Owls in the San Luis Valley of Colorado near the town of Crestone. One nested in my backyard, near Allenspark. I am aware of several nests near Estes Park, Colorado. I've seen owls in New Mexico, Wyoming, and Montana. In Canada, I've observed them in Banff, Jasper, and Yoho National Parks. They are where you find them.

Photographing captive birds is another way to obtain images of this magnificent creature. Wildlife rehabilitators, as well as licensed falconers, may have an owl. A donation is often greatly appreciated. State and federal wildlife agencies maintain a list of individuals licensed to rehabilitate and handle raptors. (See Appendix I.)

At least one organization conducts a "birds of prey" workshop, where, for a fee, participants can photograph Great Horned Owls and other raptors. The birds are taken into the wild and placed in natural settings, where participants are encouraged to take all the photographs they want. One program is conducted in early spring and the other when fall colors are at their peak. (See Appendix I.)

The following locations have breeding populations of Great Horned Owls.

CAMAS NATIONAL WILDLIFE REFUGE, IDAHO

Great Horned Owls nest in the refuge's tall cottonwood trees. Carefully search each tree for signs of their presence, including whitewash, and pellets.

For directions and additional information, see Chapter 3.

KOOTENAI NATIONAL WILDLIFE REFUGE, IDAHO

Great Horned Owls are common in the refuge. Search the tall cottonwoods along the Kootenai River, paying particular attention along the refuge's northern boundary.

For directions and additional information, see Chapter 3.

MONTOUR WILDLIFE MANAGEMENT AND RECREATION AREA, IDAHO

More than 1,000 acres of cattail marshes, flooded fields, grassy meadows, and woodlands provide excellent habitat for a variety of birds, including the Great Horned Owl. Carefully scrutinize each tree growing near the wildlife area's eastern boundary. This is where the owls build their nests and raise their young.

From Boise, go north 29 miles along State Highway 55 to the town of Horseshoe Bend. Turn left, following State Highway 52 for 8 miles to its intersection with the Sweet/Montour Road. Turn left and go 1 mile to the Payette River, the northern boundary of the Montour WMRA.

Some areas in Montour are closed during spring for the protection of certain nesting species. For information, contact the U.S. Bureau of Reclamation (208-334-1060) or the Idaho Department of Fish and Game (208-327-7025).

KELLY ISLAND, MISSOULA, MONTANA

Great Horned Owls, the "hunters of the night," nest in the cottonwood bottoms of Kelly Island. Search for their large, bulky nests. For directions and additional information, see Chapter 3.

Burrowing Owl

DESCRIPTION – Brownish; spotted with barring; white eyebrows; rounded head; long legs.

SCIENTIFIC NAME – *Athene cunicularia*

FAMILY – Owls (Strigidae)

NESTING BEGINS – Mid-May to mid-June

INCUBATION – 21 to 28 days; 6 to 11 eggs (usually 7 to 9)

TIME TO FLEDGE – 28 days

The Burrowing Owl is the small, long-legged owl of the prairies and open spaces. It is often observed in the plains, sitting on the side of a prairie-dog burrow or atop a fence post.

Owls are present from mid-March until early November. Nesting activity usually begins sometime in mid-May and continues until the third week in June.

The female lays seven to nine, glossy white eggs, usually in an abandoned prairie-dog burrow. Ground-squirrel burrows are sometimes enlarged, or a new burrow is excavated. The male often returns to the same burrow in succeeding years.

The female remains mostly inside the burrow during the three-week incubation period. During this time and for a month after the young are born, the male brings her food. The family often moves to a new burrow two or three weeks after the young owlets emerge from the old burrow. The adults and their young will remain together into the month of September.

Food consists mainly of insects and small rodents. The owls hunt day or night. An active nesting burrow is identified by the presence of regurgitated pellets.

PHOTOGRAPHIC TECHNIQUES

Like the varying personalities of people, individual personalities often are very different in other species. This fact has been brought home time and again while photographing Burrowing Owls. Certain individuals have allowed me to crawl within 10 feet on my hands and knees, and have exhibited complete indifference to my presence. Others have bolted the moment I stopped my car.

Respect these diverse personalities. Do not pressure Burrowing Owls that are skittish. Find another subject.

These small owls are most easily photographed during the nesting phase, while rearing their young.

If a blind is necessary, approach it with a partner. After you're in the blind and have set up your equipment, your assistant can leave. This may fool the birds into thinking you have left the blind. Do not approach the blind if the owls are visible at their nest site.

I recommend a 500 mm or 600 mm telephoto lens, which will allow a comfortable working distance from your subject.

TIME OF YEAR

Burrowing Owls nest throughout most of the region between mid-May and mid-June, and can be photographed during this time. Young owlets are highly photogenic. They can be photographed after emerging from their nest burrow, extending the period of photography into mid-July.

PHOTOGRAPHIC HOT SPOTS

BOSQUE DEL APACHE NATIONAL WILDLIFE REFUGE, NEW MEXICO

Burrowing Owls are not common here as they once were. Since prairie dogs have been extirpated from the area, Burrowing Owl populations have declined. However, they still nest in the refuge.

CAUTION: The refuge is home to the western diamondback rattlesnake. Watch where you place your feet.

For directions and additional information, see Chapter 3.

MAXWELL NATIONAL WILDLIFE REFUGE, NEW MEXICO

Burrowing Owls nest in burrows excavated by prairie dogs. Seven miles of road provide easy access to the refuge's prairie dog towns. Stop at refuge headquarters to get acquainted, and inform the staff of your intentions. For directions and additional information, see Chapter 3.

PAWNEE NATIONAL GRASSLANDS, COLORADO

The Pawnee National Grasslands were formed from land bought by the federal government from bankrupt farmers during the dust-bowl days of the 1930s. It is administered by the U.S. Forest Service today, and close to 30 percent of the area is owned by the federal government.

In the grasslands, prairie-dog or ground-squirrel burrows are favored nesting sites for burrowing owls. Search areas inhabited by these small rodents for nesting owls.

One such location can be reached by traveling west from Fort Collins for 36.5 miles along State Highway 14. Just before Briggsdale, turn left on Road 77. Go 3 miles, then turn left on Road 96. After 4 miles, turn right onto Road 69. After continuing approximately 3.5 miles, look for a windmill on your right. Burrowing owls nest in the prairie-dog town 200 yards east of the windmill.

For additional information, contact the U.S. Forest Service (303-353-5004) or the Colorado Division of Wildlife (970-484-2836).

SEEDSKADEE NATIONAL WILDLIFE REFUGE, WYOMING

While not common, Burrowing Owls regularly nest in the refuge. However, their populations have decreased dramatically. Fortunately, many people are working to protect these small owls. Following protective guidelines, refuge personnel may, on a case-by-case basis, allow individuals to photograph the owls. If they're convinced you know what you're doing, they are more likely to be of assistance.

For directions and additional information, see Chapter 3.

BENTON LAKE NATIONAL WILDLIFE REFUGE, MONTANA

Almost 200 species of birds find their way into the refuge, including the Burrowing Owl. These small owls are often seen perched atop an abandoned ground-squirrel burrow or badger den.

For directions and additional information, see Chapter 3.

EASTLICK POND, BIG LAKE WATERFOWL MANAGEMENT AREA, MONTANA

Across the dirt road from Eastlick Pond, known locally as Corral Pond, is a black-tailed prairie-dog town. Burrowing Owls consistently nest here. There are no guarantees in life, especially when it comes to photographing wildlife. However, this location is about as dependable as it gets for photographing Burrowing Owls.

From Billings, drive west along Rimrock Road. After connecting with State

Highway 302, continue west to the town of Molt. Just before reaching Molt; turn left onto Eastlick Road. Go 2 miles, then turn right on Lakeview Road. Go 100 yards and stop. The prairie-dog town is situated west of the road. Another prairie-dog town is on the east side of the road, near the top of the hill.

For additional information contact the Montana Department of Fish, Wildlife and Parks (406-252-4654).

UL BEND NATIONAL WILDLIFE REFUGE, MONTANA

How do you classify UL Bend? As blue-ribbon real estate for Burrowing Owls! A little windy, perhaps, but the far-reaching prairie grasslands and vast prairie-dog towns of the refuge are the ideal home for these small owls.

So, where do you find the owls? The best location is the prairie-dog town in the Hawley Flat area, near Road 319. A refuge map is essential. Obtain one before you go by contacting U.S. Fish & Wildlife offices in Fort Peck, Jordan, or Lewiston.

CAUTION: Prairie rattlesnakes inhabit this portion of Montana. Watch where you step.

From the town of Malta, in northeast Montana, drive southwest 25 miles along U.S. 191. Turn left onto Dry Fork. Drive 15 miles, then connect with Road 212. Drive south 1.5 miles. Turn left and follow Road 201 south to the UL Bend section of Fort Peck Reservoir.

Do not visit this refuge when roads are wet. A four-wheel-drive vehicle is highly recommended. For road conditions and other information, contact UL Bend National Wildlife Refuge (406-538-8706).

LAKE NEWELL, ALBERTA

Burrowing Owls are found in the grasslands surrounding Lake Newell. To reach the lake and Kinbrook Island Provincial Park, go east from Calgary along the Trans Canada Highway for 182 kilometers (109 miles). At the town of Brooks, turn right onto Highway 873. Go 30 kilometers (18 miles), following the signs to Kinbrook Island Provincial Park.

For additional information, contact Kinbrook Island Provincial Park (403-362-2962), or the Alberta Fish and Wildlife Division in Lethbridge (403-381-5281).

Broad-tailed Hummingbird

DESCRIPTION – Male: metallic green above; whitish below; red gorget

Female: speckled throat instead of red gorget

SCIENTIFIC NAME – *Selasphorus platycercus*

FAMILY – Hummingbirds (Trochilidae)

NESTING BEGINS – Early June to mid-July

INCUBATION – 14 to 17 days; 2 eggs

TIME TO FLEDGE – 21 to 26 days

With its brilliant metallic green crown and iridescent, magenta gorget, the Broad-tailed Hummingbird is aptly known as the "Crown Jewel of the Rockies."

During winter, broad-tails find food and stay warm in the highlands of Mexico and as far south as Guatemala. But come spring, they're casting their spell in the Rocky Mountains, from New Mexico to southern Montana.

Typical breeding habitat is willow thickets and open forests along mountain streams. Broad-tails are probably most numerous between 6,000 feet and 8,500 feet. In late summer, after nesting, they are often observed flitting about the flower-strewn slopes of alpine meadows.

A characteristic nest location is a low, horizontal tree branch, shielded by an overhead limb, and, in many cases, overhanging a mountain stream. The cup-shaped nest, built by the female, consists of plant fibers, moss, and lichens. Into it the female deposits two white eggs, no bigger than the tip of your little finger. It's hard to imagine a young bird developing in anything so tiny. Yet, three weeks after hatching the young are full-sized, flying hummers.

It is not uncommon for the female to return year after year to the same area for nesting.

The loud, trilling whistle produced by the male broad-tail as he flies is the result of air rushing past his outermost primary feathers, causing them to vibrate. The female produces a low-pitched buzzing when she flies. To hear her, one must be quite close.

PHOTOGRAPHIC TECHNIQUES

Hummingbirds nests, being very small and well camouflaged, are often difficult to locate. The low-pitched buzzing sound produced by the female when she is flushed from her nest often will disclose the general nesting area. Although some nests can be quite high, most tend to be seven feet or less above the ground. Nests often appear to be nothing more than a swollen area on the limb. If a stream is nearby, search the overhanging limbs. There will almost always be a protective branch a foot or less above the nest.

Once you've located a nest, the photography part is easy. Hummingbirds are incredibly tolerant of humans. A 200 mm lens is usually sufficient. I recommend the use of fill-flash to lighten up the shadows.

A point to remember: In all likelihood, the female will select a nest site in the same general area several years in a row.

Male broad-tails are highly territorial. For establishing and protecting their territory against intruders, they will select several vantage points as lookouts. These favorite perches are used over and over. Focus on one of these perches and wait. Sooner or later — usually sooner — you'll be taking pictures of your subject. You'll need a 500 mm or 600 mm telephoto, and a fill-flash is helpful for bringing out the iridescent colors.

To photograph feeding hummers, the first order of business is establishing a feeding station. Position several hummingbird feeders in the area. Use a mixture of one part sugar to four parts water, by volume. Bring the water to a boil, then stir in the sugar. Cool to room temperature before feeding the hummers. Do not use red coloring. It is harmful to the birds, and is not necessary. Once the feeding station is visited regularly, it's time to proceed to the next step.

For this you need the following: blooming plants, two flash units, a suitable backdrop, a mixture of sugar water (prepared as above), and your camera mounted with a 500 mm or 600 mm lens. (I use my 200-400 mm f4, with a 1.4X teleconverter; this combination provides 560 mm.) One flash unit should be linked to your camera via a PC cord, and the other triggered by a slave unit.

To support my backdrop, I've made a frame from half-inch PVC pipe. For the backdrop, I use three different colors of cloth: sky blue, forest green, and medium brown.

Set up the back drop and place the flowers several feet in front of it. If they're placed too close, shadows will show. Place one of the flash units on each side of the flower arrangement. Set up your camera and prefocus on the flowers. Next, remove the hummingbird feeders. After all the commotion has settled down, the hummingbirds will return in search of their feeders. Not finding them, they will go to the flowers. This is the opportunity you've been waiting for. With certain flowers, I have found it necessary to place sugar water in them to keep the hummers coming back.

I almost forgot! I also employ a comfortable lawn chair and sometimes a thermos of hot coffee or a cold beer — depending on the weather, of course. One time, I had a bag of peanuts, and, not being the stingy type, I shared them with "Charlie," one of our resident red squirrels. Nothing like having the comforts of home.

TIME OF YEAR

Broad-tails find their way into the southern portions of the region sometime in April. Several weeks may follow before they finally reach southern Montana.

In Colorado, nesting activity usually begins in early June and continues through late July. In New Mexico, it may begin as early as mid-May. However, in Wyoming, nest building is delayed until the middle of June.

It is usually mid-September before hummers leave southern Montana and Wyoming on their return trip to Latin America.

PHOTOGRAPHIC HOT SPOTS

PECOS RIVER CANYON, SANTA FE NATIONAL FOREST, NEW MEXICO

Cold mountain streams and aromatic evergreen forests — that pretty well describes the Pecos River Canyon.

The Pecos River headwaters flow down the canyon, alongside New Mexico Highway 63. The community of Pecos is near the base of the canyon. Find a location along the river that suits your fancy, and set up camp. Hang your hummingbird feeder. As soon as the hummers locate it, you're in business. Now that's what I call the easy life!

To reach Pecos from Santa Fe, go east on Interstate 25. Turn left 2 miles east of the Glorietta exit, and go 7 miles to Pecos. From Pecos, follow State Road 63 into the Santa Fe National Forest. It's about 12 miles to Terrero, which is a pretty good area for camping and photographing hummingbirds.

For more information, contact the Santa Fe National Forest (505-988-6940).

GOLDEN GATE CANYON STATE PARK, COLORADO

Mountain meadows, aspen groves, and pine-covered hills greet visitors to Golden Gate Canyon State Park. Panorama Point provides vistas of the Continental Divide, including Mount Evans, Longs Peak, and the Indian Peaks Wilderness Area.

Hummingbirds can be attracted to your camp site. Set up your hummingbird feeders and photography equipment next to your tent or camper. I recommend the Aspen Meadows Campground or the Rifleman Phillips Group Campground.

The park is 16 miles northwest of Golden. To reach the park, drive west along State Highway 46 from its intersection with State Highway 93, 2 miles north of Golden. Follow the signs to the Visitor Center.

For more information, contact the Golden Gate State Park (303-592-1502).

GRIZZLY CREEK CAMPGROUND, ROUTT NATIONAL FOREST, COLORADO

Beaver ponds and lakes, surrounded by evergreen forests, characterize the Grizzly Creek Campground area. Broad-tailed Hummingbirds are everywhere. Set up camp. Then, set up your hummingbird feeders and equipment nearby, and get ready for action.

From the community of Hebron, approximately 13 miles southwest of Walden along State Highway 14, travel southwest along Road 24 for 11 miles to the campground. For additional information, contact the U.S. Forest Service (970-723-8204).

ROCKPORT STATE PARK, UTAH

Rockport State Park, in north-central Utah, is comprised of juniper woodlands and marshes along the shore of Rockport Reservoir.

Broad-tailed Hummingbirds are common spring and summer residents. Place your feeders in the riparian area near the reservoir, and wait for the hummers to arrive. Like the monkey said when the train ran over his tail, "It won't be long now."

From Wanship, 26 miles east of Salt Lake City on Interstate 80, drive south along U.S. 189 for 6 miles. Turn left into the park.

For additional information, contact the Utah Division of Parks and Recreation (801-336-2241).

Red-naped Sapsucker

DESCRIPTION — Red crown; red nape patch; black and white barring on back.

SCIENTIFIC NAME — *Sphyrapicus nuchalis*

FAMILY — Woodpeckers (Picidae)

NESTING BEGINS — Mid-May to late June

INCUBATION — 12 or 13 days; 3 to 7 eggs (usually 4 or 5)

TIME TO FLEDGE — 25 to 29 days

"Chief caretaker — physician and surgeon — of the tree world." These are the honors bestowed on the woodpecker by Enos Mills in his book *The Spell of the Rockies*. The Red-naped Sapsucker lives up to these words, and then some.

The Red-naped Sapsucker is a fine physician, surgically removing insects harmful to trees. He is also truly chief caretaker of the woods, providing nesting cavities for many species unable to excavate their own, to say nothing of the sapsucker wells that benefit many squirrels, hummingbirds, and warblers. These wells, or small holes, are drilled by the sapsucker and eventually fill with sap and attract many insects. The sapsucker and other species then feed on the insects and drink the sap itself.

For the Red-naped Sapsucker, home is where the aspens are. Although one may nest occasionally "on the wrong side of the tracks" in an evergreen tree, they prefer aspen glades.

In Rocky Mountain National Park, nest excavation usually begins in mid-May. In New Mexico, it often starts several weeks earlier. And, in Alberta and British Columbia nesting activities are often delayed until early June.

Females invariably return to the same nesting area year after year, although not necessarily to the same cavity. Both male and female are actively involved with nest excavation, incubation, and rearing the young.

During courtship, the female signals with a steady drumming roll on a tree trunk, punctuated at intervals by loud drum beats. The male responds by drumming. This activity continues throughout the courtship period.

PHOTOGRAPHIC TECHNIQUES

Red-naped Sapsuckers are easily photographed at the entrance to their nest, bringing food to their offspring.

Sapsucker nests are easy to locate. After finding a mature aspen grove, search individual trees for cavities. Once you've located a potential nest site, listen for the "wheezy" cries of young sapsuckers, coming from within the tree as they beg for food. If incubation is still in progress, all will be quiet. Keep searching until you locate nestlings.

Should you happen upon a cavity where you suspect incubation is in progress, retreat to an inconspicuous area and watch for any activity that would confirm your suspicions. Return to this cavity when you believe the young have hatched, taking into consideration the incubation interval of 12 to 13 days.

Another clue to the presence of sapsuckers are parallel rows of holes drilled in aspen trees.

A blind is unnecessary for photographing Red-naped Sapsuckers. All that's needed is a 500 mm lens to provide a comfortable working distance. Find an unobtrusive location and wait for the activity to begin.

TIME OF YEAR

In Rocky Mountain National Park, nesting usually begins during mid-May and continues until early June. Allow 12 or 13 days for incubation. In Montana, nestlings have been reported from late June until mid-July.

As a general rule, June and July are the best months throughout the region for photographing Red-naped Sapsuckers.

PHOTOGRAPHIC HOT SPOTS

ROCKY MOUNTAIN NATIONAL PARK, COLORADO

Red-naped Sapsuckers are typically found in mature aspen groves. My favorite location is a small grove in Endovalley. Driving west from Horseshoe Park, turn right onto Fall River Road. On your right you will see a parking area. As you stand in the parking lot and face south, you will notice an aspen grove across the road and slightly to your right. Several species of cavity nesters, including the Red-naped Sapsucker, raise their young in these trees.

For directions and additional information, see Chapter 3.

TELEPHONE TRAIL, UNCOMPAHGRE NATIONAL FOREST, COLORADO

The Telephone Trail wanders through many stands of old-growth aspens and ponderosas. The area is known for its abundance of cavity-nesting birds, including Red-naped Sapsuckers.

From the Carson Hole picnic area, follow the 3-mile trail southwest along La Fair Creek, searching mature aspens for the presence of cavities.

This area can be reached from Grand Junction by going south along U.S. 50. Turn right at Whitewater, following State Highway 141 to Forest Road 402, a distance of 15 miles. Turn left and go 10 miles to the Carson Hole picnic area and Telephone Trail Trailhead.

For additional information, see Chapter 3.

KOOTENAI NATIONAL WILDLIFE REFUGE, IDAHO

Red-naped Sapsuckers nest in aspen groves near the base of the Selkirks, along the refuge's western boundary. For directions and additional information, see Chapter 3.

GLACIER NATIONAL PARK, MONTANA

Red-naped Sapsuckers can be photographed along the Red Eagle Trail. This 7-mile hike meanders through grasslands, deciduous woodlands, and verdant evergreen forests on its way to Red Eagle Lake. You should be able to locate sapsuckers without hiking the entire trail. Search the aspen groves, and don't overlook the mature cottonwoods, some of which attract cavity-nesting birds.

The Red Eagle Trail begins at the ranger station near the east end of St. Mary Lake.

For complete directions and additional information, see Chapter 3.

RED ROCK LAKES NATIONAL WILDLIFE REFUGE, MONTANA

Red-naped Sapsuckers can be photographed in many of the refuge's aspen groves. The Upper Lake Campground should provide plenty of photo opportunities. Also, check out the isolated aspen grove 2 miles west of Lakeview, along Red Rock Pass Road.

For directions, road closures, and additional information, see Chapter 3.

WATERTON LAKES NATIONAL PARK, ALBERTA

Red-naped Sapsuckers nest in the aspen groves located near the Bertha Trailhead, adjacent to the Townsite Campground. This is near the southern edge of Waterton Townsite.

For additional information, see Chapter 3.

Barn Swallow

DESCRIPTION — Iridescent, bluish black upper parts; buff-cinnamon underparts; long, deeply forked tail.

SCIENTIFIC NAME — *Hirundo rustica*

FAMILY — Swallows (Hirundinidae)

NESTING BEGINS — Mid-May to mid-July

INCUBATION — 13 to 17 days; 4 to 7 eggs (usually 4 or 5)

TIME TO FLEDGE — 18 to 23 days

Barn Swallows, known for their acrobatic flight, are found virtually worldwide. North American populations winter from Panama and Puerto Rico all the way to the southern tip of South America.

The Barn Swallow, dressed in its dazzling, iridescent blue cape and cinnamon vest, is the only swallow on the continent to sport a deeply forked tail.

Barn Swallows have become closely associated with humans, all but abandoning their natural nesting locations in favor of barns, culverts, and bridge structures — even the front porches of suburban homes.

The swallow's cup-shaped nest is assembled from mud pellets, scooped up by both male and female, mixed with plant fragments. It is usually found stuck against a vertical wall or ledge. Construction time for a new nest is one to two weeks. However, old nests are often refurbished. A nest may be solitary or built among other nests to form a colony.

Four or five white eggs, marked with reddish brown splotches, are laid around the middle of May. Nesting usually continues through mid-July, and appears to be somewhat uniform throughout the range. Both male and female share incubation duties, as well tending the young.

Food primarily consists of insects, with an occasional berry thrown in for dessert.

During the first day or two after the young swallows hatch, the parents eat the fecal sac of their young. Then, for a while, the parents carry the sacs off. After about the 12th day, the young swallows become "house broken;" they back up to the edge of their nest, and ... just be careful where you walk!

PHOTOGRAPHIC TECHNIQUES

Photographing Barn Swallows is easiest at the nest. They will readily accept your presence. In a crowded situation, I once used a 135 mm lens and obtained frame-filling images.

Obviously, the first order of the day is to locate a nest. The eaves of old buildings and the undersides of bridges are likely places to look. Many park visitor centers boast Barn Swallow nests under the eaves of their overhanging roofs.

During nest-building, it is fun to watch swallows dive to the edge of a lake or stream and scoop up a mouthful of mud. Swallows constantly flying back and forth to the same location provide a major clue that a nest is under construction. Follow them as they carry their load to the construction site. After their eggs have hatched, the parents spend hours catching insects for their young, and occasionally resting on telephone lines. The nest and their young will not be far away.

Once you've located a nest, the rest is easy. You'll need a medium-sized step ladder to position your camera slightly above the nest. A fill-flash will fill in the shadows and bring out the color of your subjects. For a lens, I find my 80-200 mm, f2.8, autofocus to be ideal.

Your best images will come after the young have hatched. You also place less stress on the adults at this time.

TIME OF YEAR

June and July are the best months for photographing Barn Swallows and their young. Nesting typically begins in mid-May. Allow two weeks for the eggs to hatch.

PHOTOGRAPHIC HOT SPOTS

BOSQUE DEL APACHE NATIONAL WILDLIFE REFUGE, NEW MEXICO

The Barn Swallow is a common sight in many parts of the refuge. I recommend searching for nests around refuge structures. For directions and additional information, see Chapter 3.

Golden Gate Canyon State Park, Colorado

Mountain meadows, aspen groves, and pine-covered hills greet visitors to Golden Gate Canyon State Park. Panorama Point provides vistas of the Continental Divide, including Mount Evans, Longs Peak, and the Indian Peaks Wilderness Area.

Barn Swallows attach their mud nests to a number of structures in the park. One location you'll definitely want to investigate is the park maintenance building near Kriley Pond. Don't overlook nests under the eaves of restroom facilities.

The park is 16 miles northwest of Golden. To reach the park, drive west along State Highway 46 from its intersection with State Highway 93, 2 miles north of Golden. Follow the signs to the visitor center.

For more information, contact the Golden Gate State Park (303-592-1502).

Seedskadee National Wildlife Refuge, Wyoming

Barn Swallows are familiar sights around the refuge during the summer. You should have no problems photographing them among the refuge buildings, where they attach their nests to almost any suitable structure. For directions and additional information, see Chapter 3.

Red Rock Lakes National Wildlife Refuge, Idaho

Barn Swallows are common inhabitants of the refuge, attaching their mud nests to any suitable structure. Explore the community of Lakeview, searching likely places for nest sites. Interpretive displays and restroom facilities throughout the refuge should also be investigated for nesting activity.

For directions, road closures, and additional information, see Chapter 3.

Benton Lake National Wildlife Refuge, Montana

The refuge is host to almost 200 species of birds, including the Barn Swallow. Barn Swallows may be photographed feeding their young in nests attached to light fixtures beneath the roof of refuge headquarters. For directions and additional information, see Chapter 3.

Tree Swallow

DESCRIPTION — Iridescent blue-black upper parts; white underparts.

SCIENTIFIC NAME — *Tachycineta bicolor*

FAMILY — Swallows (Hirundinidae)

NESTING BEGINS — May and June

INCUBATION — 13 days; 4 to 6 eggs

TIME TO FLEDGE — 16 to 24 days (usually 20)

Tree Swallows, the Olympic ice skaters of the skies, thrill the crowds as they wheel, turn, and gracefully pirouette in pursuit of airborne insects. Wintering along the Gulf Coast and southward into Central America, Tree Swallows are the first of the swallows to reappear in the Rockies in the springtime.

Tree Swallows are frequently found along woodland edges; they appear to be especially fond of aspen groves, because of the abundance of nesting cavities. Nearby water is a bonus. This species is noticeably absent in treeless areas.

The nest site is prepared by both the female and the male, often in an abandoned woodpecker cavity or unoccupied bluebird house. May and June are peak nesting months. Nest building for Tree Swallows is a slow process, occasionally taking up to a month to complete; two or three weeks would be more typical.

The four to six white eggs are guarded by the male while the female is feeding. She waits for him to appear before leaving her nest. As soon as she departs, he enters the nest and sticks his head out of the entrance while he waits for her return.

Strangely, Tree Swallows sometimes abandon their nesting area briefly. One day a dozen or so swallows may be present, and the next day none. They have been known to disappear for three or four days. Where they go, no one knows. It has happened during courtship, egg-laying, and incubation without any detrimental effects. The incubation period is extended, but that is all.

PHOTOGRAPHIC TECHNIQUES

Tree Swallows are easiest to photograph during their nesting phase. During this time, the male can often be seen perching on a limb near the nest cavity. Both parents spend a great deal of time bringing food to their offspring, providing many opportunities to photograph one of the adults perched at the nest entrance, waiting to go inside.

Until the young are a week or so old, the adults spend very little time outside the nest entrance. Instead, they arrive at the nest with food for their offspring and go immediately inside. After feeding the young, they momentarily stick their head out, but the next thing you know they're gone.

As the offspring approach fledgling size, they tend to meet their parents at the entrance. This allows the parents to feed the young without going inside, giving you more time to trip the shutter.

Locating Tree Swallow nests is simply a matter of searching aspen groves during nesting season. Swallows flying about or perched in nearby trees are dead giveaways of nesting activity. Find a comfortable place to sit down where you can observe the swallows' activity. A blind is not necessary. Within a few minutes, you will know which cavities are active. Set up your equipment and begin shooting.

Be sure to check out any bluebird nest boxes. Tree Swallows use them as much, if not more, than bluebirds.

As with most bird photography, I recommend a 500 mm or 600 mm telephoto lens.

TIME OF YEAR

May through July is the time to photograph nesting Tree Swallows throughout the region.

PHOTOGRAPHIC HOT SPOTS

ROCKY MOUNTAIN NATIONAL PARK, COLORADO

Tree Swallows are typically found in mature aspen groves. My favorite location is a small aspen grove in Endovalley. Driving west from Horseshoe Park, turn right onto Fall River Road. On your right you will see a parking area. As you stand in the parking lot and face south, you will notice an aspen grove across the road and slightly to your right. Several species of cavity nesters, including the Tree Swallow, raise their young in these trees.

For additional directions and information, see Chapter 3.

MANTI-LA SAL NATIONAL FOREST, UTAH

The La Sal Loop, a portion of which negotiates the Manti-La Sal National Forest, traverses desert scrub, juniper, aspen, riparian, and mountain habitats. Tree Swallows nest in many of the aspen groves of the national forest. I recommend working the groves surrounding Warner Lake Campground.

For directions and additional information, see Chapter 3.

YELLOWSTONE NATIONAL PARK, WYOMING

Tree Swallows can be photographed at many locations throughout the park. The aspen stands along Blacktail Plateau Drive, approximately halfway between Mammoth and Tower Junction, are accessible and should provide outstanding photo opportunities.

For directions and additional information, see Chapter 3.

KOOTENAI NATIONAL WILDLIFE REFUGE, IDAHO

Situated in the Idaho panhandle only 20 miles from Canada, this refuge is bounded by the Kootenai River on the east and the Selkirk Mountains on the west. Look for Tree Swallows nesting in aspen groves at the base of the Selkirks.

For directions and additional information, see Chapter 3.

GLACIER NATIONAL PARK, MONTANA

Tree Swallows can be photographed along the Red Eagle Trail. The trail meanders through grasslands, aspen groves, cottonwoods, and verdant evergreen forests on its way to Red Eagle Lake, a 7-mile hike. Search the aspen groves, and don't overlook the cottonwoods, some of which attract cavity-nesting birds. There should be numerous photo opportunities long before you reach the lake.

The Red Eagle Trail begins at the ranger station along the east end of St. Mary Lake. For additional directions and information, see Chapter 3.

WATERTON LAKES NATIONAL PARK, ALBERTA

Look for mature aspen groves with trees containing natural cavities or cavities made by woodpeckers. It is among such groves that you will find Tree Swallows. One such location is close to the Bertha Trailhead, on the south side of Waterton Townsite. For additional directions and information, see Chapter 3.

Clark's Nutcracker

DESCRIPTION—Gray body; black wings and tail.

SCIENTIFIC NAME—*Nucifrga columbiana*

FAMILY—Jays, Crows, Magpies (Corvidae)

NESTING BEGINS—Late February to late April

INCUBATION—16 to 18 days; 2 to 6 eggs (usually 2 to 4)

TIME TO FLEDGE—18 to 21 days

The Clark's Nutcracker, a member of the crow family, is common in high-elevation forests throughout the Rocky Mountains, from northern New Mexico all the way to central Alberta and British Columbia. They are well-known to visitors for their habit of begging handouts.

The name "nutcracker" comes from their method of opening pine nuts. The nut is held in place with one foot and cracked open with the beak. Pine nuts, along with fast-food handouts from people, comprise a major portion of their diet.

The Clark's Nutcracker begins laying eggs in late February, when the snow is still deep. Nests are typically located in conifer forests, often near treeline. Both males and females are actively involved in nest construction. By the end of April, nesting is normally complete.

Two to four pale-green eggs, with small, brownish specks, are typical. Incubation, taking approximately 17 days, and rearing of the young are accomplished by both parents.

The call of the Clark's Nutcracker is an unmistakable, raspy, crow-like khrr-a-a. They are often observed in flocks, moving from tree to tree with a gliding, undulating flight.

The Clark's Nutcracker is named after Captain William Clark, the well known member of the Lewis and Clark Expedition of 1803-1806, who is credited with its identification. It is truly amazing that this bird had never been observed by Native Americans living in the area before the expedition arrived. Perhaps Captain Clark would have missed out on a measure of fame and fortune had the bird been known as the Shoshone Nutcracker or the Chief Seattle Nutcracker.

PHOTOGRAPHIC TECHNIQUES

Look for Clark's Nutcrackers among picnic tables and at parking areas at higher elevations. They appear to have little fear of people and often beg for handouts. This makes for easy photography. Simply locate your subject and begin shooting.

A 135 mm telephoto lens is often sufficient. However, for all-around use you'll be better off with something in the 300 mm range.

TIME OF YEAR

The easiest way to photograph Clark's Nutcrackers is to concentrate on areas where they beg for handouts. Since national park visitation is at its highest between June and August, I would recommend these months.

Photographing nesting birds can be difficult, because it occurs at high elevations when deep snow is still on the ground. To reach a nesting area requires snowshoeing long distances and gaining several thousand feet in elevation.

PHOTOGRAPHIC HOT SPOTS

ROCKY MOUNTAIN NATIONAL PARK, COLORADO

I have two favorite locations for photographing the Clark's Nutcracker: Many Parks Curve and Farview Curve. Both overlooks are along Trail Ridge Road. Many Parks is on the east side of the Continental Divide, while Farview Curve is on the west. Nutcrackers, habituated to receiving handouts at these locations, are unafraid of people and easy to photograph.

For additional directions and information, see Chapter 3.

MIRROR LAKE NATURE TRAIL, WASATCH NATIONAL FOREST, UTAH

The Mirror Lake Nature Trail encircles scenic Mirror Lake, amid verdant evergreen forests in the heart of the Wasatch National Forest. You should have plenty of opportunities to photograph Clark's Nutcrackers around the campground, and along the interpretive nature trail surrounding the lake. This mountainous location, 10,200 feet above sea level, is normally open from June through September.

From the town of Kamas, drive east along State Highway 150 approximately 31 miles. Turn right at the Mirror Lake Campground sign. For additional information, contact the U.S. Forest Service (801-783-4338).

Yellowstone National Park, Wyoming

The Clark's Nutcracker is a familiar sight to visitors in many areas of the park. I particularly recommend two locations: the Grand Canyon of the Yellowstone and Mount Washburn.

Several overlooks at Canyon Village provide breathtaking views of the Grand Canyon of the Yellowstone. The area surrounding these overlooks will provide many photo opportunities.

Mount Washburn is approximately 5 miles north of Canyon Junction. Two different trails will take you to the summit. The first trail begins at Dunraven Pass. It is a 3.6-mile, moderately easy hike to the summit of Mount Washburn, with almost 1,400 feet in elevation gain. If you prefer, continue past Dunraven Pass another 4 miles until you see a road on the right and a sign proclaiming "Mt. Washburn." Don't get too excited. The road leads to the Chittenden parking area. From there, it is still a 3-mile hike to the summit.

If you're having a good day, you may not have to hike to the summit before seeing any nutcrackers. If so, and you get some nice images before completing this hike, you might also consider buying a lottery ticket the same day.

For additional directions and information, see Chapter 3.

Glacier National Park, Montana

The Clark's Nutcracker frequents scenic overlooks and picnic areas, scrounging handouts from park visitors. I recommend working the Fish Creek Picnic Area and Campground. This location should provide many photo opportunities. For additional directions and information, see Chapter 3.

Waterton Lakes National Park, Alberta

Clark's Nutcrackers can be photographed along the Goat Lake Trail. The trailhead is at Red Rock Canyon. To reach this area, go 3 kilometers (1.8 miles) northeast of Waterton Townsite to Red Rock Parkway. Turn left onto the parkway and go to the end. For additional directions and information, see Chapter 3.

Yoho National Park, British Columbia

Clark's Nutcrackers can be photographed in the Takakkaw Falls area. I recommend working both the campground and the picnic area. Due to snow conditions, the road is only open from mid-June to mid-October. To reach the falls from Field, go northeast along the Trans Canada Highway for 3 kilometers (1.8 miles). Turn left, following the signs to the falls. For additional information, see Chapter 3.

Common Raven

DESCRIPTION — Glossy black feathers; large bill with curved upper surface; shaggy neck feathering.

SCIENTIFIC NAME — *Corvus corax*

FAMILY — Jays, Crows, Magpies (Corvidae)

NESTING BEGINS — Mid-April to late June

INCUBATION — 18 to 21 days; 3 to 7 eggs (usually 4 to 6)

TIME TO FLEDGE — 38 to 44 days

According to the seafaring Tlingits of the Pacific Northwest, the Common Raven stole the sunlight from a rich man whose purpose was to keep everyone in darkness — thus, light was brought into the world.

Ravens are commonly associated with wilderness areas, preferring mountains and forests with nearby rocky cliffs for nesting. However, in the absence of rocky places they are very adaptable and may construct their nests in tall conifers. In Jackson Hole, Wyoming, for example, roughly 90 percent of all raven nests are in trees.

The male and female work together on nest construction. Three to five feet in diameter, the nest consists of a large mass of sticks and takes two to three weeks to complete. It is not uncommon for ravens to repair and reuse an old nest for several years. However, a pair usually has several nest sites and plays "musical chairs" among them.

Peak egg laying and nesting activity occurs during May. Four to six bluish green eggs, marked with brownish blotches, make up the typical clutch. The male feeds his mate while she incubates her eggs. Both parents actively care for their brownish, downy offspring. The pair stays together for life.

The Common Raven has a rather large vocal repertoire, including various animal imitations. The most common call is the low-pitched, guttural quork.

Often seen scavenging road-kills, ravens are both scavengers and predators. Their primary diet of carrion is supplemented with small vertebrates, insects, bird eggs, and nestlings.

Pair bonding is strong. Pairs stay together not only throughout the year, but for life.

PHOTOGRAPHIC TECHNIQUES

Raven nest photography is possible, providing, 1) you can locate an active nest, and 2) it is accessible for photography.

Network with birding groups, biologists, and other photographers. They can often speed the process of locating a nest. I recommend national forest land for photographing nesting ravens.

Ravens provide several clues that assist in locating nest sites. During breeding season, the pair performs flight displays in unison. They often touch wing-tips while soaring together over their chosen nest site. Only freshly broken sticks are used in nest construction. The birds invariably drop some of them when constructing their nest, and these remain on the ground under the nest site. The presence of freshly broken twigs in a nest identifies it as active.

Providing you have a good camera angle, it will probably be easier to photograph cliff-nesting ravens than trees nesters. Construct your blind 25 to 30 feet away, using dead limbs and sticks. A 500 mm or 600 mm lens will give you frame-filling images of these large Corvids.

In some of our national parks, ravens have been conditioned to begging for handouts from well-meaning but poorly informed visitors. These birds are unafraid of people and come quite close. As a photographer, you can take advantage of situations like these and, with very little effort, get some impressive images. Search the scenic overlooks, picnic areas, and campgrounds for these "junk-food junkies." The raven image illustrating this section was taken of just such a bird in Yellowstone National Park. To get this image, I used my 80-200 mm, f2.8, autofocus lens.

TIME OF YEAR

Courtship begins between late March and early April. Nest building follows a few weeks later, sometime in mid-April. With two to three weeks for nest construction, incubation of close to three weeks, plus another six weeks before the young ravens fledge, nest photography can be conducted at least until the end of July.

"Junk-food junkies" are best photographed from May through September, peak visitor times in our national parks.

PHOTOGRAPHIC HOT SPOTS

ROCKY MOUNTAIN NATIONAL PARK, COLORADO

The picnic area at Sprague Lake is one of the better locations in the park for photographing ravens. From the Beaver Meadows Entrance Station, take the first left turn. This is Bear Lake Road. Follow it until you see the entrance road into the Sprague Lake area on your left. Follow the signs. For additional information, see Chapter 3.

YELLOWSTONE NATIONAL PARK, WYOMING

Ravens are common throughout the park. Any of the picnic areas or overlooks should provide photo opportunities. The raven illustrating this piece was photographed at an overlook between Tower Junction and Tower Falls. If you hurry, you may be able to photograph the same bird — after all, ravens have a rather long life span.

For directions and additional information, see Chapter 3.

GLACIER NATIONAL PARK, MONTANA

Ravens are easy to photograph in picnic areas where they often receive handouts from park visitors. For directions and additional information, see Chapter 3.

BANFF NATIONAL PARK, ALBERTA

Picnic areas are great locations for photographing ravens — generally, the more people, the better your chances of obtaining images. For directions and additional information, see Chapter 3.

YOHO NATIONAL PARK, BRITISH COLUMBIA

Ravens are frequently observed throughout the park. Of particular note are two locations near the park's western boundary: the Hoodoo Creek Campground and the Wapta Falls Picnic Area. These spots are 4 to 6 kilometers (2.4 to 3.6 miles) east of the park's western boundary. For additional directions and information, see Chapter 3.

Mountain Bluebird

DESCRIPTION – Male: sky blue above; lighter below.
  Female: bluish gray

SCIENTIFIC NAME – *Sialia currucoides*

FAMILY – Thrushes (Muscicapidae)

NESTING BEGINS – Early May to late July

INCUBATION – 13 or 14 days; 4 to 8 eggs (usually 5 or 6)

TIME TO FLEDGE – 22 to 23 days

The Mountain Bluebird, a piece of sky that fell to earth, is one of nature's jewels. Nesting typically occurs above 5,000 feet in open woodlands. Aspen containing numerous cavities, especially aspen groves near water, are favored nesting sites. An old woodpecker nest, natural tree cavity, or bird box is selected for egg laying. Bluebirds raised in nest boxes tend to raise their young in similar houses. Once in a while, a hole in a earthen bank is chosen as a nest site.

Nest preparation is managed by both the male and the female. Egg laying begins in early May and continues through July in the northern portions of the region. The long nesting season is the result of two broods. The female will often leave the first brood in the care of the male, while she begins her second brood. Five or six glossy, pale blue eggs are customarily laid. Hatching occurs within two weeks. After three weeks, the young are able to fly and are on their own.

Mountain Bluebirds are particularly fond of insects, but occasionally indulge in a fruit dessert, especially in winter.

PHOTOGRAPHIC TECHNIQUES

It's easiest to photograph Mountain Bluebirds after the eggs have hatched and before the young have fledged. As soon as the young hatch, the male becomes actively involved with their feeding, repeatedly bringing food to the nest cavity. Adult bluebirds constantly visiting their nest, holding insects in their beaks, are sure signs the eggs have hatched. During this time, the birds accept the presence of a considerate photographer, and a blind is not necessary. Moreover, less stress is placed on the adults when photography is conducted after their eggs have hatched.

When photographing bluebirds at a nest box, place a natural-looking limb in an upright position near the nest. The birds will frequently land on this prop before entering the nest.

You will find a 500 mm or 600 mm telephoto lens helpful when photographing the Mountain Bluebird.

TIME OF YEAR

The first clutch can usually be photographed from mid-May through the first week of June. Add one to two weeks for birds in Alberta and British Columbia. Birds rearing second clutches can be photographed through the month of July.

PHOTOGRAPHIC HOT SPOTS

ROCKY MOUNTAIN NATIONAL PARK, COLORADO

Mountain Bluebirds often nest in mature aspen groves. My favorite location is a small aspen grove in Endovalley. Driving west through Horseshoe Park, turn right onto Fall River Road. On your right you will see a parking area. As you stand in the parking lot and face south, you will notice an aspen grove across the road and slightly to your right. Several species of cavity nesters, including the Mountain Bluebird, raise their young in these trees.

For directions and additional information, see Chapter 3.

SEEDSKADEE NATIONAL WILDLIFE REFUGE, WYOMING

Mountain Bluebirds are easily photographed as they come and go from the many nest boxes fastened to fence posts along the tour route, close to refuge headquarters. For directions and additional information, see Chapter 3.

CORRAL CREEK, CHALLIS NATIONAL FOREST, IDAHO

Corral Creek, in the upper reaches of Idaho's scenic Pioneer Mountains, is home to a range of birds and mammals. In the town of Ketchum, turn northeast from U.S. 75 onto Forest Road 408, known as Trail Creek Road. Follow the road 5 miles to Corral Creek Road. Follow the bluebird nest box trail located along Corral Creek Road. Mountain Bluebirds raise their young in nest boxes lining Corral Creek.

For additional information, contact the U.S. Forest Service (208-622-5371), or visit the Sawtooth National Recreation Area Visitor Center and Headquarters, 7 miles north of Ketchum along Highway 75.

RED ROCK LAKES NATIONAL WILDLIFE REFUGE, MONTANA

Mountain Bluebirds are frequently observed along Red Rock Pass Road, between the community of Lakeview and Shambo Pond. Two miles east of Upper Lake Campground, look for a willow bog along the north side of Red Rock Pass Road. A few miles east of the bog, the road makes a 90-degree turn to the north. Bluebirds are common between the bog and the 90-degree turn.

A number of bluebird houses have been placed on fence posts and trees in the refuge. All of these will supply you with many photo opportunities. Don't overlook the aspen groves. Natural tree cavities or those produced by woodpeckers are frequently used as nest sites.

For directions, road closures and additional information, see Chapter 3.

Mountain Bluebird

Common Yellowthroat

DESCRIPTION — Black mask, yellow throat and breast, olive gray upperparts

SCIENTIFIC NAME — *Geothlypis trichas*

FAMILY — Warblers, Sparrows (Emberizidae)

NESTING BEGINS — Late May to late June

INCUBATION — 12 days; 3 to 6 eggs (usually 3 to 5)

TIME TO FLEDGE — 10 days

The Common Yellowthroat, masked songster of the cattails, sings its cheery melody for all who will listen. Wintering as far south as Panama, male yellowthroats arrive in the Rockies a week or so ahead of the females and immediately establish their territory, singing while they work.

As soon as the females arrive, all singing stops. She fabricates her nest of grasses, leaves, and strips of bark into a bulky cup, while the male shadows her work. Once the project is finished, the male ceases following her around and resumes his singing.

In Colorado, males begin arriving in May, although early arrivals have been observed in mid-April. In Montana and southern Alberta, weather delays their arrival about a month.

A typical nest site of the Common Yellowthroat — invariably near wet areas — is among willows along a stream or pond, or perhaps hidden in a cattail marsh. Seldom will it be more than three feet above the ground or water. Often it is mere inches off the ground.

The three to five creamy white eggs, marked with brownish splotches, take 12 days to hatch. Only the female incubates the eggs. However, both parents care for their nestlings. Still unable to fly, the young birds leave their nest when they are only seven or eight days old. They seek cover nearby until they are able to fly.

Although yellowthroats are sometimes difficult to see, their distinctive song immediately betrays their whereabouts. Their most common song is either a two-syllable whi-chi whi-chi whi-chi, or a three syllable whi-chi-te whi-chi-te whi-chi-te. The lyrics are often a combination of two and three syllable songs and vary from area to area, and sometimes even from bird to bird.

The Common Yellowthroat is among the most common warblers. Getting acquainted with and photographing this colorful, pint-sized avian representative will be time well spent.

PHOTOGRAPHIC TECHNIQUES

Photographing Common Yellowthroats during courtship and nesting is the only way to go.

Your first step is that all-important networking — talking with knowledgeable individuals, such as local birders, biologists, and park personnel. They can direct you to areas where populations of yellowthroats exist.

Once you are in the right area, the birds will provide clues to their location. Obviously, their song is an immediate give-away. After their presence has been established, you can set up your blind and call them to you. I use the Johnny Stewart Game Caller, which plays cassette tapes and has a remote-controlled speaker that can be operated with a small, portable transmitter. (See Appendix I.)

I have used tapes of both a yellowthroat call and a screech owl call. I've had more success using the owl call. In fact, the bird in the image illustrating this piece was called using a screech owl call.

Another method is to "squeak" them into photographic range. Simply suck air through the space between your index and middle finger, close to where your fingers join your hand. A little practice is all it takes. Don't overdo it. A couple of squeaks — not too loud — every 10 or 15 seconds should do it.

CAUTION: Calling during the nesting phase can be harmful if the nest is left unprotected for long. Do not keep the adults away from their nest for more than 10 minutes at a time. Wait at least 20 minutes between photo sessions when calling the adults away from their nest.

Photographing birds on the nest is your other option. As before, the male's singing will give you a general idea of where the nest is located. If you approach the female too closely while she is building the nest, the male will repeatedly dive at her until she departs the vicinity of the nest. Likewise, if you get too close to the nest, the female will scold you with a sharp, repeated steeek.

Your next step is to locate the nest itself. Get down on your hands and knees, and systematically search the area. The nest will typically be within a foot of the ground, and almost never higher than three feet. The most likely place will be near water.

CAUTION: Wait until the young have hatched before making any images. This reduces stress on the adults.

As with most bird photography, a high-powered telephoto usually comes in handy. For this small, diminutive species, I recommend using one of the "bazookas" — at least a 600 mm lens, if not a 800 mm lense.

TIME OF YEAR

June is the month of peak activity — nest building, incubation, and rearing of nestlings — throughout most of the region.

Eggs have been observed in Colorado and Wyoming from June 9 until June 25. Active nesting in Montana has been reported from May 28 until June 29.

PHOTOGRAPHIC HOT SPOTS

BOSQUE DEL APACHE NATIONAL WILDLIFE REFUGE, NEW MEXICO

Bosque del Apache National Wildlife Refuge, embracing more than 57,000 acres of marshes, grasslands, and desert uplands, straddles the Rio Grande in the shadow of the Magdalena Mountains.

Work the willows near the marshes and along drainages. The songs of the Common Yellowthroat will direct you where to look.

For directions and additional information, see Chapter 3.

SEEDSKADEE NATIONAL WILDLIFE REFUGE, WYOMING

The yellowthroat is common throughout most of the refuge's wetlands. You will find them among the willows near the marshes and along the river. For directions and additional information, see Chapter 3.

CAMAS NATIONAL WILDLIFE REFUGE, IDAHO

The Common Yellowthroat nests among the willows near the shallow marshes. Investigate these areas, while listening for their distinctive song. For additional information, see Chapter 3.

KOOTENAI NATIONAL WILDLIFE REFUGE, IDAHO

With more than 800 acres of wetlands in the refuge, Common Yellowthroats have plenty of habitat to choose from. They are common throughout most wetland locations. One of the more convenient locations for photographing them is along the Island Pond Wild Trail.

For directions and additional information, see Chapter 3.

BENTON LAKE NATIONAL WILDLIFE REFUGE, MONTANA

Almost 200 species of birds find their way to the refuge, including the Common Yellowthroat. Yellowthroats can be photographed throughout most of the 5,000 acres of shallow marsh known as Benton Lake.

For directions and additional information, see Chapter 3.

RED ROCK LAKES NATIONAL WILDLIFE REFUGE, MONTANA

Common Yellowthroats can be photographed among the willows along the shore of Upper Red Rock Lake, near the campground. The willows near Wigeon and Culver Ponds, along Elk Lake Road, also host respectable yellowthroat populations. For road closures, directions, and additional information, see Chapter 3.

Spotted Towhee

DESCRIPTION – Male: black hood; white-spotted black back, cinnamon sides; white breast; red eyes; long tail
   Female: pale version of male

SCIENTIFIC NAME – *Pipilo maculatus*

FAMILY – Warblers, Sparrows (Emberizidae)

NESTING BEGINS – Mid-May to late July

INCUBATION – 12 to 13 days; 2 to 6 eggs (usually 3 or 4)

TIME TO FLEDGE – 10 to 12 days

The Spotted Towhee, the avian world's Mad Hatter, encourages all who listen to join him for tea, as he sings, drink-your teeeeee, drink-your teeeeee. In the Rockies, however, Towhees do not always sing the first two notes of this song; quite often, only the last teeeeee is pronounced. Likewise, the chewink alarm call of eastern birds becomes a cat-like meow, similar to that of the Gray Catbird, in the West.

Spotted Towhees were formerly considered to be a western subspecies of the Rufous-sided Tohee. In early 1996 they were reclassified as a separate species.

The towhee is found through a wide elevation range. In Colorado, for example, they can be observed from the plains at 4,000 feet to over 8,000 feet in the mountains. Population densities tend to be higher near the foothills. Forest undergrowth, riparian thickets, and brushy fields are typical breeding habitats. In the foothills, scrub-oak thickets and shrubby ravines are especially favored nesting locations.

During spring migration, the males are the first to appear. In Colorado, they begin arriving during early March from as far south as Guatemala. Peak migration in the state occurs during early May. The first birds do not reach Montana until sometime during the latter part of April.

The male establishes his territory soon after arrival. Within a few days, the female shows up. Courtship, mating, and egg-laying soon follow.

Nesting begins during mid-May in the south and mid-June in the north. In New Mexico, the first eggs are laid approximately May 15, and egg laying continues into July. Alberta has a much shorter nesting season, beginning during the second week in June and coming to a halt near the end of the month.

Nest location and construction are handled by the female. The well-hidden, cup-shaped nest is typically placed on the ground in a small depression scratched out by the female. It is generally located near the base of a wild rose, mountain mahogany, or scrub oak, and hidden beneath the plant's branches. The rim of the nest rests at ground level. Occasionally, the female will construct her nest slightly above ground in one of the plants mentioned above or in a brush pile or tangles of vines. In any case, the nest is hardly ever more than a few feet above the ground. Construction materials include grasses, dead leaves, and shredded bark.

The female lays three or four creamy-white eggs, speckled and spotted with brown markings. Young towhees hatch out in 12 or 13 days. At this time, the male begins frequenting the nest to bring food to his mate and their offspring. After a few days, these chores are shared by the female. The young birds may leave the nest a day or two before they learn to fly.

Two broods are often produced in the southern portions of the region. The same pair produces both broods, with the first egg of the second brood laid one to three weeks after the first brood has fledged. This second brood accounts for the longer nesting season in these areas.

PHOTOGRAPHIC TECHNIQUES

There are two basic options for obtaining Spotted Towhee images: photographing them at a bird feeder or at their nest site.

Bird-feeder photography requires less work, but does not always produce desirable results. The main problem is that, like most small passerines (perching birds), the Spotted Towhee does not stay still for very long. Simply put, they will not pose for you.

The best way to photograph this species at a feeder, as with most species, is to sit for a while and observe. Certain branches are frequently used for perching as the birds go to and from the feeder. Prefocus on one of these branches, and wait for your subject to arrive.

Your other option — nest photography — can produce wonderful results. The problem is locating a nest.

As always, networking is all-important. Inquire with visitor center personnel. If they can't supply the needed information, ask for referrals to someone who can help. Local birding groups can be very helpful, as well as university ornithologists, U.S. Fish & Wildlife biologists, and state wildlife biologists.

Go to the foothills during late spring and early summer, after the males have established their territory and before egg-laying begins. Search the ravines for wild roses, mountain mahogany, and other shrubs, and for scrub-oak thickets. Listen for the rustling of leaves in the underbrush as the towhees noisily forage, scratching with both feet. Listen for the songs of the male.

Search for the female, whose movements will lead you to her nest. If you get too close, and she feels danger is near, she will avoid going to the nest. Use binoculars to watch from a distance. Listen as she scolds — most likely the cat-like meow alarm call will be heard — when you get too close to her nest. Or, she may act injured if you get too close, a tactic used to lure predators away from her nest. In either case, the nest will be nearby.

Even after you have identified the general location of the nest, it blends well with its surrounding environment and can still be difficult to locate. Get down on your hands and knees, as if you were searching for the proverbial needle in a haystack.

During egg-laying and incubation, the male stays away from the nest and stops singing. Locating the nest during this period becomes more difficult. Once the eggs hatch, the male resumes his visits to the nest, bringing food to the young and his mate.

After the nest has been located, the rest is a piece of cake. Wait until the eggs have hatched before making pictures. This will reduce stress on the adults. Although the adults are quite approachable once their offspring have hatched, I still recommend using a blind to reduce stress on the new family.

A 400 mm telephoto lens is all you will need when photographing this colorful bird on its nest. However, I recommend a 500 mm or 600 mm lens for photographing near a bird feeder. Since heavy cover and low-light levels are often involved, I highly recommend the use of a fill-flash.

TIME OF YEAR

Many New Mexico birds are year-round residents, and nesting activity begins there in early May.

In Colorado, peak migration occurs in early May. Nesting follows two to three weeks thereafter.

In Alberta and British Columbia, early arrivals show up in early May, but most birds do not arrive until almost a month later, with peak nesting following in a couple of weeks.

Males begin establishing territories within a few days of arrival on their breeding grounds. The females arrive a few days later, and courtship begins in a day or so. After a two-week courtship, nesting begins.

A nest site is usually chosen approximately a week after the commencement of courtship. This is the time to begin your search for nests. In the warmer portions of the region, this usually takes place in mid- to late April. In the northern areas, pairing of the sexes typically begins in early June.

PHOTOGRAPHIC HOT SPOTS

BOSQUE DEL APACHE NATIONAL WILDLIFE REFUGE, NEW MEXICO

You will find the Spotted Towhee in most brushy areas of the refuge. They are very common. You might begin your search by hiking the Indian Well Trail, listening for the towhee's songs along the way.

For directions and additional information, see Chapter 3.

BEAR CREEK CANYON REGIONAL PARK, COLORADO

Gambel oak, mountain mahogany, and juniper blanket the hillsides, and cottonwoods mark the course of a creek through this county park in the foothills of the southern Rockies. A self-guided nature trail winds it way through the various habitats. A bird-feeding station along the trail, near the creek, attracts the Spotted Towhee, among other species. Set up your equipment at the feeding station and wait. Your patience will reward you.

You might want to take time to explore the interpretive exhibits and live-animal displays at the nature center.

To reach the park from Colorado Springs, take Exit 141 off Interstate Highway 25. Go west on U.S. 24 to 26th Street. Turn left, and follow the signs to the park. For additional information, contact El Paso County (719-520-6387).

LEWIS AND CLARK CAVERNS STATE PARK, MONTANA

This 2,700-acre state park, widely known for it spectacular limestone caverns, hosts a variety of songbirds. Several locations within the park should provide photo opportunities for the Spotted Towhee. Although you will pass several good areas along the 3-mile drive between the park entrance and the visitor center, I particularly recommend the picnic area and the nature trail.

Be sure to advise park personnel of your intentions. They can provide information that will save you much time and effort.

CAUTION: The park is home to a number of species of wildlife, including the prairie rattlesnake. Leave them alone and they will leave you alone. Besides, they were here first.

From the town of Three Forks, located along Interstate 90 in southwestern Montana, drive west along State Highway 2 for 19 miles to the park entrance. The park is open from May 1 until September 30. For additional information, contact the Montana Department of Fish, Wildlife and Parks (406-287-3541).

MEDICINE ROCK STATE PARK, MONTANA

In extreme eastern Montana lies Medicine Rock State Park — a land of open grasslands, ponderosa woodlands, sandstone buttes...and prairie rattlesnakes. Remember, if you don't bite them, they won't bite you!

The grasslands are host to a variety of songbirds, including the Spotted Towhee. The towhees inform visitors of their presence in the brushy fields with a cheery drink-your-teeeeee!

From the town of Baker, drive south along State Highway 7 for 25 miles to the state park. For additional information, contact the Montana Department of Fish, Wildlife and Parks (406-232-4365).

WRITING-ON-STONE PROVINCIAL PARK, ALBERTA

Sandstone, cottonwoods, and the picturesque Milk River mark one of Alberta's most fertile wildlife locations, Writing-On-Stone Provincial Park. The park, located 178 kilometers (107 miles) southeast of Lethbridge, has recorded up to 60 species of nesting birds, including the Spotted Towhee.

From Lethbridge, go southeast on Highway 4 to the town of Milk River. At Milk River, turn left (east) onto Highway 501 and travel 42 kilometers (25 miles). At this point, the roadway becomes gravel. Turn south and go 8 kilometers (4.8 miles), then east 2 kilometers (1.2 miles) to the park entrance.

The southern portions of the park are restricted, with access only by tour. For additional information, contact Provincial Park Service (403-647-2364), or the Alberta Fish and Wildlife Division in Foremost (403-867-3826).

Dark-eyed Junco

DESCRIPTION—Four subspecies are common in the Rocky Mountains:

Oregon: black hood; brown back, pinkish sides
Pink-sided: gray, brown back; pinkish sides
Gray-headed: gray, pinkish sides
White-winged: gray upper; two white wing bars
Winter: all white, red eye-comb and black bill and eyes are visible

SCIENTIFIC NAME—*Junco hyemalis*

FAMILY—Warblers, Sparrows (Emberizidae)

NESTING BEGINS—May to July

INCUBATION—12 or 13 days; 3 to 6 eggs (usually 3 to 5)

TIME TO FLEDGE—9 to 13 days

The Dark-eyed Junco, avian harbinger of winter snow and ice in the southern portions of its range, is the "snow bird" of North America. The junco is common throughout the United States and Canada, with four subspecies represented in the Rocky Mountains: the Oregon, Pink-sided, Gray-headed, and White-winged forms. Breeding in open woodlands, they are seasonal or permanent residents throughout most of the region covered by this book.

Favored habitat includes ponderosa woodlands, aspen forests, and pinon-juniper stands. The junco is a ground nester and forager, and areas with suitable cover for escape are considered choice real estate.

Nest sites are typically selected on steep, rocky outcrops or exposed stream banks within a woodland clearing. Occasionally a nest is placed under a shrub or beneath a brush pile. Nearby cover, such as bushes or trees, is critical.

The nest, made of coarse grasses, moss, and bark, is placed in a cup-shaped depression with some type of overhead protection, often adjacent to a nearly vertical surface. Construction is by the female, with occasional help from the male.

Three to five white eggs, with varying amounts of brownish spotting, are incubated by the female for almost two weeks. After hatching, the nestlings are tended by both parents.

The diminutive Dark-eyed Junco can brighten a cold and dreary winter day for anyone maintaining a winter bird-feeding station.

PHOTOGRAPHIC TECHNIQUES

Dark-eyed Juncos are easy to photograph at a bird-feeding station; they like platform feeders or ground feeding. Several days may be required before they locate a new feeder. Time can be saved by obtaining permission to photograph at an established feeding station. Most people have no problem with this, as long as you ask permission and, perhaps, offer an enlargement of one of the images made at their feeder.

Nest photography is your other option. The easiest way (if there is such a thing) to locate a junco nest is to watch for adults with food or nesting material in their mouths. Once you've spotted such a bird, observe from a distance using your binoculars. They will not fly directly to their nest. Instead, they will land in the general vicinity and, with great stealth and slyness, creep through cover until they reach the nest. As with all ground nesting birds, the nests are difficult to locate. Get down on your hands and knees, and search every square foot of the area until you find the nest.

CAUTION: Be extremely careful when searching for juncos' nests. It is easy to accidentally destroy the eggs and nest.

Once you've located the nest, erect your blind nearby. It's best to do this while the birds are away. Enlist the aid of someone who will see you to your blind and then leave once you're inside. This fools the birds into believing no one is nearby.

Although you can often obtain nice images of this species with a 400 mm lens, you'll be better off with something in the 600 mm range.

TIME OF YEAR

As a year-round resident in most areas, the Dark-eyed Junco can be photographed any time. Winter shots of juncos in the snow are worth considering, as are shots containing fall colors.

In the mountains, March is typically the month of heaviest snowfall. Fall colors peak in late September or early October in the southern locations. In Alberta and British Columbia, fall comes much earlier, usually in early September.

Nestlings and their parents can be photographed beginning in mid-June and continuing through July in most areas covered by this book.

In Rocky Mountain National Park, juncos are present year-round. Breeding has been confirmed in the park.

In Kootenai National Wildlife Refuge, they are common during spring and fall. During summer, they are often present but are not certain to be seen. During winter they are only seen a few times. Breeding does occur within the refuge.

Juncos are common in Red Rock Lakes National Wildlife Refuge from spring through fall. However, they are sighted only a few times during the winter. Nesting is common.

In Waterton Lakes National Park, juncos are common during spring and summer. In fall, they are observed somewhat infrequently, and winter sightings are rare. Nesting has been confirmed.

Yoho National Park boasts sizable populations from March through October. During winter they become scarce. Nesting occurs in suitable habitat throughout the park.

PHOTOGRAPHIC HOT SPOTS

ROCKY MOUNTAIN NATIONAL PARK, COLORADO

I have frequently observed Dark-eyed Juncos along the Wild Basin Trail, between the trailhead and Calypso Cascades. Look for the flash of their white-edged tails, as they flit about in search of food. To reach the trail, go south from Estes Park 12 miles along State Highway 7. Look for the Wild Basin sign. Turn right and follow signs to the trailhead.

For additional directions and information, see Chapter 3.

MOUNT NEBO SCENIC LOOP, UINTA NATIONAL FOREST, UTAH

Mount Nebo Scenic Loop, a 35-mile drive connecting several life zones, provides wildlife photographers with a variety of opportunities to photograph birds and mammals.

Dark-eyed Juncos are common sights along many trails on Mount Nebo. With 15 trailheads along the route, you will find paths leading into a number of different habitats. The ones heading into lower montane forests will probably offer good photo opportunities for juncos.

From Interstate 15 in Nephi, go east 5 miles along State Highway 132. Turn left, following the signs to the Mount Nebo Scenic Loop. The road is typically free of snow from May through October.

For additional information, contact the U.S. Forest Service (801-798-3571).

KOOTENAI NATIONAL WILDLIFE REFUGE, IDAHO

Kootenai National Wildlife Refuge, situated in the Idaho panhandle only 20 miles from Canada, is bounded by the Kootenai River on the east and the Selkirk Mountains on the west. The Dark-eyed Junco can be photographed in the conifer forests along the base of the Selkirks. Search for them along the trails.

For directions and additional information, see Chapter 3.

RED ROCK LAKES NATIONAL WILDLIFE REFUGE, MONTANA

The Dark-eyed Junco will typically be found among the aspen and conifer forests south of Red Rock Pass Road. However, I also have observed them in the Upper Lake Campground. Bird feeders around the community of Lakeview also attract juncos.

For directions, road closures, and additional information, see Chapter 3.

WATERTON LAKES NATIONAL PARK, ALBERTA

Juncos are usually present along the trail at Cameron Lake. To reach the lake, take the Akamina Parkway from Waterton Townsite. The lake is located at the end of the parkway.

For additional directions and information, see Chapter 3.

YOHO NATIONAL PARK, BRITISH COLUMBIA

Dark-eyed Juncos are quite common along the trail to Laughing Falls. Access the trailhead from the Takakkaw Falls parking area. Also scout the townsite of Field. Scan the trees near the Visitor Center in Field, and investigate areas surrounding bird feeders.

For directions and additional information, see Chapter 3.

White-crowned Sparrow

DESCRIPTION – Black and white striped crown, brownish back and wings; gray underparts; pink or orange bill.

SCIENTIFIC NAME – *Zonotrichis leucophrys*

FAMILY – Warblers, Sparrows (Emberizidae)

NESTING BEGINS – June to August

INCUBATION – 11 to 14 days (usually 12); 2 to 6 eggs (usually 3 to 5)

TIME TO FLEDGE – 7 to 12 days

The White-crowned Sparrow, adorned with a flashy crown of black and white, welcomes visitors to the land above the trees. The white-crown is common throughout most of the region where suitable habitat is available, as either a summer visitor or permanent resident. During winter, some migrate vertically from high mountain meadows to the plains, while others may winter as far south as southern Mexico.

Colorado White-crowned Sparrows are year-round residents. In Wyoming, spring migrants do not show up until the middle of April. In southern Alberta, it's usually the end of April before the birds begin appearing. Nesting begins approximately a month and a half after their arrival on the breeding grounds.

Nesting occurs in moist willow thickets above 9,000 feet, as well as krummholz forests (a German word meaning "crooked wood") and thickets of alpine willows above treeline.

The cup-shaped nest, built of coarse grass stems, leaves, and shredded bark, is typically located either on the ground at the base of a shrub, or hidden in its branches no more than a few feet above ground. The site is selected by the female.

Three to five greenish blue eggs, with reddish brown mottling, are incubated by the female for two weeks. The young nestlings, attended by both parents, fledge between one and two weeks of age. Those raised in more northern zones fledge sooner.

Non-migratory White-crowned Sparrows commonly stay pair-bonded for life.

The song of the White-crowned Sparrow consists of one or more melodious notes, followed by a "buzzy" trill. The alarm is a simple pink.

PHOTOGRAPHY TECHNIQUES

White-crowned Sparrows are easily located among krummholz (dwarfed subalpine fir or limber pine) and alpine willow stands. If you have any problems locating your subject, simply listen for their songs.

By advancing slowly and cautiously, you should be able to approach to the point that a 500 mm or 600 mm lens will supply the necessary magnification.

Nesting birds are easily photographed from a portable blind. Once the blind is erected, white-crowns readily accept its presence. Again, a 500 mm or 600 mm lens works best.

The first step in finding a nest is to locate an adult taking food to its offspring. An adult with food in its beak will not fly directly to the young, but instead will land nearby and try to sneak to the nest site. Search the area with a fine-tooth comb until you locate the nest.

TIME OF YEAR

In Colorado, White-crowned Sparrows are permanent residents. However, from Wyoming northward into Alberta and British Columbia, they are present only during spring and summer.

In Wyoming, spring arrivals show up during mid-April. In Canada, the birds typically arrive two to three weeks later. It may be several weeks after the birds arrive before the snows melt from the higher elevations and the white-crowns ascend to their alpine breeding grounds.

The season for nest photography begins in early June in Colorado and Wyoming, and from mid- to late June in Montana and Canada. In Colorado and Wyoming, opportunities for nest photography generally end around mid-July. In Montana, the season often extends into early August. Nest activity in Canada usually comes to an end sometime in early July.

PHOTOGRAPHIC HOT SPOTS

MOUNT EVANS, ARAPAHO NATIONAL FOREST, COLORADO

Echo Lake should be the first stop on your way to the summit of Mount Evans. Hike the area around the lake listening for the songs of the White-crowned Sparrows which frequently nest among the willows.

Continuing up Mount Evans, watch for gnarled, wind-blown bristlecone pines growing on Mount Goliath, just before reaching the open alpine tundra. Search the area, looking and listening for white-crowns among the willows.

For directions and additional information, see Chapter 3.

ROCKY MOUNTAIN NATIONAL PARK, COLORADO

My favorite location in the park for photographing the White-crowned Sparrow is along Trail Ridge Road near Rainbow Curve. From Rainbow Curve, go west approximately 2 miles. A parking area will be on your left. Cross the road and search the alpine willows along the sides of Sundance Mountain.

For directions and additional information, see Chapter 3.

MOUNT NEBO SCENIC LOOP, UINTA NATIONAL FOREST, UTAH

Mount Nebo Scenic Loop, a 35-mile drive connecting several life zones, provides wildlife photographers with a variety of opportunities.

White-crowned Sparrows are common sights on Mount Nebo. With 15 trailheads along the route, you will find paths leading into a number of different habitats. Willow thickets near treeline should produce the most photo opportunities.

From Interstate 15 in Nephi, go east 5 miles along State Highway 132. Turn left, following the signs to the Mount Nebo Scenic Loop. The road is typically free of snow from May through October.

For additional information, contact the U.S. Forest Service (801-798-3571).

GLACIER NATIONAL PARK, MONTANA

Glacier National Park is home to song birds of all descriptions, including White-crowned Sparrows. I highly recommend Two Dogs Flats, an open prairie carpeted with colorful wildflowers. From the Saint Mary Visitor Center, go west 4 miles along Going-To-The-Sun Road. The "flats" will be on your right.

For additional directions and information, see Chapter 3.

WATERTON LAKES NATIONAL PARK, ALBERTA

White-crowned Sparrows are common in suitable habitat throughout the park. One such location is the area around Linnet Lake, along the entrance road across from the Visitor Information Center.

For additional information, see Chapter 3.

Yellow-headed Blackbird

DESCRIPTION — Male: Black body; rich-yellow head and cape; white wing patches.
    Female: dusky brown; dull yellow breast and throat.

SCIENTIFIC NAME — *Xanthocephalus xanthocephalus*

FAMILY — Warblers, Sparrows (Emberizidae)

NESTING BEGINS — Mid-May to mid-July

INCUBATION — 11 to 13 days; 3 to 5 eggs (usually 4)

TIME TO FLEDGE — 9 to 12 days

The Yellow-headed Blackbird — head thrown back, voice unmusical, racous and rasping — proclaims his niche among the cattails for all the world to hear. Surely someone dropped the ball when singing voices were handed out to this strikingly beautiful blackbird. Distinctive? Yes! Beautiful? Hardly. The blackbird's song, if you can call it that, is a harsh, raspy squeak followed by a long, loud buzz.

The Yellow-headed Blackbird inhabits southern Canada from British Columbia to Manitoba, the western half of the United States, and, in winter, all the way to southern Mexico.

Yellowheads prefer marshes with stands of bulrushes or cattails. The birds often share these marshes with their close relatives, the Red-winged Blackbirds. However, yellowheads prefer the deeper recesses of the marsh, forcing the red-wings to nest near its outer fringes.

Male yellowheads establish territories weeks before the arrival of the females. Once the females arrive, nest building commences; the males watch and give "moral support." Construction takes anywhere from two to four days.

The nest, typically constructed of finely woven cattail blades, is lined with finer materials. It is truly a work of art. Nest building is usually delayed until new cattail growth reaches a size sufficient to support the weight of the nest.

Egg laying is usually complete by June; four bluish white eggs, heavily marked with purplish brown specks and mottling, normally are laid. The eggs hatch 12 days later. At this time, nests by reservoirs and canals are vulnerable to rising water due to agricultural demands. Many nests, and young blackbirds, are destroyed by high water.

Ten or 11 days after hatching, the young fledglings climb out of the nest onto a nearby branch, ready to fly. Up to this point, most of the responsibility of caring for the young has been borne by the female. After fledging, these young get the attention of both parents.

Males are polygamous. Mating occurs three times on average during the breeding season. Males begin breeding when the first female arrives in his territory. She then begins nesting. Later, another female arrives, breeding occurs, nesting begins, and the process is repeated.

An interesting thing happens with yellowheads each August. The birds disappear — or so it seems. In reality, they fade into the deeper recesses of the marshes, where they keep out of sight of predators while they go through their annual molt, losing their flight feathers. Once the molt is complete, the birds reappear, just prior to their fall migration into the southern portions of the United States and Mexico.

PHOTOGRAPHIC TECHNIQUES

Photograph Yellow-headed Blackbirds during nesting season. Network with birders, park and refuge personnel, and other photographers. They can save you time in locating marshes supporting yellowhead populations. Finding the birds is easy once you're in the field; the birds' singing will pin-point their location.

Photographing yellowheads also is easy. A blind is unnecessary. I prefer to use chest-high waders to wade around in marshes. The birds will allow you to get reasonably close. A 500 mm or 600 mm lens will provide a comfortable working distance.

TIME OF YEAR

Yellow-headed Blackbirds begin arriving in the spring around mid-March. In the fall, the last birds leave sometime during late September.

Nesting activity in Colorado begins in mid-May and continues until mid-June. In Wyoming, nesting may begin a few days later and extends until early July. In Montana and southern Canada, nesting does not begin until late May and ends around the middle of June.

PHOTOGRAPHIC HOT SPOTS

ARAPAHO NATIONAL WILDLIFE REFUGE, COLORADO

Several reservoirs are located along the refuge's Self-Guided Auto Tour. Yellow-headed Blackbirds occupy one of the reservoirs along the western edge of this area. You cannot miss seeing and hearing them as you drive the loop. I've been able to obtain a few images of these birds from the window of my Cherokee.

For directions and additional information, see Chapter 3.

SEEDSKADEE NATIONAL WILDLIFE REFUGE, WYOMING

Yellow-headed Blackbirds are common sights and sounds in the refuge during the summer. Photograph them among the cattail marshes south of refuge headquarters. For directions and additional information, see Chapter 3.

CAMAS NATIONAL WILDLIFE REFUGE, IDAHO

The unmistakable song of the Yellow-headed Blackbird betrays their position among the cattails growing in the refuge's ponds and marshes. Off-road travel is prohibited between February 1 and July 15. For directions and additional information, see Chapter 3.

BENTON LAKE NATIONAL WILDLIFE REFUGE, MONTANA

Yellow-headed Blackbirds can often be photographed from your car as you drive the 9-mile Prairie Marsh Wildlife Drive. Don't overlook the Prairie Marsh Trail Boardwalk. For additional information and directions, see Chapter 3.

TYRRELL AND RUSH LAKES, ALBERTA

Tyrrell Lake, Rush Lake, and the adjacent marsh lands form a major staging area for shore birds and waterfowl. The marshes also provide habitat for nesting Yellow-headed Blackbirds.

This area can be reached by going southeast from Lethbridge along Highway 4 for 38 kilometers (23 miles) to the town of New Dayton. Continue past New Dayton for 3 kilometers (1.8 miles) along Highway 4, and you will find access to Tyrrell Lake. Highway 36, to the west, provides additional access into the area. For additional information, contact the Alberta Fish and Wildlife Division in Lethbridge (403-381-5281), or St. Mary's River Irrigation District in Lethbridge (403-328-4401).

Evening Grosbeak

DESCRIPTION — Male: yellow body; black wings and tail; pale-green, conical bill
  Female: grayish tan, with pale-yellow wash

SCIENTIFIC NAME — *Coccothraustes vespertinus*

FAMILY — Finches (Fringillidae)

NESTING BEGINS — Early June to late July

INCUBATION — 11 to 14 days; 2 to 5 eggs (usually 3 or 4)

TIME TO FLEDGE — 13 or 14 days

The Evening Grosbeak, moving about in large flocks one year and disappearing the next, is the colorful wizard of the Rocky Mountain forests. Perhaps the varying availability of its favorite foods — willow buds and the seeds of box elder, maple, and conifers — account for the Evening Grosbeak's abundance one year and total absence in the same area the following year.

The Evening Grosbeak breeds across the entire southern portion of Canada, and in the United States from New England to central California. Winter populations extend throughout most of the United States.

In the Rockies, subalpine spruce, fir, and lodgepole forests are favored breeding habitats. Heavy snows force many birds into the foothills and nearby plains during the winter.

Breeding begins in early June and continues into late July. The cup-shaped nest, built by the female, is typically placed near the end of a branch, high in the tops of a tall conifer. Appearing like an accumulation of twigs and sticks thrown together at the last minute, the nest is often concealed from predators by foliage.

Three or four greenish blue eggs, marked with purplish brown scrawls, are incubated between 11 and 14 days. During this time, the male feeds the female.

PHOTOGRAPHIC TECHNIQUES

Evening Grosbeaks are relatively tame birds and make good photographic subjects. They are easily photographed at bird-feeding stations, and prefer platform feeders liberally stocked with sunflower seeds. These birds wander irregularly, and the secret is locating feeders being visited by them.

If you do not live in an area frequented by Evening Grosbeaks, you will have to locate someone who does, and obtain permission to photograph the birds at their feeder. Network with owners and patrons of stores selling bird-feeding supplies, such as Wild Bird Center or Wild Birds Unlimited. If nothing turns up, your next step is to place a notice on the store's bulletin board, seeking the whereabouts of the species and your desire to photograph them.

Since platform feeders do not always provide pleasing photo backdrops, locate a small, photogenic tree or branch, and place it nearby. Tie it in place if necessary. The birds will land on this prop as they come and go, providing a more natural-looking perch.

TIME OF YEAR

Evening Grosbeaks frequent platform feeders during the winter, between December and March. If you are intent on photographing a nesting pair of Evening Grosbeaks, breeding season begins in early June and continues until late July.

PHOTOGRAPHIC HOT SPOTS

There are no specific photographic hot spots for photographing Evening Grosbeaks. However, since they are present in the following parks, network with businesses selling bird-feeding supplies in nearby towns.

ROCKY MOUNTAIN NATIONAL PARK, COLORADO

Inquire at stores selling bird-feeding supplies in Grand Lake, Estes Park, and Boulder. Talk with park personnel. The more you inquire, the better your chances of finding feeders being frequented by Evening Grosbeaks. For additional information, see Chapter 3.

YELLOWSTONE NATIONAL PARK, WYOMING

Evening Grosbeaks can be located through networking at stores selling bird seed and feeders in the Wyoming towns of Jackson and Cody, or the Montana towns of West Yellowstone, Gardiner, Silver Gate, and Cooke City.

For additional information, see Chapter 3.

GLACIER NATIONAL PARK, MONTANA

Visit stores near Glacier that sell bird seed and feeders. On the east side of the park, call on stores in the towns of Babb and St. Mary. On the west side, go to Columbia Falls, Kalispell, and Whitefish. Through these contacts you should be able to locate Evening Grosbeaks.

For additional information, see Chapter 3.

BANFF NATIONAL PARK, ALBERTA

Go to Banff Townsite and inquire at stores selling bird-feeding supplies. Find out who is seeing Evening Grosbeaks at their bird feeders. Talk with the personnel at the park information center, located at the corner of Wolf and Banff. Also, don't overlook the Banff Park Museum, at the intersection of Lynx and Bear. For additional information, see Chapter 3.

WATERTON LAKES NATIONAL PARK, ALBERTA

Talk with store owners and salespeople at businesses selling bird-feeding supplies in the nearby towns of Cardston and Pincher Creek. Don't overlook Waterton Townsite businesses. Talk with employees and volunteers at the visitor information center in town. Most park personnel put out bird feeders. For additional information, see Chapter 3.

APPENDIX

RESOURCE CONTACTS

North American Nature Photography Association
10200 West 44th Avenue, Suite 304
Wheat Ridge, Colorado 80033
(303) 422-8527
(Committed to the photography of
our environment)

National Forests

Fishlake National Forest
Beaver Ranger District
190 N 100 E
Beaver, Utah 84713
(801) 438-2436

Moab Ranger District
Manti-La Sal National Forest
2290 S. West Resource Blvd.
Moab, Utah 84523
(810) 259-7155

National Parks

Arches National Park
30 South 100 East
Moab, Utah 84532
(801) 259-8161

Banff National Park
P.O. Box 900
Banff, Alberta T0L 0C0
(403) 762-1550

Canyonlands National Park
125 West 200 South
Moab, Utah 84532
(801) 259-7164

Grand Teton National Park
P.O. Drawer 170
Moose, Wyoming 83012
(307) 733-2880

Glacier National Park
West Glacier, MT 59936
(406) 888-5790

Jasper National Park
P.O. Box 10
Jasper, Alberta T0E 1E0
(403) 852-6176

Kootenay National Park
P.O. Box 220
Radium Hot Springs
British Columbia V0A IM0
(604) 347-9615

Rocky Mountain National Park
Estes Park, Colorado 80517
(970) 586-1399

Waterton Lakes National Park
Waterton Park, Alberta T0K 2M0
(403) 859-2224

Wind Cave National Park
Hot Springs, South Dakota 57747
(605) 745-4600

Yellowstone National Park
Yellowstone National Park, WY 82190
(307) 344-7381

Yoho National Park
Box 99
Field, British Columbia V0A 1G0
(604) 343-6324

National Wildlife Refuges

Arapaho NWR
P.O. Box 457
Walden, CO 80480
(970) 723-8202

Bear River Migratory Bird Refuge
866 S. Main
Brigham City, Utah 84302
(801) 723-5887

Benton Lake NWR
P.O. Box 450
Black Eagle, Montana 59414
(406) 727-7400

Bosque del Apache NWR
P.O. Box 1246
Socorro, New Mexico 87801
(505) 835-1828

Camas NWR
HC 69, Box 1700
Hamer, Idaho 83425
(208) 662-5423

Grays Lake NWR
74 Grays Lake Road
Wayan, Idaho 83285
(208) 574-2755

Kootenai NWR
HRC 60, Box 283
Bonners Ferry, Idaho 83805
(208) 267-3888

Maxwell NWR
P.O. Box 276
Maxwell, New Mexico 87728
(505) 375-2331

Monte Vista NWR
9383 El Rancho Lane
Alamosa, Colorado 81101
(719) 589-4021

National Bison Range
132 Bison Range Road
Moiese, Montana 59824
(406) 644-2211

National Elk Refuge
P.O. Box C
Jackson, Wyoming 83001
(307) 733-9212

Ouray NWR
1680 West Highway 40
Suite 112-C
Vernal, Utah 84078
(801) 789-0351

Red Rock Lakes NWR
Monida Star Route
Box 15
Lima, Montana 59739
(406) 276-3536

Rocky Mountain Arsenal
National Wildlife Area
Building 111
Commerce City, Colorado 80022
(303) 289-0232

Seedskadee NWR
P.O. Box 700
Green River, Wyoming 82935
(307) 875-2187

UL Bend NWR
P.O. Box 110
Lewiston, Montana 59457
(406) 538-8706

State Parks

Fort Kearney State Park
Route 4
Kearney, Nebraska 68847
(308) 234-9513

Golden Gate Canyon State Park
3873 Highway 46
Golden, CO 80403
(303) 592-1502

Greycliff
Prairie Dog Town State Park
Parks Division of Montana
Department of Fish, Wildlife & Parks
2300 Lake Elmo Drive
Billings, Montana 59105
(406) 252-4654

Miscellaneous Canadian Agencies

Fish & Wildlife Division
Alberta Forestry, Lands and Wildlife
Main Floor, 9945-108 St.
Edmonton, Alberta T5K 2G6

Miscellaneous Federal Agencies

Bureau of Land Management
3380 Americana Terrace
Boise, Idaho 83706
(208) 384-3000
(Snake River Birds of Prey Area)

U.S. Bureau of Reclamation
Canyon Ferry Field Office
7661 Canyon Ferry Road
Helena, Montana 59601
(for info on Bald Eagles viewing)

U.S. Fish & Wildlife Service
1745 West 1700 South
Salt Lake City, Utah 84104
(801) 524-5630
(801) 538-7220

U.S Fish & Wildlife Service, Region 1
911 NE 11th Avenue
Portland, OR 97232-4187
(Contact for falconer and
rehab facility listing - for Idaho)

U.S. Fish & Wildlife Service, Region 2
Migratory Bird Permits Division
P.O. Box 709
Albuquerque, NM 87103-0709
(Contact for falconer and
rehab facility listing - for New Mexico)

U.S. Fish & Wildlife Service, Region 6
Migratory Permit Office
P.O. Box 25486
Denver Federal Center
Denver, CO 80225
(Contact for falconer and rehab facility
listing - for Colorado, Utah, Montana, Wyoming)

Miscellaneous State Agencies

Colorado Division of Wildlife
6060 Broadway
Denver, Colorado 80216
(303) 297-1192

Jim Haskins
District Wildlife Manager
Colorado Division of Wildlife
Hayden, Colorado
home (970) 276-3338
(for info on Sharp-tailed Grouse leks)

Idaho Department of Fish and Game
600 S. Walnut
Boise, Idaho 83707
(208) 334-3700

Montana Department
of Fish, Wildlife and Parks
P.O. Box 200701
1420 East 6th Avenue
Helena, Montana 59620
(406) 444-1276

New Mexico Department of Game and Fish
Villagra Building
State Capitol
Santa Fe, New Mexico 87503
(505) 841-8881

Utah Division of
Wildlife Resources
1596 West North Temple
Salt Lake City, Utah 84116
(801) 596-8660

Utah Division of
Parks & Recreation
1636 West North Temple
Salt Lake City, Utah 84116
(801) 538-7220

Wyoming Game and Fish Commission
Commission Headquarters Building
Cheyenne, Wyoming 82006
(307) 777-4600

Bird Rehabilitation Facilities

Rocky Mountain Raptor Program
Colorado State University
Veterinary Teaching Hospital
300 W. Drake
Fort Collins, Colorado 80523
(970) 491-0398

Game farms

Absolutely Wild
3200 S. Foothills
Boulder, Colorado 80303
(303) 499-1400

Animals of Montana
14752 Bracket Creek Road
Bozeman, Montana 59715
(406) 686-4979

Red Feather Lakes
Wildlife & Photography Center
20490 West County Road 74 East
Red Feather Lakes, Colorado 80545
(303) 881-2216

Triple "D" Game Farm
P.O. Box 5072
Kalispell, Montana 59903
(406) 755-9653

Wild Eyes Photo Adventures
894 Lake Drive
Columbia Falls, Montana 59912
(406) 387-5391

Miscellaneous Contacts

Lillian Annette Rowe Sanctuary
National Audubon Society
Route 2, Box 146
Gibbon, Nebraska 68840
(308) 468-5282

Platte River Whooping Crane Trust
2550 North Diers Avenue, Suite H
Grand Island, Nebraska 68803
(308) 384-4633

Kearney Visitors Bureau
P.O. Box 607
2001 Avenue A
Kearney, Nebraska 68848
(308) 237-3101

Grand Island Visitors Bureau
P.O. Box 1486
309 West 2nd
Grand Island, Nebraska 68802
(800) 247-6167, Ext 625

Lou Wyman Elk Ranch
Box 278
Craig, Colorado 81626
(970) 824-6431
(Sharp-tailed Grouse)

Great Bear Adventures
10555 Highway 2 East
Coram, Montana
(406) 387-4290
Mailing Address:
P.O. Box 190611
Hungry Horse, Montana 59919
(Drive-thru bear park)

Chamber of Commerce Visitor Center
Jackson Hole Chamber of Commerce
P.O. Box E
532 North Cache
Jackson, Wyoming 83001
(307) 733-3316

National Bighorn Sheep Interpretative Center
P.O. Box 1435
907 West Ramshorn
Dubois, Wyoming, 82513
(307) 455-3429

For Yellowstone reservations...
TW Recreational Services, Inc.
Yellowstone NP, Wyoming 82190-9989
(307) 344-7311

The Peregrine Fund
World Center for Birds of Prey
5666 West Flying Hawk Lane
Boise, Idaho 83709
(Non-profit raptor research organization)

Wheat Ridge Parks & Recreation Dept.
P.O. Box 638
Wheat Ridge, Colorado 80034
(303) 423-2626
(Wheat Ridge Greenbelt)

Suppliers

Bogen Photo Corporation
565 E. Crescent Avenue
Ramsey, New Jersey 07446-0506
(Suppliers of Bogen and Gitzo tripods)
For the money, Bogen tripods are the best
buy on the market.

Cabela's
812 13th Avenue
Sidney, Nebraska 69160
1 (800) 237-4444
(Camo clothing, etc.)

Johnny Stewart Game Calls
P.O. Box 7594
Waco, Texas 76710
(817) 772-3261

Kirk Enterprises, Inc.
107 Lange Lane
Angola, Indiana 46703
1 (800) 626-5074
(Specialized photo equipment)

Leonard Rue Enterprises
138 Millbrook Road
Blairstown, New Jersey 07825
(908) 362-6616
(Products for photographers)

Protech
5710-E General Washington Drive
Alexandria, Virginia 22312
(Dalebeam products)

Woods Electronics Inc.
14781 Pomerado Road, Suite 197
Poway, California
(619) 486-0806
(Shutter-Beam)

Wildlife Preserves

Mission: Wolf
P.O. Box 211
Silver Cliff, Colorado 81249
(719) 746-2919

Prairie Wind
Wild Animal Refuge
22111 County Road 150
Agate, CO 80101
(303) 621-2304

SELECTED REFERENCES

Birder's Guide to Colorado, by Holt and Lane
(L & P Press)
This is a very detailed guide, listing species, and detailed locations. Worth the money. Guides for other states are also available.

Birder's Guide to Montana, by Terry McEneaney
(Falcon Press)
Another detailed guide that should be in every wildlife photographer's library.

Birder's Handbook, by Ehrlich, Dobkin, and Wheye (Simon & Schuster)
Lists info that will inform and allow you to decide the best times to photograph nestlings. Chocked full of natural history info.

Birding Crane River: Nebraska's Platte, by Gary Lingle (Harrier Publ.)
Excellent guide on where to go, and what you will see when you get there.

Birding Jasper National Park, by Kevin Van Tighem (Parks and People)
This book is a MUST for people visiting Jasper.

Birds of Colorado, by Bailey and Niedrach
(Denver Museum of Natural History)
A very comprehensive two-volume series. Excellent for research. Out of print. A good used book store can get you a set for around $150.

Birds of the Rocky Mountains, by Paul Johnsgard
(Colorado Associated University Press)
Supplies nesting dates, abundance, and breeding info for U.S. and Canadian Rockies. With this book, you will know when to begin looking for nesting birds.

Field Guide to Mammal Tracking, by James Halfpenny (Johnson Books)
Jim talks not only about tracking, but also includes info on scat.

Field Guide to the Birds of North America
(National Geographic Society)
The is the best field guide for birds.

Field Guide to the Nests, Eggs, and Nestlings, by Colin Harrison (Stephen Greene Press)
An excellent ID book.

Guide to the National Wildlife Refuges, by Laura/William Riley (Macmillan)
Don't be without this book. It provides info on every refuge.

Hawks In Flight, by Dunne, Sibley, and Sutton
(Houghton Mifflin)
Identifying raptors can sometimes be difficult. Not if you use this book. It takes all the mystery out of raptor identification.

How To Call Wildlife, by Byron W. Dalrymple
(Outdoor Life Books)
Out of print. It's worth trying to obtain a copy.

How To Spot An Owl, by Patricia and Clay Sutton
(Chapters Publishing)
This book will get you to thinking like an owl, and increase your owl sightings.

Large Mammals of the Central Rockies, by Stephen Torbit (Bennet Creek)
Supplies a tremendous amount of natural history, listing habits, sign, breeding information, etc.

Peterson Field Guide Series/Animal Tracks, by Olaus Murie (Houghton Mifflin)
Olaus set the standard. For years this has been THE BOOK on animal tracking.

Rocky Mountain Mammals, by David Armstrong
(Rocky Mountain Nature Association)
From the deer mouse to bighorn, this book furnishes natural history and distribution of mammals found in Rocky Mountain National Park.

Stokes Nature Guides/Bird Behavior, by Donald and Lillian Stokes (Little, Brown and Company)
I can not say enough good things about these books. Unfortunately only three books are in the series at this time. EXCELLENT behavioral info on birds.

Stokes Nature Guides/Animal Tracking and Behavior, by Donald and Lillian Stokes (Little, Brown and Company)
This is another MUST HAVE selection including tracks and signs, plus an inside look at animal behavior.

BT Journal (quarterly journal for wildlife photographers, by B. Moose Peterson) Mail inquires to:
Sharon Peterson
Wildlife Research Photography
P.O. Box 3628
Mammoth Lakes, California 93546
(619) 924-8632

Birds of North America
P.O. Box 687
Holmes, Pennsylvania 19043
(800) 345-8112
(Bimonthly species accounts)

First Light
P.O. Box 11066
Englewood, Colorado 80151
(303) 762-8191
(Monthly newsletter for wildlife and nature photographers)

Photograph America Newsletter
1333 Monte Maria Avenue
Novato, California 94947
(Bimonthly photo travel newsletter)

Photo Traveler
P.O. Box 39912
Los Angeles, California 90039
(Bimonthly photo travel newsletter)

PERSONAL INVITATION

Weldon Lee Wildlife Photo Tours
P.O. Box 487
Allenspark, CO 80510
(303) 747-2074

Dear Reader,

I would like to extend this invitation to join me on one of my models workshops, or wildlife photo tours to Colorado, Alaska, or Africa.

Some of the species available during the models workshops are eagles, owls, red fox, wolves, bobcat, mountain lion, and black bear.

In addition, I also conduct personalized one-on-one photo sessions focusing on photography basics, flowers, landscapes, wildlife, or models.

The choice is yours!

Weldon Lee

Profile of a Wildlife Photographer/Writer

photo by Linda Buehring-Lee

Weldon Lee has a special way of communicating with wildlife, and seems to have the unique ability of capturing the essence of their personalities on film.

He has traveled throughout this great country of ours, from Alaska to Texas to Florida, including the Rocky Mountains from New Mexico to British Columbia, photographing and writing about wildlife.

His work has been published in various periodicals including *National Parks Magazine, Backpacker, Nature Photographer, Texas Highways, Colorado Outdoors, Idaho Wildlife, Montana Magazine, New Mexico Wildlife, Bird Watcher's Digest,* and several publications by National Park Network, as well as appearing in books by publishers such as Roberts Rinehart, Falcon Press, and Macmillan. His images have also been exhibited in the Denver Museum of Natural History and The Carnegie Museum of Natural History in Pittsburgh. He already has one book to his credit, *Watchable Birds Of The Rocky Mountains,* which was published by Mountain Press. He worked for a year as contributing editor for *Rocky Mountain Photographer,* writing about wildlife photography. In addition to his own stock photo business, he is also represented by Stock Imagery, Inc., of Denver. In January, 1995, he was elected Chair of the Education Committee of the North American Nature Photography Association.

Long before becoming a photographer and writer, Weldon was a naturalist. As such, he is actively involved in wildlife preservation, giving slide lectures and outdoor education workshops. He also maintains a busy schedule teaching nature photography workshops and conducting wildlife photography tours.

"Wildlife photography, to me, is more than capturing an image," explains Weldon, "It is the opportunity to preserve on film the feeling, the mood, the drama of a fleeting moment in the life of a particular specie. When I am fortunate enough to capture one of those moments, I begin to realize that I am touching something greater than life itself. Today, many species of wildlife are being threatened with extinction. If they are to survive, then we...as humans...must learn to coexist with them. Wildlife photography and writing gives me the opportunity of fostering an appreciation of the uniqueness of all life forms which will hopefully lead to their survival."